D0169036

Ernest Hemingway

Revised Edition

Twayne's United States Authors Series

Kenneth Eble, Editor

University of Utah

TUSAS 41

ERNEST HEMINGWAY
(1899–1961)
Photograph courtesy of Ted Sato
and the John and Mable
Ringling Museum of Art

Ernest Hemingway

Revised Edition

Earl Rovit

City College of the
City University of New York

Gerry Brenner

University of Montana

TWAYNE PUBLISHERS
An Imprint of Simon & Schuster Macmillan
NEW YORK

Prentice Hall International
LONDON · MEXICO CITY · NEW DELHI · SINGAPORE · SYDNEY · TORONTO

Ernest Hemingway, Revised Edition

Earl Rovit and Gerry Brenner

Copyright © 1995 Simon & Schuster Macmillan
All Rights Reserved
Twayne Publishers
An Imprint of Simon & Schuster Macmillan
1633 Broadway
New York, NY 10019-6785

Copyediting supervised by Lewis DeSimone
Book production by Elizabeth Todesco
Book design by Barbara Anderson

Typeset in 11 pt. Garamond
by Modern Graphics, Inc., Weymouth, Massachusetts

Printed on permanent/durable acid-free paper
and bound in the United States of America

Library of Congress Cataloging in Publication Data

Rovit, Earl H.
Ernest Hemingway.

(Twayne's United States authors series; TUSAS 41)
Bibliography: p. 194
1. Hemingway, Ernest, 1899–1961—Criticism and
interpretation. I. Brenner, Gerry, 1937–
II. Title. III. Series.
PS3515.E37Z78   1986   813'.52   85-28916
ISBN 0-8057-7455-6
ISBN 0-8057-7468-8 (pbk.)

Contents

About the Authors

Earl Rovit, a member of the English department at the City College of New York, is the author of *Herald to Chaos,* a study of the novels of Elizabeth Madox Roberts, and *Saul Bellow.* Along with many articles on American literature and culture, he has published three novels.

Gerry Brenner, a member of the English department at the University of Montana, is the author of *Concealments in Hemingway's Works* and a number of articles on American and British literature.

Preface to the Revised Edition

This revision of a text written twenty-three years ago was undertaken with two goals in mind. We wanted to include within our overview of Hemingway's work the primary materials in the canon that appeared either in the last years of Hemingway's life or posthumously. We also wanted to indicate at least the tip of the titanic iceberg of scholarship and criticism that has been building so vigorously in Hemingway studies in the last three decades. Accordingly, chapter 9 provides a summary study of *A Moveable Feast, Islands in the Stream, The Dangerous Summer,* and *African Journal.* Further, we have compiled a new bibliography of primary and secondary sources, including detailed catalogs of audiovisual materials. And, finally, we have refurbished and extensively amplified the original notes and references. In our judgment, these revisions make this edition a concise and useful handbook that attempts to reflect the range, depth, and multidirections of Hemingway studies.

And while we have the opportunity of doing so, let us—more personally—commend the community of Hemingway scholarship. Since the 1963 publication of the original edition, we have met directly or indirectly most of the scholars whose names appear in the notes and bibliography. Markedly heterogeneous in their opinions, methodologies, and sensibilities, they possess, we believe, a genuine kinship in their passion for literature and their zeal to express and share that passion. We all have literary heroes and heroines besides Hemingway—in many cases, writers whom we may even more esteem—and yet around the heat and brilliance of his work we have found, communally, a clean, well-lighted place. As scholars fully aware of our debts to those who have worked before and alongside of us, we want to express our appreciation of their labors. And, lastly, we take pleasure in citing with special gratitude Jo August Hill, the first curator of the Hemingway Collection at the Kennedy Library.

Earl Rovit
*City College of the
City University of New York*

Gerry Brenner
University of Montana

Preface to the First Edition

My original intentions for the structure of *Ernest Hemingway* were to dispose of Hemingway the man in the opening chapter and to survey his work chronologically in the succeeding chapters. Two things happened to make this sensible plan impossible. After I had disposed of Hemingway in chapter 1, he wouldn't stay out of the succeeding chapters. At first I fought against him, but ultimately I capitulated. My plans to treat his work in successive chronological fashion likewise met with disaster. The whole body of Hemingway's writing proved to be of such a single piece that individual fictions written twenty years apart demanded to be treated together. Again I fought, and again I surrendered unconditionally. If it were possible to blame something besides my own cowardly irresolution, I would claim that Hemingway and his books determined the composition of my book. It is not likely that such a claim would be honored.

In general the structure of this study proceeds along the following lines. Chapter 1 introduces Hemingway and makes an initial attempt to place him in the context of his times and to follow the course of his life. Chapter 2, which deals with the formation of his prose aesthetic, investigates such matters as his aesthetic concern with emotion, the major influences on his characteristic techniques up to the time of his earliest publications, a preliminary investigation of his style, and a discussion of his attitude toward his audience. Chapter 3 is an extended investigation of his typical characters—heroes and heroines—and an attempt to see how these fit into his aesthetic. Chapter 4 studies the characteristic structures of his fiction and tries to relate these structures to the overriding aesthetic. In chapter 5 the famous Hemingway "code" is analyzed extensively, and there is an attempt to fit this code into the cumulative context of the aesthetic that has been developing from chapter 2. Chapter 6 deals almost exclusively with Hemingway's metaphysic of time and its relation to the code and the aesthetic; there is also a further examination of Hemingway's style in this chapter, which attempts to relate the style to the aesthetic in a more complex manner than did the earlier investigation. Chapter 7, an essay in literary exegesis on *The Sun Also Rises,* is designed to be an illustrative exemplar of the critical hypotheses drawn from the first six chapters. And chapter 8 attempts to sum up the results of the introductory survey and to indicate the shape of Hemingway's achievements, as well as his significance in literary history.

Inserted within the general discussion are fairly detailed explications of many of Hemingway's fictions; these include "Big Two-Hearted River," "In Another Country," "The Undefeated," "A Clean Well-Lighted Place," "Fifty Grand," "The Snows of Kilimanjaro," "The Short Happy Life of Francis Macomber," *A Farewell to Arms, For Whom the Bell Tolls,* and *The Old Man and the Sea.* Unlike the discussion of *The Sun Also Rises,* the exegeses of the other fictions are usually subordinate to the illustration or examination of some specific point in the discussion. I have been more interested in investigating the total contour of Hemingway's fiction than in providing a series of readings of his individual fictions. The reader is referred to the index for citations of specific stories.

I should like to acknowledge the generosity of the University of Louisville Research Fund Committee, which accorded me a grant through which I was able to secure the necessary time to prepare this study.

Earl Rovit

August 1962
Louisville, Kentucky

Acknowledgments

Quotations from the following works of Ernest Hemingway are used by permission of Charles Scribner's Sons and Jonathan Cape Ltd.: *The Sun Also Rises*, copyright 1926, Charles Scribner's Sons; copyright renewed 1954, Ernest Hemingway. *A Farewell to Arms*, copyright 1929, Charles Scribner's Sons; copyright renewed 1957, Ernest Hemingway. *Death in the Afternoon*, copyright 1932, Charles Scribner's Sons; © renewed 1960, Ernest Hemingway. *Green Hills of Africa*, copyright 1935, Charles Scribner's Sons; © renewed 1963, Mary Hemingway. *To Have and Have Not*, copyright 1937, Ernest Hemingway; © renewed 1965, Mary Hemingway. *The Fifth Column and the First Forty-Nine Stories*, copyright 1938, Ernest Hemingway; © renewed 1966, Mary Hemingway. *For Whom the Bell Tolls*, copyright 1940, Ernest Hemingway; © renewed 1968, Mary Hemingway. *Across the River and into the Trees*, copyright 1950, Ernest Hemingway; © renewed 1978, Mary Hemingway. *The Old Man and the Sea*, copyright 1952, Ernest Hemingway; © renewed 1980, Mary Hemingway. *A Moveable Feast*, © 1964, Ernest Hemingway, Ltd.

Quotations from the following works are used by permission of Charles Scribner's Sons: *Islands in the Stream*, © 1970, Mary Hemingway. *The Dangerous Summer*, © 1960, Ernest Hemingway; © renewed 1985, Mary Hemingway, John Hemingway, Patrick Hemingway, and Gregory Hemingway. "African Journal, " in *The Enduring Hemingway*, © 1974, Charles Scribner's Sons; © 1974, Mary Hemingway.

The authors are grateful for permission to quote from "The Hollow Men," copyright 1925, T. S. Eliot, Harcourt Brace & World, Inc.

The authors wish also to acknowledge the imagination, courage, and intelligence of Joseph Salzman and Jacob Steinberg whose energetic midwifery brought TUSAS into existence.

The authors wish finally to thank Ted Sato for permission to use his photograph for the frontispiece; it originally appeared in the 1953 *Ringling Brothers and Barnum and Bailey Circus Magazine and Program*.

Chronology

1899   Ernest Hemingway born 21 July in Oak Park, Illinois, son of Dr. Clarence E. and Grace Hall Hemingway.

1917   Graduates from Oak Park High School. Works as a reporter on the *Kansas City Star*.

1918   Drives ambulance for the Red Cross in Italy. 8 July, severely wounded under mortar fire at Fossalta di Piave.

1920–1924   Reporter and foreign correspondent for *Toronto Star* and *Star Weekly*. Meets Sherwood Anderson (1920–21); marries Hadley Richardson (1921); publishes *Three Stories and Ten Poems* in Paris (1923). Works with Ford Madox Ford on *transatlantic review*, and is friendly with Gertrude Stein and Ezra Pound. As correspondent, covers Greco-Turkish War (1922) and interviews Clemenceau and Mussolini. Publishes *in our time* in Paris (1924).

1925   Publishes *In Our Time* in U.S.

1926   *The Torrents of Spring* and *The Sun Also Rises*.

1927   Divorces Hadley Richardson; marries Pauline Pfeiffer. *Men Without Women*.

1928–1938   Sets up housekeeping at Key West, Florida; this home becomes the base of his various peregrinations. Begins the hobby of sports-fishing on Gulf Stream.

1929   *A Farewell to Arms*, his first major commercial success.

1930   Hurt in automobile accident in Montana.

1932   *Death in the Afternoon*.

1933–1934   *Winner Take Nothing* (1933). First safari to Africa; also visits Paris and Spain.

1935   *Green Hills of Africa*.

1936–1938   Covers the Spanish Civil War for the North American

Newspaper Alliance. *To Have and Have Not* (1937). Helps prepare film, *The Spanish Earth* (1938). *The Fifth Column and the First Forty-Nine Stories* (1938).

1939–1958   Buys Finca Vigía at San Francisco de Paula, Cuba, his home until just before Castro overthrows Batista.

1940   Divorced by Pauline Pfeiffer; marries Martha Gellhorn. *For Whom the Bell Tolls.*

1942–1946   War correspondent in Europe, flies with the Royal Air Force, participates in Normandy invasion, fights his own private war to liberate Paris, and attaches himself to the Fourth Infantry Division. Divorces Martha Gellhorn (1945); marries Mary Welsh (1946).

1950   *Across the River and into the Trees.*

1952   *The Old Man and the Sea.*

1953–1954   Revisits Africa; suffers two airplane crashes; is reported dead in the world press. Receives the Nobel Prize for Literature in 1954.

1961   Commits suicide at his home in Ketchum, Idaho, on 2 July.

1964   *A Moveable Feast.*

1970   *Islands in the Stream.*

1972   *The Nick Adams Stories.*

1985   *The Dangerous Summer.*

Chapter One
The Juggler and His Masks

The pragmatic code of Johnson J. Hooper's great rogue-creation, Simon Suggs, was crystallized in his favorite ethical motto: "IT IS BEST TO BE SHIFTY IN A NEW COUNTRY."[1] The life, the work, and perhaps even the self-inflicted death of Ernest Hemingway may be viewed as an extended twentieth-century adaptation of Suggs's comically conceived stance against the world. But where Simon Suggs practiced shiftiness in order to exploit and victimize, Hemingway seems to have learned the Suggs attitude as a desperate means of survival. The new country that Hemingway was born into was global and was riven by wars, civic and domestic violence, and mercurial changes in loyalties and in definitions of right conduct. Stability in such a country was the ineluctable mark of "the sitting duck"—of the grotesque parade of "potted" German soldiers who follow one another in regular cadence over the garden wall at Mons.

Stability also meant the fixed virtues of Oak Park, Illinois, or of the Oklahoma town to which Krebs returns ("Soldier's Home") after World War I. "But the world they were in," Krebs realizes, "was not the world he was in."[2] When his mother tells him that "God has some work for every one to do" and that "there can be no idle hands in His Kingdom," Krebs must voice the deepest truth he knows: " 'I'm not in His Kingdom,' Krebs said" (SS, 151). Hemingway's life, a romantic series of evasive actions with stopovers at such places as Kansas City, Fossalta di Piave, Toronto, Paris, Pamplona, Key West, Nairobi, Madrid, Havana, Venice, and Ketchum, Idaho, took place in a continually new, or other country; and his art records his gradually improvised techniques of defense and temporary survival in a changing and dangerous country that is not in His Kingdom.

Hence the multiple masks that Hemingway exuberantly offered to the world; hence also the bewildering sleight of hand with which he juggled the images of Hemingway the man, the artist, the public personality, and the legend. He was the limping twenty-one-year-old ex-*Tenente* Ernesto Hemingway, recipient of the Medaglia d'Ar-

1

gento al Valore and the Croce ad Merito di Guerra, who had 227 pieces of shell fragment taken from his leg; the Richard Harding Davis war correspondent covering the Greco-Turkish war and sending back dispatches on the massive refugee evacuation across the Maritza River; the shy young man with "passionately interested" eyes who studied the craft of writing with Gertrude Stein and Ezra Pound and helped Ford Madox Ford edit the *transatlantic review*. He was the "spokesman" of The Lost Generation whose two volumes of short stories (*In Our Time* and *Men Without Women*) and two novels (*The Sun Also Rises* and *A Farewell to Arms*) fixed the accents of two generations into a theatrical clipped dialogue of understatement, and created a prose instrument that was later to be praised by the Nobel Prize Committee for its "forceful and style-making mastery of the art of modern narration." He was the bullfight aficionado, the skier, the big and little game hunter, the fisherman, the prize-fighter and shadow-boxer, the short-time darling of the Loyalist sympathizers in the Spanish Civil War, the bearded soldier of fortune miraculously transported through time to ride missions with the Royal Air Force, to land in Normandy on Fox Green Beach, to liberate Paris ahead of the columns of General Leclerc, and to fight with the Fourth Infantry Division from the Schnee-Eifel operation to the Huertgen Forest. He was the Santa Claus figure of *Field and Stream* who survived two airplane crashes in Uganda in 1954 and sneered at his own obituaries, which intimated that they had been expecting his death for a long time; and he was the sad-eyed isolate figure whose self-inflicted death on 2 July 1961, in Ketchum, Idaho, shocked a world that may have been expecting his death for a long time, but could not believe it when it actually happened.

Hemingway's biography, of course, has been written, and the memoirs and reminiscences appear without stint;[3] but even when all the documents are collected and collated, the enigma of the man will doubtless remain. Although he was the most autobiographical of writers,[4] obsessively concerned with himself and with his own experiences in a way that brings Whitman inescapably to mind, he is—like Whitman—wonderfully hidden in the midst of his own creation. He is so many men and so many personalities, each sharply etched and wonderfully consistent, that the total dramatis personae of his own character-making suggests that the actual man, Hemingway, is not to be found in the sum of his images, but rather in the hidden center. For each image was undeniably a true one. There was the almost ascetic apprentice to the trade of letters whom John Peale Bishop found in Montparnasse in 1922 with an "innate and genial honesty which is the very chastity of talent."[5] The Hemingway of "the loose disquisitions, arrogant, belligerent and boastful," Edmund Wilson excoriated as "the worst-invented character to be found in the author's work";[6] this image, a shadow in *The Torrents of Spring,* makes a full appearance in *Death in the Afternoon* and in *Green Hills of Africa,* and then returns with a noisy vengeance in Lillian Ross's *New Yorker* Profile[7] and in *Across the River and into the Trees.* The Hemingway of the Spanish Civil War, "big and lumbering, with the look of a worried boy on his round face," whom Arturo Barea describes in Madrid in 1937,[8] is as valid a persona as the intrepid, swashbuckling Hemingway who risked his life daily in the filming of *The Spanish Earth* and who presided nightly over the carefree parties in his shelled hotel room in the Hotel Florida (see *The Fifth Column*).

Hemingway was at times all of these figures and more. He was a craftsman dedicated to the art of letters who rarely wavered in his adherence to the highest standards of artistic probity and who significantly influenced twentieth-century writing on all levels through his aesthetic pronouncements and the principles of professionalism which he introduced and lived.[9] But he was also a night-club roisterer; a slick and chromatically unreal advertisement in the rotogravures; unfailingly "good copy" for the gossip columnists; public brawler and braggart;[10] and the "batter'd, wreck'd old man" who appeared to Seymour Betsky and Leslie Fiedler in November 1960 as "an unsure schoolboy," desperately uncertain and frail.[11]

It would be easily possible to multiply almost endlessly the paradoxes of Hemingway's biographical identity. Born into an upper-middle-class milieu that seems almost a caricature of late nineteenth-century Protestant respectability and conventionality,[12] he single-handedly revivified the Byronic stereotype of the artist-adventurer. The foremost publicizer of metaphysical nada in our time, consistently preaching the importance of determining values on the basis of one's honest empirical experience, he converted to Roman Catholicism after the Italian campaign in World War I, and referred to himself for the rest of his life as "a rotten Catholic." Although he regarded the end of a marriage as a personal defeat,[13] he married four times—and each time to a Midwestern American woman who was seemingly quite unlike the docile European heroines whom he and Hollywood made famous through his fiction.[14] The outstanding advocate of contempt for such obscene words as "glory, honor, courage, and sacrifice,"[15] his novel on the Spanish Civil War unashamedly rests on the very basis of "glorious sacrifice" implied in the title quotation *(For Whom the Bell Tolls)*. An insatiable student of literature and painting, the anti-intellectualistic bias of his temperament made him a most usable proponent for the vulgar anti-intellectual position.[16] This list could be prolonged interminably, but without adding substantially to the multiple confusions that radiate from an attempt to locate the coordinates of Hemingway's character. A giant in twentieth-century literature, he can be made to seem a pygmy in many aspects of his blustering, adolescent career. And, conversely, a carefully angled study of his life and works can make him seem "the dumb ox" of letters[17] and a paragon of courage and generosity in his nonliterary life.[18]

And yet, in a curious sense, Hemingway's life and work is of a single piece, possessing total human congruity within the remarkable poses, the paradoxes, the violent shifts in attitude. His response to the terrors and uncertainties that contemporary life appeared on the verge of launching against him was the aggressive defense of guerrilla warfare—a ruthless behind-the-lines infiltration, ambush, espionage, and counterespionage. If it is best to be shifty in a new country, it is also possible to become practically invisible there by projecting so many contradictory images of one's self that one can ultimately become concealed in the center. We are reminded of the practice of dispatching surrogate kings to feudal battlefields so that the enemy might exhaust itself on their armor. And for Hemingway, fiercely competitive in everything he did, all that was not himself (animals, terrain, weather, other people, Nature, life itself) and some things, indeed, that were himself (his ambition, his talents, his ineffaceable tenderness and sensitivity, his sadistic and even his sensual desires) were potentially or actually of the enemy camp.

Although he does not formally codify the irreconcilable conflict until *A Farewell to Arms* (1929), this view is foundational in his writings from 8 July 1918 (the date of his first wound),[19] and it is retrospective from that to the memories of his earliest childhood:[20] "If people bring so much courage to this world the world has to kill them to break them, so of course it kills them. The world breaks every one and afterward many are strong at the broken places. But those that will not break it kills. It kills the very good and the very gentle and the very brave impartially. If you are none of these you can be sure it will kill you, too, but there will be no special hurry" (249). W. M. Frohock points up this overwhelming sense of hostile isolation as a cardinal element in Hemingway's work: "From the beginning he has been concerned less with the relations between human beings than with the relations between himself, or some projection of himself, and a harsh and mainly alien universe in which violence, suffering, and death are the rule, and which, in terms of what the human being expects of it, stubbornly refuses to make sense."[21] This donnée of unappeasable isolation was to shape his art as thoroughly as it shaped the direction of his life and personality, but we must reserve discussion of the former for chapter 2 and concentrate for the moment on the man with the many masks.

Implicit in the quoted passage from *A Farewell to Arms* is the controlling metaphor of the game, or the contest: "The world breaks every one and afterward many are strong at the broken places. But those that will not break it kills." This statement indicates that it behooves man to learn how to be broken that he may mend himself for his savage encounter with the world. This also suggests that some rules guide the contest, ruthless and unjust as it may be: "You did not know what it was about. You never had time to learn. They threw you in and told you the rules and the first time they caught you off base they killed you" (327). The epigraph that Hemingway wrote for his volume of short stories, *Winner Take Nothing* (1932),[22] develops the game metaphor further: "Unlike all other forms of lutte or combat the conditions are that the winner shall take nothing; neither his ease, nor his pleasure, nor any notions of glory; nor, if he win far enough, shall there be any reward within himself."

A year earlier, in *Death in the Afternoon*, he had described the significant difference between the *suertes* of a good bullfighter and those that were without emotion and relevance:

It is the difference between playing cards with an individual who, giving no importance to the game and having no sum at stake, gives no attention to the rules and makes the game impossible and one who having learned the rules, through having them forced on him and through losing; and now, having his fortune and life at stake, gives much importance to the game and the rules, finding them forced upon him, and does his best with utmost seriousness. It is up to the bullfighter to make the bull play and to enforce the rules. The bull has no desire to play, only to kill.[23]

From 1918 until the end of his life (and also probably long before 1918), Hemingway gave his utmost concentration to the rules, playing his game for survival with all the means at his disposal. His rootlessness is a matter of public legend; freed from the financial necessity of holding a regular job by the commercial success of *A Farewell to Arms,* he and his retinue roamed through four continents—to the delight of the photographers—in search of excitement and new sensations, but also to keep from being trapped in one place.[24]

His record of unsuccessful marriages and his often violently shattered friendships (particularly with Sherwood Anderson and Gertrude Stein),[25] as well as his occasionally unprovoked attacks on relatively harmless individuals,[26] project a picture of a man hypersensitively ready to strike out against a potential foe before he himself is struck. And it may be significant that, in all of his fiction, Hemingway—who is, after all, our modern poet of camaraderie—nowhere depicts a really mutual friendship. The closest is perhaps between Frederic Henry and Rinaldi in *A Farewell to Arms,* but even there the two characters move through their own self-propelled orbits; they share little except wine and bright conversation. The pattern is similar between Jake Barnes and Bill Gorton of *The Sun Also Rises* and between Thomas Hudson and Roger Davis of *Islands in the Stream;* and, although some of the later fiction chronicles with delicacy a relationship of mutual respect between persons (Robert Jordan and Anselmo, especially), the evidence suggests that Hemingway was not a man inclined to expose himself to the trust that friendship requires.[27]

In this context his notorious female characterizations ("There isn't any me. I'm you. Don't make up a separate me." [*F,* 115]), in which the beloved is totally subservient to the intermittent desires of the lover, offer added evidence. A love affair can conceivably expose the man to the shock of his partner's impregnating personality; for this to happen, however, there must be at least a relaxing of the taut barriers with which the male protects his inmost self. Hemingway's lovers—Frederic Henry, Harry Morgan, Robert Jordan, Philip Rawlings, Richard Cantwell—are genuinely moved by the pleasure and devotion their respective sweethearts generously proffer upon them; they are profoundly disturbed by the impersonal malice of life in those instances where death or duty put abrupt ends to their happy affairs; but in no case does the private circle of their most personal experience of themselves seem seriously affected.[28] They all seem to have taken strongly to heart the advice of the Major of "In Another Country" that a man must not marry: "He should not place himself in a position to lose. He should find things he cannot lose" (*SS,* 271).

Not surprisingly, then, Hemingway's instinctual need to defend himself in a hostile world and his device of multiple personality-screens led to the creation of a series of images—personal, fictional, and legendary—that would have a profound appeal for his fellow writers and his readers between 1926 and 1941. The mood that marked the 1920s—of expatriation and alienation, of massive disillusionment with traditional values of all kinds, of deep-rooted distrust of any sort of collective venture—was tailor-made for the young romantic iconoclast who was learning to write above a carpenter shop in the rue de Notre Dame des Champs.[29] He had certain distinct personal advantages to offer: he was attractive, athletic, and quick to learn languages; his journalistic background and his instinctive concern with how things work gave him at least the appearance of the insider's expertise in a foreign situation; he had the bizarre experience of having served, been wounded, and decorated in a foreign army. And his rebellion against the conventional mores of American rural-and-village life patterns antedated the disenchantment of World War I. (Hemingway had run away from home several times while in high school, and, of course, had never attended college.)[30]

On top of this he was patiently teaching himself the craft of fiction. Working with Gertrude Stein and Ezra Pound and with the horrors of his own experience, Hemingway was carving out a prose style that would be (in Ford Madox Ford's phrase) as new and clean as "pebbles fresh from a brook."[31] It is not surprising, therefore, that such contemporaries as Edmund Wilson, John Peale Bishop, and F. Scott Fitzgerald should see in the Hemingway of 1925 a potential new Moses (or at least a Joshua) who might lead American art out of the arid deserts of the nineteenth century into a Promised Land beyond imagining.

The images and texture of his fiction also insured him a favorable reception with the reading audiences of the 1920s and 1930s. His prose was fast and violent enough to make excellent barbershop reading; his dialogue—especially in *The Sun Also Rises*—was sophisticatedly clever enough to recall the balmy days of *The Smart*

Set. There was the delight of a well-told action story with sensationalism and forbidden sex for the common reader; for the uncommon reader the discovery of a new aesthetic for approaching literature
and evaluating life. With the publication of *A Farewell to Arms*
Hemingway's reading audience was secured, and it remained only
for him to maintain a supply of new material for its consumption.[32]
For we must remember that Hemingway's immense popularity during his lifetime took place on two distinct levels. From the October
1924 *Dial* review of *In Our Time*[33] to the *Life* magazine installments
of *The Dangerous Summer*,[34] Hemingway's work was subject to constant critical evaluation and appreciation on the most serious levels
even as it was lustily consumed by an unsophisticated mass-audi-
ence.[35] No other serious writer of Hemingway's stature in the twentieth century commanded as large and as responsive a readership
through all levels of society as he did.

Several speculations may suggest the reasons for Hemingway's
mass popularity through the 1930s which continued with *For Whom
the Bell Tolls* (1940) and with *The Old Man and the Sea* (1952). The
psychological effects of the world-wide depression of the 1930s are
far too complicated to trace in detail, but surely one effect of the
massive economic paralysis of the times was a strengthening of the
total bureaucratization of life and an increasing sense (individually
felt) of the impotence and helplessness of the single unit, man. The
traditional notion of the possibilities of heroism—in the capacity
of man to front the world with a certain degree of success, using
only the powers and resources that were his own natural inheritance—this concept of heroism had almost disappeared in serious
fiction. Readers were invited to identify with bewildered, frustrated
victims of one sort or another—Leopold Bloom, Joseph K.—or
with heroes who were unsuccessful, broken rebels—Jay Gatsby, Joe
Christmas.

Hemingway was, as Sean O'Faolain said, "the only modern writer
of real distinction for whom the Hero does in some form still live."[36]
Even though Hemingway's heroes are in a sense winners who take
nothing, they *are* winners, and the manner of their taking is individually self-generated, within situations largely of their own
choosing, and under circumstances in which their native resources
for physical action and courage are given every possibility of expression. The radical significance of the individual as an important
integer in the struggle for existence, largely denied or neglected in

the fiction of the 1920s and 1930s, is a salient first factor in Hemingway's mass popularity.

A second reason for his popularity may well be the vicarious excitement of physical and sensuous experience that Hemingway offered in abundance to an audience increasingly urban-oriented, increasingly desensitized and immunized from a physical life of full sensory response.[37] Hemingway's talent for evoking physical sensations, for transmuting into prose how it is to taste, to see, to hear, to smell, to feel in a great varity of ways is a staple ingredient of his prose. And these sensations are typically presented within a framework of physical or psychological stress, in which the narrative perspective is left open-ended so that the attentive reader is forced to serve as the "ground" for the powerful prose-currents of the presented action. That is, the sensations are not merely described, but presented within a controlled frame of dramatic awareness, and the reader is invited to participate in, as well as to observe, the bombardment of sensory stimuli. The effect of the prose on this level is a cumulative one, but perhaps the following short passage from "Big Two-Hearted River: Part II" may give a partial demonstration of this involvement:

On the left, where the meadow ended and the woods began, a great elm tree was uprooted. Gone over in a storm, it lay back into the woods, its roots clotted with dirt, grass growing in them, rising a solid bank beside the stream. The river cut to the edge of the uprooted tree. From where Nick stood he could see deep channels, like ruts, cut in the shallow bed of the stream by the flow of the current. Pebbly where he stood and pebbly and full of boulders beyond; where it curved near the tree roots, the bed of the stream was marly and between the ruts of deep water green weed fronds swung in the current. (*SS*, 227–28)

The Hemingway protagonist, like Nick in this excerpt, is actively engaged in some form of purposive activity; and the reader has no choice except to join him in the activity. At the same time, the activity of the protagonist takes place within an ambience of external activity: the grass is actively growing, the stream is actively running, the weed fronds are actively swinging, etc. If it is possible for prose to coerce vicarious sensory response at all, Hemingway's prose, with its intense concentration on action and active response, is admirably suited to secure such an effect.[38]

And finally, Hemingway the public personality (who gradually merges into Hemingway the legend) became an additional contributing element to excite the unparalleled avidity with which his stories and even his casual remarks were received. Hemingway became for a great number of readers not only the describer of heroism and physical activity but also the actual hero himself. His exploits in all forms of sport—and later his military activities—were duly recorded, improved upon, and ground out in the publicity mills of the world press. It is irrelevant that the largest part of his alleged achievements have been factually corroborated; the point is that the public life of the writer overwhelmed his writings and reentered his prose as a substantiating force for the aesthetic validity of those works. In the case of no other serious American writer except Mark Twain and Walt Whitman had the writer's personality become such an intrusive and confusing factor in the judgment and reception of his works.[39] A cursory examination of the criticism primarily directed against or in defense of the reputed Hemingway personality will give ample evidence of the confusions to which literary critics are quite justifiably susceptible.[40]

But if this consequence was a frustrating impediment to a dispassionate evaluation of Hemingway's works, it was also a final stimulus for his commercial popularity. The distinction between life and literature tended, in his case, to blur and merge. Reading Hemingway was as informative as reading the newspapers, and much more exciting. And the vision of heroism, the proof that the individual could still wage solitary battle against the elemental forces that oppress mankind, could be found not only in the breezy, tight-lipped dispatches that the legendary Hemingway sent back to *Collier's*, to *Ken*, or to *Esquire*, but also in the strained expressions of grim grandeur with which Gary Cooper sighted along the barrel of his machine gun at the Fascist cavalry lieutenant, or with which Spencer Tracy reeled in the big marlin.

Meanwhile there was an actual flesh-and-blood Hemingway behind all the masks. The poses, the shiftings of personality, the sporadic outbursts of frightened aggressiveness were the means through which Hemingway the man might survive, might forestall the destruction that he felt awaited American writers. But merely to survive was not enough. The rules of the game called for total competition—unconditional surrender on one side or the other. And the weapon that Hemingway selected—the weapon that all his personality machinations were designed to protect—was his capacity to create art: "A country, finally, erodes and the dust blows away, the people all die and none of them were of any importance permanently, except those who practised the arts. . . . A thousand years makes economics silly and a work of art endures forever . . ." (*GH*, 109). To write a prose with "nothing that will go bad afterwards" would be to achieve importance; to secure a small piece of almost tangible immortality; to gain a handsome victory over life in which, even though the winner takes nothing for himself, the mere survival is made to yield a product that will endure forever.

Undisputed champion in 1929, Hemingway's publications of the next decade did little to increase his literary stature. Except for a half dozen short stories, his volumes of the 1930s were generally inferior productions. Although *Death in the Afternoon* (1932) can be defended on special grounds and although interesting things can be found in *Green Hills of Africa* (1935), it was difficult for even his fiercest partisans to find much to applaud in *To Have and Have Not* (1937) or *The Fifth Column* (1938). On top of this, the chilly winds of social and political doctrines had virtually dispelled the pleasant laissez-faire airs of aestheticism that had nurtured Hemingway's original emergence into the literary scene in the 1920s.[41] The lone-wolf Hemingway hero and the lone-wolf Hemingway, hunting luxuriously in Africa and Wyoming and fishing the Gulf Stream for sport while millions were unemployed and the world seemed to be organizing itself toward total collapse, were not palatable images for many critics and intellectuals of the mid-1930s, although it is doubtful that the common reader was disturbed. Hemingway's partial renunciation of "the separate peace" in his decision to go to Spain and his publication of *For Whom the Bell Tolls* (1940), followed by the war years (1941–45), gave a temporary surcease to the critics and probably also to Hemingway's struggles for immortality.

But the game he had elected to play was a relentless one. Santiago, in *The Old Man and the Sea,* could very well be speaking for his author as he describes his attitude in the face of the new encounter: "The thousand times that he had proved it meant nothing. Now he was proving it again. Each time was a new time and he never thought about the past when he was doing it."[42] Nor was there any possibility for Hemingway to avoid the new encounters; to live meant to struggle with all that was not himself, and this in turn required him to write continually a prose that would not go bad.

It is hard for us to believe that he could have judged *Across the River and into the Trees* (1950) to be superior to *A Farewell to Arms*.[43] And we wonder whether his statement to the Nobel Prize Committee that "it is because we have had such great writers in the past that a writer is driven far out past where he can go, out to where no one can help him,"[44] is either literary cliché or the proclamation of a terrifying desperation and loneliness. Our own notion would hold the latter to be true since it yields some explanation of the last seven years of Hemingway's life. The magic capacity to turn out prose would seem to have gone bad;[45] and, with the collapse of the ultimate weapon against life, the ironic control over the masks and poses must have been lost.

He who was so careful to guard his inmost privacy during his flourishing times would not be prone to expose himself in his hurt. Nevertheless, Hemingway's family, friends, and assorted hangers-on have violated that privacy and have let us glimpse the last years of his life, years of a very special kind of agony under which he was only sometimes brave under the agony.[46] And although it is inexcusably arrogant to theorize on such matters, it is possible to find his death predictable and in keeping with the total pattern of his life. All readers of Hemingway know his special concern with suicide (his father had shot himself in 1928); it provides a theme for "Fathers and Sons" and an undercurrent for Robert Jordan's reminiscences in *For Whom the Bell Tolls*. Suicide appears in most of Hemingway's works as a complete abrogation of the rules of the game. It is even worse than dying badly, which is in accordance, at least, with the rules. His views on death were aggressively expounded to Lillian Ross in May 1950: "I'll make the prettiest corpse since Pretty Boy Floyd. Only suckers worry about saving their souls. Who the hell should care about saving his soul when it's a man's duty to lose it intelligently, the way you would sell a position you were defending, if you could not hold it, as expensively as possible, trying to make it the most expensive position that was ever sold. It isn't hard to die. . . . No more worries. . . . It takes a pretty good man to make any sense when he's dying."[47]

Perhaps it is fair to assume that Hemingway's death was his way of selling a position that could no longer be held, and that for him this was the most intelligent way to handle the necessary transaction. Having chosen to do battle with nothing less than eternity on a day-to-day basis, it may have been his way of complying with the rules insofar as the rules required the unconditional surrender of one of the combatants. It is also possible that his death was Hemingway's calculated punishment of that aspect of himself that had failed him in his need. Just as his creativity had been his prime resource in the struggle for a small piece of immortality, so death would strike with unerring accuracy at the part that had offended—at the creativity itself. And finally, without negating these two possibilities, there is always the chance that his death was Hemingway's final act of personality prestidigitation. The master juggler, in danger of having his whole spinning world fall in shambles at his feet— himself naked and powerless to control—could in one final manipulation of a new mask put a triumphant crown to his whole glittering career. These are, of course, unfounded speculations, but there is no need to assume that Hemingway was any less shifty in the new country that he left, than he was when he entered. Nor is it idle sentimentality to suppose that if any man could make sense—in Hemingway's terms—when he was dying, it would be Hemingway himself.

Chapter Two
The Real Thing

In the preceding chapter we noticed that the act of writing performed at least two functions for Hemingway: it was his weapon against an alien universe—the means by which he kept himself alive; and it was the battlefield in which he struggled for a small piece of immortality. Both of these are good personal reasons for a man to become a writer, and both have long and respectable antecedents in the history of literature.[1] But neither reason throws much illumination on the underlying principles that govern Hemingway's typical artistic approach and technique. These reasons have relevance solely to Hemingway, but they suggest no connection between Hemingway and the rest of the world.

If we can discover what it is that he intends his fictions to accomplish—what it is that they must do to be "right"—we will be in a better position to examine and properly judge the results. And Hemingway has been characteristically both forthright and deceptive in his statements about his artistic purposes; he has stated frequently and positively that he is concerned with capturing "truth," with transcribing accurately "the way it was." "Let those who want to save the world if you can get to see it clear and as a whole. Then any part you make will represent the whole if it's made truly" (*D*, 278).[2] His statements have an impressive authoritarian ring, but *truth*—one of Hemingway's favorite words—is a protean entity in a metaphysic founded on incessant conflict where the winner takes nothing. It may, then, be more sensible to approach Hemingway's aesthetic from a roundabout direction and to ignore for the moment his excessive protestations of the "true."

As a starting point we may note that Hemingway's consistent test for the authenticity of an art object is the involuntary subjective response of the perceiver. When Robert Jordan in *For Whom the Bell Tolls* repeats to himself the dying speech of Maria's mother, "He knew it was good because it made a tingle run all over him when he said it to himself" (355). Similarly, watching his first bullfight before he had trained himself to discriminate between good and bad bulls, or good and bad bullfighters, Hemingway recalls being profoundly moved by the kill: "I remembered in the midst of this confused excitement having a great moment of emotion when the man went in with the sword." He is careful to point out that it was not just the act of killing, but the properly administered (aesthetically correct) act of killing that caused his emotion, since he watched the slaughter of some fifty more bulls before this emotion was elicited again (*D*, 234–35). It is perhaps relevant to note that at late as 1954, Hemingway subjected his writing to the same kinetic test; if his writing raised gooseflesh on Miss Mary's (his wife's) arms, he knew it must be good.[3] We suppose all artists invoke some variety of kinetic test, but Hemingway seems to have taken this more seriously than most—seems, indeed, to have made the stimulation of an emotion in the reader a cardinal point in his aesthetic. The consequences of this—the primacy of *feelings* in his notion of morality as well as art—will become obvious and far-reaching.

The first effect is to give the artist a special role in human affairs, a role that will separate him from his audience as decisively as the *barrera* separates the paying spectators from the brave matador. And given Hemingway's temperamental obsession with himself and his insatiate need to be an "insider," a professional who performs rather than a customer who watches, this separation between artist and audience has a strong tendency to turn into a competition between them and, indeed, to become even an assault in which the artist has all the good cards in his hands. It is difficult to discuss this concept without overstating the case; but, if we overstate it now for the sake of clarity, we can make the proper redresses later. Typically Hemingway will use the metaphors of games, sports, bullfights, and wars to describe his views on life. The Passion of Christ is described within the values of prizefighting terminology ("Today Is Friday"), as is the prowess of military leaders and great artists. Baseball, football, horse racing, hunting, and fishing provide him with his consistent metaphors for expression.[4] But the significance of this use goes deeper than colorful atmosphere and the often-noted aggressive competitiveness that marked Hemingway's literary and nonliterary career. The metaphor of violent games provided Hemingway with a structure in which he could cast his aesthetic—present again and again his portraits of the artist as hunter, fisherman, matador, soldier, prizefighter, and gambler.

One of the few extraneous scenes in *The Sun Also Rises*—and, at the same time, a passage that seems to be so honestly felt that it obtrudes from the carefully controlled "theatricalness" of the main narrative—concerns itself with the appearance of Juan Belmonte in the Pamplona bull ring. Belmonte has returned from retirement, sick and forced to battle the legend of his former prowess as well as the bulls:

The public, who wanted three times as much from Belmonte, who was sick with a fistula, as Belmonte had ever been able to give, felt defrauded and cheated, and Belmonte's jaw came further out in contempt, and his face turned yellower, and he moved with greater difficulty as his pain increased, and finally the crowd were actively against him, and he was utterly contemptuous and indifferent. He had meant to have a great afternoon, and instead it was an afternoon of sneers, shouted insults, and finally a volley of cushions and pieces of bread and vegetables, thrown down at him in the plaza where he had had his greatest triumphs. His jaw only went further out. Sometimes he turned to smile that toothed, long-jawed, lipless smile when he was called something particularly insulting, and always the pain that any movement produced grew stronger and stronger, until finally his yellow face was parchment color, and after his second bull was dead and the throwing of bread and cushions was over, after he had saluted the President with the same wolf-jawed smile and contemptuous eyes, and handed his sword over the barrera to be wiped, and put back in its case, he passed through into the callejon and leaned on the barrera below us, his head on his arms, not seeing, not hearing anything, only going through his pain. When he looked up, finally, he asked for a drink of water. He swallowed a little, rinsed his mouth, spat the water, took his cape, and went back into the ring.[5]

Hemingway seems to have felt the significance of this scene so strongly that he was unable to eradicate it from the narrative, where it serves only as a contrasting foil for Pedro Romero's success.[6] The centrality of this image to his thinking can be seen when we remember how many of his heroes are winners who perform valiantly only to have their prizes taken away or scorned. Manuel of "The Undefeated" has the same contempt and indifference for the crowd as Belmonte does, and suffers even greater disdain. Francis Macomber stands before the charge of the buffalo in perfect accord with the hunting code; and his wife—the *only* nonprofessional observer—rewards him by blasting out his brains. Richard Cantwell (*Across the River and into the Trees*) makes a career of being a good soldier and is deranked from the General Staff as a result. And Santiago lands the biggest marlin in the history of literature only to lose it, piece by piece, to the voracious sharks.

The portrait of the artist that begins to emerge is that of the individual compelled by his special talents, or sensitivities, or hurts (and at times, Hemingway would seem to equate all three) to accept life as a kind of game. This he (the artist-player) does not choose to do, if he is a serious player; the choice is forced upon him:

> It is a vast wheel, set at an angle, and each time it goes around and then is back to where it starts. One side is higher than the other and the sweep it makes lifts you back and down to where you started. There are no prizes either, he thought, and no one would choose to ride this wheel. You ride it each time and make the turn with no intention ever to have mounted. There is only one turn; one large, elliptical, rising and falling turn and you are back where you have started. (*FW*, 225)

Once he has made his commitment to the game, however, the contract is eternally binding; he is arbitrarily defined in the universe as a bullfighter (like Manuel), as a fisherman (like Santiago), as a soldier (like Cantwell), as a writer—like Hemingway. The rules of the game require that he learn his trade as swiftly and thoroughly as possible, that he strive to be better at his craft than anyone has ever been, and that he have a deep humility and respect for the materials within and against which he must practice his craft. These materials would include bulls, marlins and the sea, opposing soldiers and the terrain on which battles must be fought, wild game, words, and one's experience of the past. Nothing else, himself included, is worthy of respect.

But the conflict rarely takes place in a social vacuum. Conceivably a matador could fight bulls without an audience, even as a hunter or a fisherman goes off to the woods alone to exercise his sporting talents. Conceivably, also, a writer can wrestle with language and float his results on pieces of rice paper down the nearest river. But such a writer would have to possess a very secure sense of oneness with the universe—precisely that sense that we have seen to be severely lacking in Hemingway's orientation. Thus the composite portrait of Hemingway's artist requires an audience in order that the poetic execution of the craft can be made in some sense permanent. Let us return to *Death in the Afternoon,* which serves in so many ways as Hemingway's principles of poetic composition:

It is impossible to believe the emotional and spiritual intensity and pure, classic beauty that can be produced by a man, an animal and a piece of scarlet serge draped over a stick. If you do not choose to believe it possible and want to regard it all as nonsense you may be able to prove you are right by going to a bullfight in which nothing magical occurs. . . . But if you should ever see the real thing you would know it. It is an experience that either you will have in your life or you will never have. . . . But if you ever do see one, finished by a great estocada, you will know it and there will be many things you will forget before it will be gone. (207)

Again we find the touchstone of the kinetic experience—the something "magical" that occurs in the successful performance of an art. This is made more definite in a succeeding passage:

Now the essence of the greatest emotional appeal of bullfighting is the feeling of immortality that the bullfighter feels in the middle of a great faena and that he gives to the spectators. He is performing a work of art and he is playing with death, bringing it closer, closer, closer, to himself, a death that you know is in the horns because you have the canvas-covered bodies of the horses on the sand to prove it. He gives the feeling of his immortality, and, as you watch it, it becomes yours. Then when it belongs to both of you, he proves it with the sword. (213)

This, then, is the ideal Hemingway artist—the man who in the midst of a great *faena* makes an imperishable poem of his own body and patterned gestures, who achieves immortality through the perfection of his controlled dance with death, and who has so well educated or sensitized his audience that he can allow them to share in the immortality that he has created.

This is the ideal portrait of the artist for Hemingway, but even as an ideal it has serious deficiencies for him. The bullfight takes place in time, and the feeling of immortality is communicated in time. And although he suggests optimistically that "there will be many things you will forget before it will be gone," it is inevitable that it too will be forgotten, or falsified by memory. Thus his first problem is to discover a medium—"a fourth and fifth dimension" in prose—that will hold the emotion of immortality. Then there is the second problem of the audience. In the ideal portrait, the audience is composed entirely of aficionados like Hemingway; in actual practice—both in bull rings and among reading audiences—

the spectators are not worthy to share the Host. They are uninformed, or uninvolved, or too calloused and cynical to be receptive to mysteries. Further, they can easily become antagonistic to the artist; they will try to sap his strength and to bribe him away from the integrity of his dedication through the classic temptations of wealth, power, sex, or easy indolence. The actual audience is the great enemy for the artist because without it he is consigned to an endless narcissistic exhibitionism; but with it he is always in danger of being dragged down to its seamy, time-serving level. And the third problem with the ideal portrait is the difficulty of persuading one's self or one's audience that the artist "is playing with death, bringing it closer, closer, closer, to himself" when he is merely tapping typewriter keys or writing in longhand while he stands up to a writing-table.[7] Hemingway's efforts to solve these deficiencies, or to learn to live with them, should explain the development of his aesthetic.

Before we attempt to describe this development, we must first examine Hemingway's one careful presentation of a nonideal portrait of an artist; for against this we may test our perceptions. Although many of Hemingway's heroes might nominally qualify as artists— Jake Barnes, writer; Nick Adams, writer; Frederic Henry, architect; Richard Cantwell, expert in general; Robert Jordan, writer; Thomas Hudson, painter—only Harry of "The Snows of Kilimanjaro" is presented convincingly as a writer; and only he seems actively concerned with the problems created by his calling.[8] Structurally the story is rather simple—a variation on Ambrose Bierce's classic "An Occurrence at Owl Creek Bridge." Harry, the writer, tries to come to terms with the fact of his approaching death; he has a badly gangrenous leg which is too far advanced to be cured, even though a rescue airplane is expected on the following day to carry him out of the African bush to the nearest hospital. He spends the afternoon and early evening quarreling with his wealthy wife, berating himself for having wasted his talents, remembering sharp vignettes of the past that he had always intended to use in his writing but never did. The last section of the story (as in Bierce's model) is a description of the arrival of the airplane and its ascent to the top of Kilimanjaro: "great, high, and unbelievably white in the sun." Then the story flashes back to the dead Harry discovered by his wife, and we realize that the airplane ride was Hemingway's trick on the reader. The story is prefaced by the following epigraph: "Kilimanjaro is a snow-covered mountain 19,710 feet high, and is said to be the highest mountain in Africa. Its western summit is called the Masai 'Ngàje Ngài,' the House of God. Close to the western summit there is the dried and frozen carcass of a leopard. No one has explained what the leopard was seeking at that altitude" (SS, 52).[9]

Thematically the story is also relatively simple, and it is reminiscent of Henry James's "The Middle Years" in which another writer confronts the fact of death and berates himself and life for not having time enough to write the things he is now ready to do. If we approach "The Snows of Kilimanjaro" from the special view with which we have been concerned, we will see that Hemingway used a traditional structure and a conventional theme to achieve his own peculiar ends; and we will also see that Harry is a kind of extended portrait of the artist, similar in attitude to the portrait of Belmonte previously cited.

First, there are some obvious, paired contrasts within the story: the snow, clean and cold on the mountain top and in Harry's reminiscence, as against "the heat shimmer of the plain," which becomes associated with the ugly rotting leg. Similarly, "the dried and frozen carcass" of the leopard is contrasted to the wide-snouted hyena, which is the harbinger and final announcer of Harry's death. Through various devices, Helen is contrasted with Harry and associated with the heat, the plain, the gangrene, and the hyena. The contrasts are all neat and in balance, with the exception of Harry; he, of course, is connected to the leg, Helen, and the hyena—even as he dreams of the snow and the ascent beyond the plain. And it is Harry's character that provides the key to the story. He is not, at all, a nice man. He is a liar, a quarreler, and a traitor to himself as well as to other people. "He had sold vitality, in one form or another, all his life and when your affections are not too involved you give much better value for the money" (SS, 61). He had married Helen, he tells us, for security and comfort, and he had never loved her. And yet, "it was strange . . . that he should be able to give her more for her money than when he had really loved" (SS, 60–61).

Several things should be obvious. Harry is egocentric, hypocritical, and morally as well as physically rotten; and yet the thrust of values in the story elevates him to the snow-capped summit and forces the reader to accept him as a superior man. Helen, on the other hand, is honest, generous, and reasonably intelligent; yet she is left at the end of the story with the unbandaged leg that she cannot bear to look at. Harry disposes of her for himself and for the reader in one sentence: "She was always thoughtful, he thought. On anything she knew about, or had read, or that she had ever heard" (*SS*, 59). On normal standards of valuation, this would seem to be generous praise; but in terms of the story, it is clear that this is enough to make Helen despicable. Harry, it would seem, is thoughtful on things he does not know about, has not read, and has not ever heard. He is justly contemptuous of artists, like Julian (F. Scott Fitzgerald), who have been wrecked. He is justly contemptuous of Helen and her total milieu; he is "a spy in their country" and, by implication, a mysterious stranger in all countries save that which he shares with a frozen leopard at an altitude of almost 20,000 feet. And the only source of his marvellous superiority is that "for years it [death] had obsessed him; but now it meant nothing in itself" (*SS*, 54). That, and the fact that in the face of death, he performs his craft; he writes. [10] This is what makes him superior; this is what gives him "the feeling of immortality" which is vouchsafed to him in his ascent to the mountain.

The portrait of Harry is thus very similar to the earlier picture of Belmonte. Both are sick with disgust at their unknowing audiences (Helen is Harry's audience), but both, presumably, attain a level of inner possession which can only be called beatific. Harry differs from Belmonte in that he manages in an offhand way to satisfy his audience even with the gangrene. The remarkable tour de force of the story is that Hemingway is able to present a thoroughly upside-down world to readers who must not be very different from Helen—and to make them like it. And here we must mention the hyena in order to appreciate the full resonance of the tour de force. The hyena is introduced into the story in such a way as to connect it to the obscenely squatting vultures that sit with their "naked heads sunk in their hunched feathers," presumably waiting for Harry's death. It, like them, is called "a filthy animal" and a "bastard," and it is quickly associated with the "sudden evil-smelling emptiness" that characterizes the approach of both the gangrene and death in the narrative. But after Harry dies, the hyena appears again: "Just then the hyena stopped whimpering in the night and started to make a strange, human, almost crying sound" (*SS*, 76). He continues to do this until Helen wakes up and discovers the corpse. If the hyena were simply meant to stand for death, its continual symbolic use is a foolish distraction which dissipates the force of the story. And why the emphasis on "human," especially since the hyena's crying is almost the first "human" sound in the story?

It is possible to suggest an interpretation for the hyena that will be in keeping with the reading of the story and the portraiture of the artist that we have been examining, if we call to mind Hemingway's description of the "highly humorous" hyena in *Green Hills of Africa*. The hyena is a source of much amusement in that book because of the obscenely funny contortions that he goes through when he is shot: "the pinnacle of hyenic humor, was the hyena, the classic hyena, that hit too far back while running, would circle madly, snapping and tearing at himself until he pulled his own intestines out, and then stood there, jerking them out and eating them with relish. . . . Fisi, the hyena, hermaphroditic, self-eating devourer of the dead, trailer of calving cows, ham-stringer, potential biter-off of your face at night while you slept, sad yowler, camp-follower, stinking, foul . . . mongrel dog-smart in the face . . ." (37–38). The despicable hyena joins Helen in weeping for the dead artist, because the hyena becomes a distended identification of the audience that the artist must serve. Fickle, treacherous, stupid, and cunning at the same time, it is quick to lament the loss of the artist, even as it is quick to harry him down when he is alive. Without pushing the metaphor too far, it is fair to say that Hemingway succeeds in this story in insulting his audience beyond endurance, in making the audience eat its own wounds, and like it. There is surely a more than savage irony in the "human, almost crying sound" that ends the tale; and the reflection that Hemingway was reputed to have received $125,000 for the movie rights to this story merely compounds the irony.[11]

If this description of Hemingway's attitudes as an artist seems somewhat harsh, we should look again at the stance that Hemingway aggressively assumed against life: "You never saw a counter-puncher who was punchy. Never lead against a hitter unless you can outhit him. Crowd a boxer, and take everything he has to get inside. Duck a swing. Block a hook. And counter a jab with everything you own. Papa's delivery of hard-learned facts of life."[12]

Papa's delivery of hard-learned facts of life should teach us, then, to be chary in approaching his fiction. It will attempt to create an emotional charge of some sort, but more often than not, the charge will be exploded at the vulnerability of the unwitting reader. The success of the fiction, in part, will depend upon the author's ability to "lead" the reader, to hook him soundly, and when he is hooked and wriggling against the wall, to administer the gaff accurately and well. Many critics have noticed the tendencies of Hemingway's sporting and bullfighting descriptions to move into areas usually connotative of the writing process:

He looked down into the water and watched the lines that went straight down into the dark of the water. He kept them straighter than anyone did, so that at each level in the darkness of the stream there would be a bait waiting exactly where he wished it to be for any fish that swam there. Others let them drift with the current and sometimes they were at sixty fathoms when the fishermen thought they were at a hundred.

But, he thought, I keep them with precision. Only I have no luck any more. But who knows? Maybe today. Every day is a new day. It is better to be lucky. But I would rather be exact. Then when luck comes you are ready. [13]

We are reminded of Hemingway's evaluation of Edgar Allan Poe's work: "It is skillful, marvelously constructed, and it is dead" (*GH*, 20). Seemingly, then, the prose "that has never been written," the prose "without tricks and without cheating," the prose "with nothing that will go bad afterwards," will be like Poe's except that it will be alive. And while Hemingway was seeking this prose in the early 1920s, there was an abundance of individual writers and movements from which he could borrow, if he wanted to, and which he could easily adapt to his own ends.

For the sake of simplicity, we will restrict the discussion of Hemingway and the influences upon him to five rather arbitrarily selected areas. It must be remembered, of course, that the creation of a prose style hardly follows the mechanical principles of a cake recipe and that a writer as eagerly educable and eclectic as Hemingway is particularly unresponsive to this kind of analysis. The attempt to discuss influences is justifiable, however, in that it may give us a rough idea of what Hemingway was doing to fashion the medium that would contain "the emotional intensity" that he required and, at the same time, be subservient to the special kind of assault that seems to have been a psychological necessity for him to launch. [14]

A major discernible influence was undoubtedly Ring Lardner's, whose exploitation of the world of the sports page and savagely ironic techniques of presentation paralleled Hemingway's interests acutely.[15] Writing for *Trapeze* (the Oak Park High School literary paper), and later for *Ciao* (the newsletter intermittently distributed by the Red Cross Ambulance Unit in Italy), Hemingway consciously imitated Lardner. Hemingway adapted Lardner's poker-faced, first-person narrator's mode of presentation to the area of local interests that both chatty newspapers required. Thus, in *Ciao* we find this early Hemingway: "Well Al we are here in this old Italy and now that I am here I am not going to leave it. Not at all if any. And that is not no New Years revolution Al but the truth. Well Al I am now an officer and if you would meet me you have to salute me. What I am is a provisional acting second lieutenant without a commission but the trouble is that all the other fellows are too. There ain't no privates in our army Al and the Captain is called a chef. But he don't look to me as tho he could cook a damn bit."[16] Although it would be foolish to exaggerate their importance, we can find many likenesses to the kind of fiction that Hemingway was to produce in Lardner's *You Know Me, Al* collection and in his later short stories, "Haircut" and "Alibi Ike." There is a strong similarity in the mordant and sardonic attitudes of the two writers, as well as a common penchant for adopting a mask that will conceal the bitter, shocked responses of the authors to the cruelty and injustice of life. Hemingway's vignettes of violence in *in our time* and his pieces like "Mr. and Mrs. Elliot," "After the Storm," and "A Natural History of the Dead" have significant affinities with the structural devices of Lardner's fiction, which aim to evoke an overwhelming disgust with what they are innocuously presenting under a mask of naive or ignorant acceptance. It might not even be too far out of line to suppose that Hemingway caught in Lardner's humor his own first glimpse of that "toothed, long-jawed, lipless smile" which was Belmonte's measure of contempt for the audience he was serving. We ought also to remember that Hemingway in *The Torrents of Spring* (1926) made his feeble obeisances to the ghost of Henry Fielding and that, although traditional satire was never within the control of his talents, it is almost always an ingredient of them.[17] Thus, Hemingway could have found in Lardner an early model on which to base his experiments in colloquial speech-patterns and in modes of narrative presentation, as well as a kindred spirit in mordancy and spiritual outrage.

Another major influence in the formation of Hemingway's style was his journalistic experience on the *Kansas City Star* (1917–18) and the *Toronto Daily Star* and *Star Weekly* (1919–23).[18] It is as easy to overestimate this influence as it is to undervalue it, but certain factual observations can be made. Hemingway's seven months on the *Kansas City Star* must undoubtedly have stimulated some characteristics that were latent in him and have introduced him to a discipline not at all uncongenial to that which he later developed into a cult. The famous *Star* style sheet—"Use short sentences. Use short first paragraphs. Use vigorous English. Be positive, not negative"—and the exacting tutelage of C. G. Wellington, the assistant city editor, could have helped to train the embryonic writer—just out of high school—to a kind of stripped, nonliterary use of language where the standards of readability, accuracy, and economy would be the paramount determinants of the way scenes and events were described. Similarly, the presence of Lionel Calhoun Moise on the *Star* staff at that time, whose favorite literary advice was, "Pure objective writing is the only true form of storytelling," gives a startling anticipatory foreshadowing of the kind of story Hemingway was to make famous. Hemingway's later employment on the two affiliated Toronto newspapers where he was given freer scope to his activities, and encouraged to write "human interest" and "humorous" stories, would not have caused him to unlearn anything of value that he brought from Kansas City. What he learned would, on the other hand, give him a range of flexibility within which to experiment with prose as he could never have done on the *Star*.

There are also some less tangible areas which Hemingway's experiences as newspaper reporter and correspondent must have interlocked with the steady construction of his prose style and vision. First and obviously, he was placed in a position where he had to write on a daily earn-a-living basis. For a man who was convinced that the rules of the game required the player to learn his craft as quickly and thoroughly as possible, no better opportunity could have offered itself than the compulsory routine that journalism demanded. It is probably true that these advantages quickly reach a point of diminishing returns; but, for the apprentice Hemingway, the almost-five years of his newspaper experience gave him a training in the manipulation of words which neither a college education nor private experimentation in writing could have afforded.

Second, and certainly equal in importance, his initiation into the newspaperman's point of view must have struck a responsive chord in Hemingway's spirit. Confronting the hundreds of items of petty human behavior that stack the city desk of a major city journal every day; deliberately seeking the isolated scenes of grotesquerie, violence, and corruption that are the standard components of "the news"; and excitedly following the hospital, the police station, and the city hall beats, Hemingway must have found strong corroboration for his already developed sense of alienation. He found not only a mine of material to use effectively in his short stories, but also an episodic picture of the way life actually was.

Hemingway's newspaper experience—furthering his cynical distrust of hypocrisies of rhetoric and sharpening his critical sensitivities to men's concealed motivations—undoubtedly strengthened his insider's attitude. The assumption of the professional's expertise gained by knowing the inside story, by interviewing such international celebrities as Clemenceau and Mussolini, would incorporate his instinctive distrust into a refusal to "be taken in" by the game; and it would harden his determination to be on the side of the manipulators rather than the manipulated. In sum, Hemingway's background as a reporter did much the same for him that it had done earlier for Mark Twain and Theodore Dreiser: it supported him while he learned to write, it gave him the professional's arrogant contempt for the amateur and the tourist (who are always "innocents abroad"), it made him too knowing ever to be comfortable or acceptant in any situation, and it trained him in a special way of seeing what life was really about.

Hemingway's indebtedness to Sherwood Anderson is more difficult to assess; it is likely, in fact, that Hemingway himself overestimated the influence, which may account for the unnecessary savagery of his parody of Anderson in *The Torrents of Spring.* Hemingway told Dean Christian Gauss that he had used *Winesburg, Ohio* as his first pattern;[19] and, in spite of his disclaimers to Edmund Wilson that he had never been "inspired" by Anderson,[20] his early stories, "Up in Michigan" and "My Old Man," are Andersonian in both texture and feeling. His friendly association with Anderson in Chicago (at a time, 1920–21, when Anderson was the only successful writer in Hemingway's acquaintance) and the older man's reputation as a revolutionary pioneer in prose would have made it certain that Hemingway read Anderson's fiction with a good deal of care. He could have found there a technique of first-person narration and a concern with the living rhythms of speech that would be very useful to him. In the loose, episodic sketches of *Winesburg, Ohio,* which at their best trail off poetically into an indefinite resonance, he could have found a pattern that might shape his Nick Adams stories into complete single units. If "My Old Man" seems to have suffered from too much conscious or unconscious derivation from a story like Anderson's "I Want to Know Why," a later story like "The Battler" seems to have learned what it needed from *Winesburg*—and gone far beyond it.

Another possible area of influence on the developing Hemingway concerns his attempts to find means to transfer emotion from the neural system to the texture of a prose narrative. We have already seen that the involuntary shock of emotion is the central element in Hemingway's aesthetic concerns. And we also know from vignettes like "On the Quai at Smyrna" or his late story, "A Man of the World" (1957), that Hemingway was willing to use almost any means to gain a legitimate effect on his reader. He himself would seem to have absorbed an abnormal quantity of emotional shocks, and the transference of these to the prose was to serve as both the preserver and the release of emotional intensity. Caught and frozen in the narrative, the emotion would be safe from the fritterings of time and the distortion of memory; the author, meanwhile, would have freed himself from the overcharge of his own nervous system and be able to contemplate with a greater degree of serenity the jagged contours of his own past.

Hemingway seemed to have approached this problem with a good deal of awareness and concentration, as he explains in *Death in the Afternoon:*

I was trying to write then and I found the greatest difficulty, aside from knowing truly what you really felt, rather than what you were supposed to feel, was to put down what really happened in action; what the actual things were which produced the emotion that you experienced. . . . [T]he real thing, the sequence of motion and fact which made the emotion and which would be as valid in a year or in ten years or, with luck, and if you stated it purely enough, always, was beyond me and I was working very hard to try to get it. (2)

In his 1958 *Paris Review* interview with George Plimpton, Hemingway returns to this problem again:

What Archie [MacLeish] was trying to remember was how I was trying to learn in Chicago in around 1920 and was searching for the unnoticed things that made emotions such as the way an outfielder tossed his glove without looking back to where it fell, the squeak of resin on canvas under a fighter's flat-soled gym shoes, the grey color of Jack Blackburn's skin when he had just come out of stir and other things I noticed as a painter sketches. You saw Blackburn's strange color and the old razor cuts and the way he spun a man before you knew his history. These were the things which moved you before you knew the story.[21]

Hemingway's search for the "real thing"—the sensory detail that would trigger an emotional response in a prose narrative—happened to coincide with a considerable amount of literary activity dedicated to similar searches. Marcel Proust's experiments with the physical stimulations of the involuntary memory were coming to fruition. Joyce had successfully applied the "epiphany" in *Dubliners* and then with greater dexterity in *A Portrait of the Artist as a Young Man.* Thomas Mann's use of the leitmotiv was public currency; the followers of T. E. Hulme, the imagists, and the unaffiliated practitioners of the New Poetry were making similar struggles with a new or refurbished use of language to create affective responses. Hemingway could have been influenced in his private search by any of these movements, or even by D. W. Griffith's pioneer applications of movie-camera close-ups.

However Hemingway achieved the "real thing," he did develop a highly selective use of flat pictorial details which, by repetition, juxtaposition, and muted contrast with the violent situation they envelop, create a powerful tension and frequently succeed in shocking the reader into emotional awareness. It is interesting to note that in 1919 T. S. Eliot published "Hamlet and His Problems," an essay that contains the famous proposition of the "objective correlative": "The only way of expressing emotion in the form of art is by finding an 'objective correlative'; in other words, a set of objects, a situation, a chain of events which shall be the formula of that *particular* emotion; such that when the external facts, which must terminate in sensory experience, are given, the emotion is immediately evoked." It would be too much to suggest that Hemingway learned from Eliot how to capture emotion in prose, but Eliot's "objective correlative" makes an excellent definition of one of Hemingway's major techniques.

Hemingway's final influence, his relationship with Gertrude Stein, is the most difficult to evaluate because of the emotional smog cast over their mutual hostility in the 1930s.[22] Again we must try to remain within the limits of probable factual observation. Miss Stein's salon in the rue de Fleurus was one of the most exciting cultural classrooms in modern history; and Miss Stein was an appropriate lecturer. For Hemingway, between 1922 and 1924, no better place could have been found to round out his education. Erudite, keen in her appreciation of music and the visual arts, trained in psychology under Hugo Munsterberg and William James; and, above all, passionately, methodologically, opinionatedly absorbed in an attempt to revolutionize prose, Miss Stein was the ideal teacher to fill the gaps in Hemingway's education. It may be fair to say that she cleansed him of the false ontology of journalism by teaching him that reality in prose must be invented, not reported. Further, her concern with the simplification of language, of the heavy duty which the noun must assume, her obsessive device of repetition, and her experimentation with dialogue were all post-graduate courses which Hemingway was most eager to learn. That he might have learned them without Gertrude Stein seems beside the point. She took an interest in him, read and criticized his early manuscripts ruthlessly, and gave him practical encouragement when his submitted stories were returned to him with a regularity that must have been discouraging. It is perhaps too much the fashion today to discount Gertrude Stein as a mere eccentric and egotist; this is to forget that had she done no more than write "Melanctha," her prime place in twentieth-century fiction would be secure. And no discussion of Hemingway's development as an artist can afford to discount her unmeasurable contribution.

Thus we have the "formed" Hemingway of 1924, his palette more or less complete, his characteristic approaches to the rendering of experience almost fully assembled, and his period of tutelage come to an end with the writing of his honor's thesis—"the five finger exercises"—that are the miniatures of *in our time*. It should be instructive to examine one to see what he had learned.

They shot the six cabinet ministers at half-past six in the morning against the wall of the hospital. There were pools of water in the courtyard. There were wet dead leaves on the paving of the courtyard. It rained hard. All the shutters of the hospital were nailed shut. One of the ministers was sick with typhoid. Two soldiers carried him downstairs and out into the rain. They tried to hold him up against the wall but he sat down in a puddle of water. The other five stood very quietly against the wall. Finally the officer told the soldiers it was no good trying to make him stand up. When they fired the first volley he was sitting down in the water with his head on his knees. (SS, 127)

The most obvious characteristic of this passage is its shocking pictorial quality. The scene exists; it is startlingly, completely there. And not only is it there, but there is a compulsive sense of slow urgency in the depiction of the scene that makes the reader feel as though he is being forced to observe this thing against his will. What he is viewing is a very "theatrical" stylized stage-set—a slowly moving tableau on an almost bare stage with a small number of props. There is almost no concern in the passage for the simulation of a three-dimensional illusion of reality; there are no contours, no suggestions of depth—photographic, psychological, or social.

The scene itself is as sharp and linear as an engraving, but the "flatness" is deceptive; there is a third dimension in the scene, provided by the relationship of the semistunned narrator to the action taking place before his eyes. The reader is not immediately aware of the narrator, because the reader has been insidiously placed in his viewing and reacting position. The third dimension of the picture—the quality that provides and compels the aesthetic illusion of reality, or belief—is forced out of the reader himself. In being made to feel the shock of the description (under the guidance of the half-concealed narrator), the reader completes the current of emotion and, as it were, validates or verifies the existential reality of the scene. This is not at all "the way it was," as early commentators on Hemingway's prose argued. It is rather the way it is when the successfully sensitized reader is shocked into making an involuntary emotional response to the stimuli of the prose and thereby into creating the "truth" of the description in terms of his own pulse-beat.

It is not possible for explication to demonstrate how a prose passage like this really works; if there were tested principles of prose manipulation, then anyone could write successful prose. But explication can suggest how a particular prose passage appears to achieve its effects, and we can learn to become more aware and hence more susceptible to a writer's characteristic stylistic devices.[23] And this passage, although it appears early in Hemingway's career, is fairly representative of the kind of effect that was to become his hallmark. We may note, then, some of the more obvious patterns of movement that inform this scene. The sentences, with one minor exception, are all straight declarative statements, usually quite short in length. The diction is elaborately simple and there is a preponderance of monosyllabic words. Out of eleven sentences, only two ("Two soldiers. . . ." and "They tried. . . .") are definitely sequential; all the other sentences, to a greater or lesser extent, have a kind of fragmentary unconnectedness, one to the other. In other words, the logic of the scene construction is dependent neither on the stage-setting nor on the action that takes place within it, but on the fragmented reaction of the observer. This substitution of the logic of reaction for the logic of reported action may be one of the determinants in forcing the reader's identification with the narrator.

The simplicity of the sentence structure and of the diction is reinforced by the minimal use of adjectives and adverbs. There are no metaphors, similes, or descriptive relative clauses. In other words, the traditional techniques of achieving pictorial description have been sedulously avoided. It is important for the success of the passage that, while the scene must have intensive clarity, it must not be too solidly rooted in a situation of objective reality; it must be free to detach itself from its spatial-temporal background and come to objectification in someone's inner consciousness. Further, the careful use of repetition—repeated constructions, words, and near rhymes—which allies itself with the muted rhythmical quality of the passage, reinforces the echo of the narrator's presence. It can be only his voice that is talking, and the unvarying monotone of that voice sets the audial frame for the emotional response.

Finally, the selection of details is patently controlled by Hemingway's attempts to select just those details that will evoke and control the desired emotional response. Here the objective correlative of the emotion is defined by the rain, the pools of water in the courtyard, the wet dead leaves, and the final sordid puddle of water in which the sixth cabinet minister sits down to receive his death. This image-pattern, which moves from the pools on the ground to the sky ("It rained hard") and then back down to the ground again, is paralleled by the descent of the sixth minister ("Two soldiers carried him downstairs. . . .) who ("his head on his knees") completes the vignette in a closed, sodden collapse. The pattern of images is actually quite traditional; and, with the insertion of the "wet dead leaves," it is almost sentimental. The saving detail, which testifies to Hemingway's success in observing "the unnoticed things that made emotions," is the line: "All the shutters of the hospital were nailed shut." This, it seems to us, is the "goose-flesh" line in the sketch—the muted detail that operates on an almost subliminal level to release emotional resonance. It is stark, final ("shutters" are "shut"), and claustrophobic. The hospital—the place of restoration to health, the monument to normality—is sordidly degraded. We could even reluctantly suggest a hint of crucifixion imagery in "nailed" and a suggestion that, in the shuttering up of the hospital windows, the eyes of health and normality have been stricken with outraged blindness. The fact is that this line works; how or why it works we cannot really know, but it seems to have something to do with "the real thing" that Hemingway sought.

Stylistic analysis that attempts to be interpretative is always to some degree subjective and, whether admittedly or not, operative under a priori commitments. Yet it is interesting to project from such an analysis what kinds of attitudes, effects, limitations, and strengths we can expect in Hemingway's prose. Some of these have been discussed earlier and others implied; we will now attempt to sum up the implicit aesthetic, or—to return to an earlier metaphor—to describe more accurately the nature and design of Hemingway's weapon against the world.

On the basis of what we have seen, Robert Penn Warren's description of Hemingway is pithily accurate: "[he is essentially a] lyric rather than a dramatic writer, and for the lyric writer virtue depends upon the intensity with which the personal vision is rendered rather than upon the creation of a variety of characters whose visions are in conflict among themselves."[24] While it is not exactly fair to make the early Hemingway vignette bear the burden of so much interpretation, we can see from it that the only character of real interest in it is the narrating voice. The five docile ministers, the sick one, the soldiers, and the officer have as much but no more importance than the puddles and pools, the leaves, the hospital shutters, and the rain. They are all—animate or inanimate—counters that really do not count in the game, except as they mirror or enflesh the state of mind of the narrator.

And because of this need for a lyrical outlet for his personal vision, we will find that the typical Hemingway fiction will be of two closely related types. Either there will be an actual or an implied first-person narrator (the Nick Adams stories, *The Sun Also Rises, A Farewell to Arms*), or there will be seemingly objective third-person narrated fiction in which the reader will be coerced into the position of the reacting, unspeaking "voice" *(The Old Man and the Sea)*. We will investigate these kinds of fictional structures in detail but we may point out here that Hemingway is likely to run into trouble whenever he departs from this format. Because the Hemingway fiction generates its form and its strength from its capacity to deliver an emotional shock, or punch, the creation of a surrogate reacting character (or punching bag) will be mandatory; and the kinds of characters and situations that he can invent will be dependent on this structural determinant.

Further, because Hemingway is attempting to capture emotional intensity in time and to make it timeless—safe from the onslaughts of distorting memory and the erosion of the temporal—we can expect his fiction to take place in a world that is, as Carlos Baker suggests, "screened . . . at both ends."[25] His fictional worlds may have illusory geographical settings; they may be located on a map or in history, but this seeming objective authenticity will be a functional divertissement to engage the reader in the emotional context of the personal and not the public vision. Hence the fictional worlds will tend to be enclosed and removed, existentially rootless as surreal landscapes in which the reader and the narrator (overt or covert) may share in their inward realities. Hemingway's work has frequently been unjustly criticized on this point by critics determined to apply the measurements of objective realism (or naturalism) to materials that are simply incompatible with those measurements. The preceding miniature is a fair demonstration of this. It is devoid of social-historical reality—and purposely so. It may or may not have been based on an actual occurrence, and it may even make an indirect contribution to historical understanding. But, as it stands on the page, it is primarily a nightmare emotion, recollected or invented within an artifice of simulated shock.

In varying degrees this "out-of-space out-of-timeliness" holds true for almost all of Hemingway's fiction. Hemingway confused the issue by declaring in *Green Hills of Africa* that "where we go, if we are any good, there you can go as we have been" (109). It would be fruitless and unjust to Hemingway to invoke this as a literal test. His cherished landscapes merge together; his rivers are all pretty similar whether they flow in Spain, Italy, the Black Forest, or Upper Michigan. Mountains and meadows, villages and large cities—they are all individually believable within their own artistic-emotional contexts; but, taken out of them, they are indistinguishable, except by the place names, the slight variations in folk idiom, and the distinctive peculiarities of locale which even Hemingway could not disguise. But in a more important and valuable sense, Hemingway's declaration is quite true, especially in those descriptions where he finds the objective correlative for his reactions to places. Hemingway's exceptional forte was not to describe what he saw, but to describe himself seeing, to convey the complex of feeling that was invoked in him or in an invented character when that character was placed in an appropriate situation of tension.[26] This *there* he could and did render with wonderful precision and complex tonality; and to this *there* countless readers have been able to follow him.

The thrust of this central characteristic of Hemingway's aesthetic is to move his stories away from fiction toward fable—away from a concern with the concrete and the particular toward the universal and the symbolic. Hemingway's "lyric" need to project his personal vision of the world suggests that the personal vision may become so overriding as to supplant the "objective" world when they come in conflict with one another. Saul Bellow brilliantly perceived this danger in his review of *The Old Man and the Sea,* but the tendency is also present in Hemingway's earliest fictions: "He tends to speak for Nature itself. Should Nature and Hemingway become identical one or the other will have won too total a victory."[27] It was Nature that ultimately won the victory, but the conflict that he carried on against Nature—and it was a "total" conflict—provided him and us with the products of his art. "Let those who want to save the world if you can get to see it clear and as a whole. Then any part you make will represent the whole if it's made truly" (*D,* 278). These words, which have such an Emersonian ring, become potentially dangerous when the only test of "clearness" and "wholeness" is involuntary emotional responses. When truth, goodness, and beauty—in traditional romantic fashion—are based on the neural shudder that raises the gooseflesh on the skin, and when the skin belongs to a man hypersensitively aware of his own isolation and excessively prone to lash out from behind his many masks before he himself suffers a hurt—then the literary critic may be excused his romantic speculation that perhaps Herman Melville invented Hemingway over a century ago.

The aesthetic directions of an Ahabian vision are at least not speculative. We can expect that Hemingway's fiction will move from dramatic concerns to the enactment of myth; that his focus will concern itself less and less with men, and more and more with Man; and that Man will tend to be cast in the image of its undivine creator. We can also expect that Death, the universal antagonist of the cosmos, will have to be neutralized in some fashion by an artist who has chosen the course of antagonism against a hostile universe; and we realize that this neutralization may require a tacit truce or even a working alliance between the artist and Death.

Concerning his ideal artist-bullfighter Hemingway wrote in *Death in the Afternoon:* "A great killer must love to kill; unless he feels that it is the best thing he can do, unless he is conscious of its dignity and feels that it is its own reward, he will be incapable of the abnegation that is necessary in real killing. The truly great killer must have a sense of honor and a sense of glory far beyond that of the ordinary bullfighter. In other words he must be a simpler man" (232).

And D. H. Lawrence, summing up what seemed to him the very essence of the American spirit and the true business of the American myth, wrote:

The essential American soul is hard, isolate, stoic, and a killer. It has never yet melted.

Of course the soul often breaks down into disintegration. . . .

What true myth concerns itself with is not the disintegration product. True myth concerns itself centrally with the onward adventure of the integral soul. And this, for America, is Deerslayer. A man who turns his back on white society. A man who keeps his moral integrity hard and intact. An isolate, almost selfless, stoic enduring man, who lives by death, by killing, but who is pure white.[28]

An examination of Hemingway's aesthetic ends inevitably in a contemplation of the Lawrentian version of the true American myth.

It remains to see whether we are dealing with "the disintegration product" or the work of "a simpler man" whose soul "has never yet melted."

Chapter Three
Of Tyros and Tutors

Hemingway's vision, based on his need to relate his isolate self to all that was not-self, was, as we have seen, an intensely lyrical vision; yet he is not a poet but a writer of fiction.[1] When he says in *Green Hills of Africa* that he is striving to create a prose "much more difficult than poetry," he is not indulging in casual hyperbole. He is actually stating quite accurately the dilemma that his aesthetic demands and his storytelling talents forced upon him. Given his insatiable drive to make his identity metaphysically secure through attaching it to the things of the universe by, as it were, emotional adhesion, we might have expected him to write a prose equivalent to "Song of Myself" or *The Waste Land*. In these poems—as in the last chapter of *Death in the Afternoon,* in Harry's remembrances of things past in "The Snows of Kilimanjaro," or in the preface to Vittorini's *In Sicily*—the principles of aesthetic and metaphysical structure fuse in the device of the evocative catalog. The metaphysical selves of the artists (their identities, in the full sense) are created and realized in their recollected moments of sincere emotional response; these, in turn, are re-created artistically as the fragments they have shored against their ruins.[2]

But Hemingway differed from both Whitman and Eliot in very significant ways. Unlike Whitman, he prized the adamant separateness of his isolate self, as we can see in his choice to be an administrator of death rather than a wooer of it. He fiercely resisted any potential loss of self, even a loss that might have given him the incalculable gain of transcendent mergence. There is in Hemingway a curious deficiency in the capacity to love which becomes manifest when we compare him to Whitman; the latter could write love poems to "sweet soothing death" and become whole in the spirit of total communion; Hemingway's book on bullfighting is a kind of love song to killing that insures him the role of eternal opposition. "The kelson of the creation is love," sang Whitman. But for Hemingway the kelson had cracked right down the middle, and the creation had become a form of combat in which "the conditions are that the winner shall take nothing."

And, unlike Eliot—whose revulsion at the world was matched by his revulsion at his own sensory responses—Hemingway could not deny the fundamental joie de vivre of experiencing physical action, of delighting in the increased awareness of life and self that the operation of his five senses so abundantly offered him. Eliot could try to enter the realms of all-acceptant love by a firm denial of the self that he found so distasteful; once there, his "vision of the street" could become softened into a prayerful meditation where "the fire and the rose are one." But Hemingway's deficiencies in his powers to love are matched by his incapacity to really hate. He can be contemptuous; he can be shocked and outraged; he can be arrogantly superior. But lacking a sense of real security in the universe, he lacked also the necessary bases of self-righteousness and self-unity, the sources of hatred. And thus again, for precisely the reverse reasons as with Whitman, Hemingway was forced into the role of eternal opposition in total conflict with everything that was Other.

This introductory discussion is pertinent if it helps us to realize why Hemingway had no choice except to dramatize his lyric vision. The uncompromising split that he felt between himself and the universe could be made to yield an objective correlative of his emotions only through the tensions of the dialectic form. Action and reaction, force and shock, challenge and response—these are the relentless antagonists that will engage in dubious battle throughout Hemingway's fiction; the battlefield, the locus of contact and the point of arrest, is the willed awareness of the human spirit, Hemingway's spirit, recording with precision the attacks and counterattacks, the retreats, the acts of bravery and cowardice, the casualties and the irreparable damages. To examine the dramatic tension that provides the action of his fictions, we will have to examine in some detail the famous Hemingway "Hero" and Hemingway's "Code" within the general frame of reference that we have been developing.[3]

There are, as criticism has come slowly to recognize, not one but two Hemingway heroes; or, to use Philip Young's designations, the "Nick-Adams-hero" and the "code-hero." The generic Nick Adams character, who lives through the course of Hemingway's fiction, appears first as the shocked invisible "voice" of the miniatures of *in our time;* he grows up through Hemingway's three volumes of short stories and at least four of his novels, sometimes changing his name to Jake Barnes, Frederic Henry, Mr. Frazer, Macomber, Harry, Robert Jordan, Richard Cantwell; and he makes his final appearances (appropriately unnamed as when he first entered the fictional stage) in Hemingway's last two published stories in 1957. The code-hero also figures in Hemingway's earliest fiction. He dies of a *cogida* as Maera in *in our time,* and he is resurrected in a considerable variety of shapes, forms, and accents (usually non-American) through the bulk of Hemingway's creative output. His manifestations would include Belmonte in *The Sun Also Rises;* Manuel in "The Undefeated"; the Major in "In Another Country"; Harry Morgan; Wilson in "The Short Happy Life of Francis Macomber"; Cayetano Ruiz in "The Gambler, the Nun, and the Radio"; El Sordo; and Santiago.

For convenience sake we will refer to the Nick Adams hero as the tyro and to the "code-hero" as the tutor; for it is basically an educational relationship, albeit one-sided, that binds them together. The tyro, faced with the overwhelming confusion and hurt *(nada)* inherent in an attempt to live an active sensual life, admires the deliberate self-containment of the tutor (a much "simpler man") who is seemingly not beset with inner uncertainties. Accordingly, the tyro tries to model his behavior on the pattern he discerns. However, the tyro is not a simple man; being in fact a near projection of Hemingway himself, he never attains the state of serene unselfconsciousness—what James once called nastily "the deep intellectual repose"—that seems to come naturally to the tutor. What he can learn, however, is the appearance of that self-containment. He can laboriously train himself in the conventions of the appearance of "the code"; and he can so severely practice those external restraints as to be provided with a pragmatic defense against the horrors that never cease to assault him.

It may be salutary to digress slightly to what we can call "The Education of Nick Adams" because there is some inevitable confusion surrounding it. In one sense the education is thoroughly abortive; Nick at the end of his multicheckered career is as terrified and lost as he was, for example, in his encounter with the stark, machined horror of the Chicago gangsters in "The Killers." In the following quotation is the tyro, aged somewhere in his mid-fifties, trying to cope with the loss of his eyesight ("Get a Seeing-Eyed Dog"): "Because I am not doing too well at this. That I can promise you. But what else can you do? Nothing, he thought. There's nothing you can do. But maybe, as you go along, you will get good at it." The tyro, with his unfair inheritance from Hemingway of a particularly fecund and hyperactive imagination of disaster, has lost nothing of his capacities to be afraid—in spite of his long indoctrination in the craft of courage. In fact, he has rather increased his capacities, for his accumulated experience of horror has taught him many more things of which to be afraid. Measured pragmatically, however—and the defense never pretends to be more than a pragmatic one—Nick does survive for an astonishingly long time. He does, as Hemingway puts it, get pretty good at it as he goes along.

If we sketch briefly Nick's biography, we will be able to judge somewhat better the values of his education and to note also the varying ways that Hemingway employed him as shock absorber and seismographer of emotional stress. Nick is born, roughly at the turn of the twentieth century, somewhere in the Midwest. His father, a physician, is fond of hunting and shooting, and is concerned to teach Nick the proper ways of handling a rod and a gun. Dr. Adams has incredibly sharp eyesight and is a better wing-shot than Nick will ever be. He is also intimidated by his wife—a suspiciously indistinct character who is a blur of polite nagging and vague religious sentiments—and, on one occasion, Nick is shocked to see his father back down from a fight. The pattern of cowardice and intimidation, never actually explained, comes to a disgusting (to Nick) finale when his father commits suicide in the 1920s with Nick's grandfather's gun. The grandfather becomes elected as Nick's spiritual father—a tutorial hero because of his reputed bravery during the Civil War.

As a boy, Nick's adventures distill the excitements, perplexities, and terrors that are classically supposed to accompany adolescence. He witnesses a lynching in Ohio, a Caesarean delivery by jack-knife, and a razor suicide in an Indian camp; he has a very satisfactory initiation into sex with an Ojibway Indian girl whom he later discovers to be promiscuous. He also undergoes a puppy-love affair with a "nice" girl, which he is tremulously strong enough to break off. Unexplainedly "on the road," he comes into contact with sentimental whores, sinister homosexuals, and a vaudeville team of professional assassins. His characteristic response to these situations is open-eyed shock; he registers the events as though he were a slow-motion camera, but rarely if ever does he actively participate in them. He never gets into a fight; he does not argue; he does not retreat to protect his sensibilities. Like the camera, he has a curious masochistic quality of total acceptance and receptivity. At about this point we begin to suspect that the adventures of Nick Adams are approximately as realistic as "The Adventures of Tom Swift," although any individual episode in the serial is gratifyingly convincing. We begin to suspect that Hemingway's tyro figure is a projection into the nightmare possibilities of confusion, pain, and immolation; that his adventures are mythic fantasies, guided by the rhythms of intense fear and alienation. That, in short, Nick Adams is a sacrificial victim, bound time and time again to the slaughtering-table to be almost slaughtered in order that his creator and readers may be free of fear.

The pattern continues and proliferates when Nick joins the Italian Army fighting the Austrians in northeastern Italy. He is blown up at Fossalta di Piave, where he feels his soul go out of his body, go off, and then return. For a long time after this he has to leave the light burning at night to keep his soul in place. His convalescence at the hospital in Milan is aided and abetted by a love affair with a British nurse, but he is finally returned to the Austrian front as a morale advertisement—in spite of the fact that he is in a severe state of combat trauma. He returns briefly to the United States to go fishing, and then reembarks for Europe where he remains except for sporadic visits to hunt in Wyoming and to recuperate from an accident in a Montana hospital. Somewhere along the line he has become by profession a writer—more often a newspaperman—and he has also married. There is surprisingly little information about his domestic life, other than that he is afraid his approaching fatherhood will restrain his athletic diversions. Much later we discover that he has been married and divorced three times; but, in general, the nightmare terrors of banal marital existence are avoided in the episodes of his adventures.

We catch glimpses of his life in the 1920s—skiing in Switzerland, riding his bicycle through Paris streets, developing an air of expertise on the running of the bulls in Spain and the empty carousing of the American bohemians throughout Europe. Details of isolated horror in World War I crop up in his memories from time to time, and the action of the Greeks in breaking the legs of their baggage animals and dumping them in the harbor at Smyrna (Izmir) becomes a kind of climactic leitmotiv in the aria of his remembered terrors.

But meanwhile there has been a gradual hardening of his powers to resist the shocks that he seems desperately impelled to pursue. He slowly edges away from the margins of nervous collapse as a war convalescent who has seen too many helmets full of brains. Painfully during the 1920s, he masters his physical responses and rather proudly subjects himself to situations of violence and disgust as though (like the red-headed veteran in *To Have and Have Not*) these occasions give him an opportunity to prove that he can not only absorb punishment but also take a perverted pleasure in it.

The 1930s extend his experience to the fishing waters between Cuba and Key West, safaris to Africa, and the Loyalist front in the Spanish War. Nick, who has become increasingly resistant to shock, reacts now more as a clinical observer than as an outraged participant. In fact, there is evidence that he even manipulates events consciously to increase a stress situation, as when—through "the always dirty desire to see how people act under an emotional conflict, that makes writers such attractive friends"[4]—he triggers off a rather unpleasant series of consequences that leads to the execution of one man and the guilty shame of another. His exposures to the cynicism of political chicanery in the command levels of the Spanish War are followed by disgust with the military stupidities and vanities of the higher echelons that control the operations of World War II. The threat of old age and physical debility appears in his collection of terrors in the late 1930s, becomes a more dense specter in the 1940s, and assumes haunting proportions in the 1950s in his recurrent fear of blindness. The question of suicide, introduced in the early 1930s, remains a foreboding undercurrent in his ethical reflections through the 1940s and 1950s; and it is probably significant that his first aggressive denunciation of the act becomes reluctantly mollified. And, finally, a marginal interest in Catholic attitudes toward life and death, which appears in the 1920s, maintains its steady flow throughout his career, without seeming to engage his deeper levels of concern.

Such is Nick Adams, surely not, as one critic explains, a man whose life's story "differs in no essential way from that of almost any middleclass American male who started life at the beginning of the present century or even with the generation of 1920."[5] There is little that is realistically representative in the career of Nicholas Adams, nor is there meant to be. In a sense—which his name suggests—he is a released devil of our innocence, an enfleshment of our conscious and unconscious fears dispatched to do battle with the frightening possibilities that an always uncertain future holds over our heads. He is the whipping-boy of our fearful awareness, the pragmatic probability extrapolated into a possible tomorrow to serve as a propitiary buffer against the evils that tomorrow may or may not bring. He suffers our accidents and defeats before they happen to us. Like Tiresias, he is doomed to foresuffer them all— to witness the infidelities and deaths of our loved ones; to enact our cowardices and indecisions; to struggle against the internal and external diseases that inexorably pursue us; in short, to die the innumerable times we project our deaths in our imaginations. But for all this he is a far from impotent counter in the game in which the winner takes nothing. Hemingway plays him, the sacrificial card in his hand, to finesse the ruthless king; he is the defeated victim, but in experiencing his defeat, Hemingway (and we) can ring ourselves in invisible armor so that we will be undefeated if and when the catastrophes of our imagination do actually occur. On this level, then, the Nick Adams projection is a vital defensive weapon in Hemingway's combat with the universe.

The tutor, on the other hand, is a much less complicated figure than the tyro; but he is certainly no more realistic. If the tyro is in general a projection of the possibilities of an inadequate response to "the terrible ambiguities of an immediate experience" (Jung's phrase), the tutor is the embodied wish-fulfillment of a successful response. He is "a tough boy," which Colonel Cantwell defines as "a man who will make his play and then back it up. Or just a man who backs his play" (*A*, 48–49). The seemingly innocuous amendment to the definition underlines one distinction between the tutor and the tyro. The fully developed tyro is "the man who will make his play and then back it up." The tutor is "just a man who backs his play." The difference, so deceptively small, encompasses the whole range of man's conscious awareness of himself while engaged in action; it includes his capacities not only to reflect and to imagine but also to be aware of reflecting and imagining. This human burden the tyro must always carry, but from it the tutor is free; this, indeed, is what makes the tutor "a simpler man." He is so simple, in fact, that he is closer to brute animality than to "humanness."[6] For example, we cite Manuel of "The Undefeated" as he is facing the bull that will not charge:

He thought in bull-fight terms. Sometimes he had a thought and the particular piece of slang would not come into his mind and he could not realize the thought. His instincts and his knowledge worked automatically, and his brain worked slowly and in words. He knew all about bulls. He did not have to think about them. He just did the right thing. His eyes noted things and his body performed the necessary measures without thought. If he thought about it, he would be gone. (*SS*, 260)

Thought and action (or reaction) are simultaneous for Manuel; he is "just a man who backs his play," and hence his responses will be inevitably adequate to the challenge he is trained to accept. The tyro, as we see often in Hemingway's works, must try to stop himself from thinking. There is an inevitable hiatus between challenge and response, action and reaction; it is here, in Hemingway's diagnosis, that man's greatest danger takes place. The broken circuit, the incomplete synapse, the failure of the nerve: all these phrases designate that emotional paralysis, or shock, which Hemingway had every reason to fear, and which on a collective basis may very well be the major disease of twentieth-century man. Thus the trained tyro is "the man who will make his play and then back it up"; unable to become a fully responsive mechanism of instincts, he can try to condition himself to force the right responses under stress.

The tutor takes a surprisingly large variety of forms in Hemingway's fiction, but, in each of his manifestations, he is always "the professional." With two significant exceptions, his activities are confined to areas where he can perform within the predictabilities of his training—fighting bulls, bootlegging whiskey and Chinamen, facing lion charges, and landing large fish. The exceptional stories recount, in part, the adventures of tutors who encounter challenges beyond the jurisdiction of their professional preparations; these are in "Fifty Grand" and "In Another Country."

"Fifty Grand," one of Hemingway's most humorous stories, recalls Ring Lardner's "Champion" in tone and situation. The tutor is Jack Brennan—loutish, parsimonious, overaged welter-weight champion of the world. Believing honestly that he will lose his title to the challenger, Walcott, he bets fifty thousand dollars against himself. He does not know, however, that a gambling syndicate has arranged for Walcott to throw the fight. In the eleventh round, when it is obvious that Brennan (who has been making an honest fight thus far) will eventually lose on points, Walcott deliberately fouls him and seriously hurts him in the process. The situation is supremely comical: if Brennan abides by the rules of boxing, as well as by the imperatives of his creature instincts (he is in much pain) and his professional conditioning, he will retain his championship and lose fifty thousand dollars. Instead, he waves off the referee and brutally fouls Walcott twice, losing the fight on a foul and winning his bet. And he remarks toward the end of the story, "It's funny how fast you can think when it means that much money" (*SS,* 326).

One critic has dubbed this to be a story of the "honor-and-courage-among-thieves" variety, finding Brennan a satisfactory code hero in the peculiar milieu of his operations.[7] This interpretation, however, misses the humor and the point of the story. What we have is an exposure in veniality to the noncommitted first-person narrator (the tyro), and an indication that professionals (tutors) can be trusted only within their special areas of mastery. Brennan breaks the code in betting against himself, and when he is challenged by the foul, he is thrown like the rest of us into a decision-making problem where his training is useless. His exercise of "fast" thinking under stress transforms him from a fully responsive mechanism of instincts into an instinctive machine of avarice.

"In Another Country," surely one of Hemingway's masterpieces in the short story form, also takes a professional into a challenge situation for which he has not been prepared, but with very different results from the satiric "Fifty Grand." The Major of the story is Hemingway's most attractive tutor figure, and he is also the most intelligent and sensitive. A professional soldier, and before the war a champion fencer, he is undergoing mechanical therapy for a wound which has left his fencing hand shrunken to baby size. Disabling wounds and death are foreseeable eventualities for professional soldiers, and the Major accepts his lot with equanimity. Out of a sense of duty he reports to the hospital every afternoon to be treated by the therapeutic machines (designed to rehabilitate industrial accidents), even though he does not believe in their efficacy. When he engages the tyro (the first-person narrator) in conversation, he insists with characteristic professionalism that the boy speak Italian grammatically. As Hemingway presents him, the Major is a figure of considerable dignity and somewhat stuffy rectitude who "did not believe in bravery," presumably because, like Santiago, he chooses precision and exactness over the uncontrollable results of impulse action.

But one afternoon he comes to the hospital in an irritable mood
and provokes the tyro into a rude argument over marriage, declaim-
ing angrily that a man must not marry. "If he is to lose everything,
he should not place himself in a position to lose that. He should
not place himself in a position to lose. He should find things he
cannot lose" (SS, 271). He makes a telephone call and returns to
the room where the tyro is sitting.

He was wearing his cape and had his cap on, and he came directly toward
my machine and put his arm on my shoulder.
   "I am so sorry," he said, and patted me on the shoulder with his good
hand. "I would not be rude. My wife has just died. You must forgive
me."
   "Oh—" I said, feeling sick for him. "I am *so* sorry."
   He stood there biting his lower lip. "It is very difficult," he said. "I
cannot resign myself."
   He looked straight past me and out through the window. Then he
began to cry. "I am utterly unable to resign myself," he said and choked.
And then crying, his head up looking at nothing, carrying himself straight
and soldierly, with tears on both his cheeks and biting his lips, he walked
past the machines and out the door. (SS, 272)

One final paragraph concludes the story, in which we are told that
the Major returns for his regular treatments three days later with
mourning crepe on his uniform sleeve. The doctors had placed
photographs of wounds before and after treatment in front of his
machine. "The photographs did not make much difference to the
major because he only looked out of the window" (SS, 272).
   This is the one certain case in Hemingway's work where the tutor
rises far beyond the artificial boundaries that restrict his need to
make decisions. As we have seen, the code of professionalism with
its severe conditioning in special pragmatic skills and attitudes is
designed to minimize the multiplicity of possibilities existing in
any challenge situation. Or, to express it more simply, the professional attitude creates an arbitrary chart of the future—like a contour
map of preselected terrain—in which only a few items are considered
significant and the rest are ignored. The rationale for the adoption
of such a code is suggested in the Major's passionate cry: "[Man]
should not place himself in a position to lose. He should find things
he cannot lose." He will eventually lose everything when he loses
himself, but along the way he will be able to control his losses and

also the sequence of "holding attacks" through which he wages his battles.

If such a life code were adhered to strictly, a man would have to be either "the dumb ox" (the "simpler man") of so much Hemingway criticism or an unbelievable monster of machined egotism living, as it were, in an almost impregnable pillbox with no exits or entrances. The Major of this story is neither; his adoption of a code of life does not preclude his exposure to the risks of the incalculable in spite of his angry cry of outrage. Because he is human, he has loved; and, to continue the military metaphor, he has wittingly exposed his flanks to undefendable attack. His commitment to love and his shock at his wife's death have placed him "in another country" than the one he has prepared to defend. That other country is nothing less than the human condition itself, for the human will is always vulnerable to ruthless destruction. And Hemingway's ultimate test of human performance is the degree of stripped courage and dignity that man can discover in himself in his moments of absolute despair. It would have been quite simple for the Major to have died well; his challenge is far greater than his own death (a challenge that Hemingway has typically considered a relatively easy one to face). The Major, in losing his wife, suffers a death of himself accompanied by the absurdity of his own continued life. It is meaninglessness—*nada*—that confronts the Major in full assault.

And like Jesus in "Today is Friday," the Major is "good in there." He is badly broken, but not destroyed. He refuses to resign himself to the chaos of unmeaning, but he refuses also to deny the actuality of his fearsome defeat. He holds tight to the superficial conventions of his training—the empty forms of innate courtesy and soldierly duty—and sits within them to begin the laborious process of making the broken places within himself strong again. His response can be characterized as neither acceptance nor denial; he is neither victim nor rebel. The least and the best that can be said of him is that he survives with dignity, and it is possible that he may be considered Hemingway's most eloquent portrait of ideal heroism—unquixotic, unathletic, profoundly humanistic.

The characteristic of dignity, so important to Hemingway as to have furnished him with one of the major themes in his fiction, is relevant to our discussion at this point. The peculiar problems of twentieth-century life have made the depictions of human dignity almost anomalous in modern literature. Our characteristic heroes have been antiheroes or nonheroes, aggressive doomed men in revolt or essentially pathetic dupes at the mercy of nonmalicious and implacable victimization. Dignity in either situation is difficult to ascribe to such heroes who tend by choice to divest themselves of the traditional values of rational intelligence and moral integrity on which dignity has always rested. The great majority of modern heroes in literature are purposely grotesque—picaresque saints, rebels, victims, and underground men of all shapes and colors. Their individual value as artistic achievements and embodiments of viable life attitudes is undeniable, but dignity is a quality largely beyond their grasp.[8] Hemingway's attempt to retain the ideal of dignity without falsifying the ignobility of the modern human condition (that impulse in his work that leads many commentators to associate his beliefs with those of classical Stoicism) is one of his signal triumphs as a modern writer. And it is generally through his characterizations of the tutor figure that this quality of dignity is manifested.

Besides the Major we can find dignity in Manuel ("The Undefeated"), in Anselmo of For Whom the Bell Tolls, in the old men of "A Clean Well-Lighted Place" and of "Old Man at the Bridge," and finally in Santiago. It is probably significant that all of these examples are older men. Dignity certainly does not come automatically with age in Hemingway's fiction, but it is usually denied to youth with its passions and penchant for illusions.[9] A minimal degree of native intelligence is a basic requirement; basic also are the qualities of real humility and self-abnegation. Thus characters like Harry Morgan, Cayetano Ruiz, Wilson, or El Sordo—all in some fashion tutor figures and models of a kind of excellence—are on the lower levels of Hemingway's portraits of heroism. This point should be remembered since too many evaluations of Hemingway's life code mistakenly assume that Hemingway's code heroes can be lumped togther in an indiscriminate stereotype of brute primitivism and animal virtues.

One other point should be made concerning the tutor figure. We have noted that the great majority of them are non-American (Spanish bullfighters, Mexican gamblers, British white hunters, etc.), and that the ones of greatest excellence, of dignity, are all non-Americans and men of mature or advanced age. We also noted earlier that Hemingway's nubile heroines are likewise non-Americans and that, if they do not grow progressively younger as Hemingway writes over a period of some thirty years, they do not noticeably age either. His heroines would seem to be so many variations on his archetype, the Ojibway Trudy. These two examples of repetitive characterization offer some evidence for legitimate speculation. Just as we have seen that the Nick Adams projection can be understood as a compulsive fantasy figure closely related to one aspect of Hemingway's self-image, so these two other consistent figurations are comparable fantasy projections. It takes no great Freudian sophistication to recognize in the tutor figure a father image. Purified of the weaknesses that shame Nick in his real hunting-and-fishing father, the substitute retains the capacity to "doctor" or heal by emulation. All the tutor fathers are childless (Harry Morgan has a brood of daughters); and, in suffering the sea change of denationalization and conversion to Catholicism, they are moved by Hemingway into another country where they can be loved and respected by their tyro sons without reservation. The heroines, similarly, seem purified mother figures; at once completely satisfying and undemanding, they are handy oceanic reservoirs of temporary regression and security. The incest motif that obtrudes from *Across the River and into the Trees* can thus be seen as a rather consistent modulation on the erotic concerns in Hemingway's fiction.

The relationship between Colonel Cantwell and Renata affords an opportunity of investigating the Hemingway heroines somewhat more closely.[10] Renata is "almost nineteen," the age at which Nick Adams and Cantwell suffered the great wound at Fossalta di Piave. Cantwell refers to Renata and to her symbolic portrait as "boy" and "daughter," suggesting that Hemingway is employing the device of "symbolic doubling" (Carlos Baker's term) to make Renata not only the mother image (the daughter inversion is a standard Freudian trick) of Cantwell, but also his alter ego or anima—that is, himself some thirty years earlier. The temporary gift of the two emeralds which Renata presents to Cantwell is clearly symbolic of Cantwell's youthful virility; and Renata's name ("the reborn") would seem to make this reading decisive.

Extending this interpretation to Hemingway's other typical heroines, Catherine Barkley and Maria, we find that the double function of each is likewise present but less obvious. Each becomes absolutely identified with her lover: "There isn't any me. I'm you." And in the physical act of union—symbolically appropriate in a womblike sleeping bag or under a blanket in a Venetian gondola—the tyro figure makes a complete regression to a prenatal state of oneness with himself and the mother. Finally we may note that in *The Old Man and the Sea,* Hemingway's last published major work, the impulse to regression is complete. The tyro has split into the young boy, Manolo, and the hero, Santiago, while the Hemingway heroine (the mother and anima) has assumed its primordial symbolic shape as *la mar,* the eternal, feminine sea.

We are neither interested nor qualified to conduct a fully developed psychoanalytic study of Hemingway's fiction, several of which have been attempted;[11] but an elementary analytic reading can illuminate some of the conditions of Hemingway's art. The point worth grasping here, as we have been insisting, is that Hemingway's aesthetic concerns are not with the depiction of objective reality, but with the fantasy projections of his inner consciousness. The mirror of his art is held up to his own nature, not Nature; and, if he succeeded in casting a definition of the human condition that has been useful to twentieth-century readers, it is because his own human condition, painfully and honestly transmuted into evocative prose in a lifetime of disciplined writing, was in some way deeply representative of the condition of humanity. We can never know how aware he was of the direction his art took. We do know it was compulsively intent on recording those emotional shocks that gave him a feeling of immortality. We know also that he wrote in order that he could live, and when he could no longer "get rid of it" (the disintegrating shocks) through writing them out, he ceased to live. The pattern of his work is consistently rooted in a dramatization of the traumatic births of his tortured psyche, relentlessly struggling to rid itself of its horrors. An examination of one of the problems recurrent in Hemingway criticism may be persuasive in showing that the real pain in Hemingway's fiction is residual in his personality, and that he may very well be talking about his own theory of writing when he asks through Professor MacWalsey in *To Have and Have Not,* "why must all the operations in life be performed without an anaesthetic?"[12]

The inconsistency of Hemingway's sociopolitical beliefs has been, since the middle 1930s, a stumbling block or source of embarrassment to Hemingway's critics, both the friendly and the hostile. A writer, like everyone else, has every right to change his mind on cardinal principles of belief; but a writer, especially a great writer, is under obligation to leave a trail of evidence behind him in his shifts of opinion, so that his devious course can be followed. In the miniatures of *in our time* (1924), Hemingway proclaimed the "separate peace"; and he officially ratified it in the famous baptismal plunge into the Tagliamento River in *A Farewell to Arms* (1929):

> You had lost your cars and your men as a floorwalker loses the stock of his department in a fire. There was, however, no insurance. You were out of it now. You had no more obligation. . . .
> Anger was washed away in the river along with any obligation. . . . I had taken off the stars, but that was for convenience. It was no point of honor. I was not against them. I was through. I wished them all the luck. . . . But it was not my show anymore. (232)

Frederic Henry's political "lone-wolfism" and his disseverance from any body of authority is strictly held to through *Death in the Afternoon* (1932) and *Green Hills of Africa* (1935); if anything, his determination to be uninvolved is more pronounced. And yet, in an amazingly sudden turnabout, Hemingway renounces the separate peace with Harry Morgan's dramatically unmotivated dying speech in *To Have and Have Not* (1937): "No matter how a man alone ain't got no bloody . . . chance" (225). And the shift is spelled out as clearly as possible with Robert Jordan's voluntary enlistment against fascism in *For Whom the Bell Tolls* (1940).

The nub of the literary critical confusion in Hemingway's political shifts is that Robert Jordan submits to Communist discipline for reasons precisely antithetical to those that impel Frederic Henry's desertion. Henry stands for the concrete immediacy of experience and is "embarrassed by the words sacred, glorious, and sacrifice and the expression in vain." He concludes that only place names have dignity, and that abstract words "such as glory, honor, courage, or hallow" are obscene. Eleven years later, Robert Jordan, referring to his participation in the Loyalist Cause as a "crusade," attempts to define how he feels:

> You felt, in spite of all bureaucracy and inefficiency and party strife something that was like the feeling you expected to have and did not have when you made your first communion. It was a feeling of consecration to a duty toward all of the oppressed of the world which would be as difficult and embarrassing to speak about as religious experience. . . . It gave you a part in something that you could believe in wholly and completely

and in which you felt an absolute botherhood with the others who were engaged in it. It was something that you had never known before but that you had experienced now and you gave such importance to it and the reasons for it that your own death seemed of complete unimportance. . . . (*FW*, 235)

The disparity between Jordan's and Henry's positions can never be adequately explained by Hemingway's reactions to world events, for it is doubtful that political or social ideas seriously engaged his creative consciousness. As a man and as a newspaper correspondent, Hemingway was in a better position to assess European social and political developments than probably any other writer of the period. His dispatches and articles in the 1920s and 1930s are evidence that he possessed a keen political eye for what was important in the news; yet he rarely uses this material except in a superficial way, and none of his fictions are truly political. The significant line of development between the filing for a separate peace in 1929 and the return to brotherhood in 1940 can, however, be suggested on a psychoanalytic level of interpretation.

The interior struggle symbolized in *A Farewell to Arms* is fairly easy to follow. The tyro, Henry, undergoes a series of unjust brutalities at the hands of mysterious forces beyond his understanding. He is blown up and seriously wounded (symbolically castrated), only to be nursed back to wholeness and security by Catherine (the anima-mother). This idyllic union in the hospital is only a temporary stay, however (prefigured, in part, by the fact of Catherine's pregnancy), and the tyro returns to the war. His opportunity for rebellion arrives during the chaos of the Caporetto retreat. His ambulance unit picks up two wandering sergeants from an engineering detachment, and, when they run off, he shoots one of them, aiming at the one "who had talked the most." Neither of the sergeants is described or characterized in any detail. Henry's actual desertion takes place at the bridge when the forces of tyranny are imaged in the merciless battle police with their "beautiful detachment and devotion to stern justice" (*F*, 224). In the face of certain execution he leaps into the water and escapes to his anima-mother at Stresa. There he meets Catherine and learns that the authorities have tracked him down. During the night he and Catherine escape over the lake to Switzerland where the idyll is resumed outside of Montreux. Finally

Catherine dies giving birth to a still-born baby boy, and the tyro is left alone in the rain.

On a psychoanalytic level Henry's separate peace is attained at the expense of becoming an orphan and a half-man. Parricide, matricide, incest, and narcissistic suicide are clumsily ponderous terms to apply to anything as delicate as *A Farewell to Arms,* but they describe what happens in the symbolic construct of the novel. Henry's wholeness is attainable only through the anima-mother who is from the earliest time of their meeting inexorably doomed. The father-images are split between the engineering sergeants (one of whom Henry inexplicably kills), the ruthless battle police, and the anonymous authorities. The tyro revolts against the tutor (symbolically killing one of his manifestations, but not all of them) and indirectly destroys his mother and anima. At the end of the novel he has, it is true, a separate peace with the universe, but he is bereft of any affectional contact with it. [13]

While Hemingway was writing the second draft of *A Farewell to Arms,* he learned of his own father's suicide. [14] We have every right to expect that this fact would influence the interior drama of Hemingway's fiction. The first point we notice is that, after the publication of *A Farewell to Arms,* Hemingway's fictional output noticeably slows down. *Winner Take Nothing* (1933) contains fourteen stories, and among them are some of the bitterest in the Hemingway canon: "A Natural History of the Dead," "The Mother of a Queen," "God Rest You Merry, Gentlemen." The famous *nada* prayer of "A Clean Well-Lighted Place" and "the opium of the people" speech of "The Gambler, the Nun, and the Radio" are in this collection. The volume is also notable for its savage concern with homosexuality and castration, and it is surely remarkable that not one of the stories has a love interest. The anima-mother is nonexistent, and only in "The Gambler, the Nun, and the Radio" is there a tyro-tutor relationship. In that story, however, Cayetano Ruiz is an exceptionally inadequate father image and Mr. Frazer, the tyro, concludes the action by reaching for a bottle of "giant killer" while reflecting that anything that serves as an opiate against the pain of life is a good.

The other two volumes between *A Farewell to Arms* and *To Have and Have Not* are nonfictional treatises on the pleasures of killing. In *Death in the Afternoon* (1932) not only are there long detailed descriptions of men killing bulls and bulls killing men and horses, but a rather elaborate justification for an interest in such murders:

Killing cleanly and in a way which gives you aesthetic pleasure and pride has always been one of the greatest enjoyments of a part of the human race. One of its greatest pleasures, aside from the purely aesthetic ones . . . is the feeling of rebellion against death which comes from its administering. Once you accept the rule of death thou shalt not kill is an easily and a naturally obeyed commandment. But when a man is still in rebellion against death he has pleasure in taking to himself one of the Godlike attributes; that of giving it. This is one of the most profound feelings in those men who enjoy killing. (232–33)

Green Hills of Africa (1935), which continues the interest in killing, moves from the spectator's viewpoint behind the *barrera* to the participant, Hemingway, behind the sights of a .220 Springfield. Hemingway recounts his slaughter of a wide variety of animal life, but if there is a climax to the book, it occurs in the description of a giant sable bull that got away from him, although he had gut-shot it. Both volumes with their emphasis on compulsive killing suggest that the separate peace is still in effect. In terms of our analysis it seems likely that the tyro, desperately fragmented, can only strike out again and again in repetitive acts of destruction. That the targets of his destruction are male animals of rather noble stature is not surprising; the father image has treacherously escaped the tyro by removing himself from gun-range (although he has been "gut-shot"), and the symbolic animals must fall until the Oedipal fury is exhausted.

To Have and Have Not (1937)[15] marks, as we have seen, the clear recantation of the separate peace. And since social and political analysis must stumble over the abrupt switch in position, we are justified in searching the inward mechanisms of the novel for an indication of what has happened. Harry Morgan, whose prototype seems to have been invented in "After the Storm" (1932), is one of Hemingway's most brutalized characters. As tutor or father image, he is, on the one hand, degraded in speech patterns, utterly lacking in dignity, and morally unscrupulous; on the other hand, his elemental power is indicated by his physical strength and endurance (his delighted lust in killing, and his admirable sexual prowess with his wife). The symbolic thrust of the novel is directed to wound-castrate him (his arm must be amputated) and finally to destroy him in a carnage of gore and pain so that the fragmented tyro may become whole. However, this has been done already in Hemingway's previous two works of nonfiction at nearly the same level of intensity, and with no obvious therapeutic value. The differences may be explained as follows. The classic formula, "A man must kill his father in order to become a man," requires not only the death of the father but the death of the son-killer and his emergence as man; in his rebirth he becomes his own father. And this is the pattern in *To Have and Have Not* which is lacking in the preceding work.

In the crucial third section of this novel, Hemingway introduces the tyro figure, Emilio, the good Cuban revolutionary. Harry Morgan, a character not overly given to sentiment or affection, thinks of him as "a kind of nice kid." Emilio voices the rebellion theme, as he explains to Harry what his movement stands for: "We want to do away with all the old politicians, with all the American imperialism that strangles us, with the tyranny of the army. We want to start clean and give every man a chance" (*TH*, 166). Harry listens to him tolerantly and unmoved, reflecting that "He was a nice-looking boy all right. Pleasant talking too" (169). And then with the dispassionate efficiency of a ritual executioner, he blasts his head off. In the ensuing barrage, the three other Cubans are killed, and Harry is shot in the stomach. Like the sable bull, he is "gut-shot," but unlike the sable bull, his death has been fully propitiary. The son has become reborn in the father, and Harry's last words rejecting the philosophy of "a man alone" are the words of the son-become-father. In the chaotic, disorganized, melodramatic structure of *To Have and Have Not,* which could stand almost as an objective correlative of the disintegration of the Caporetto retreat, the tyro ceases to be a separate "piece" of the whole, and is ready for the experience of integration chronicled in *For Whom the Bell Tolls.*

But there are still several serious gaps in the symbolic drama. There is, as it were, a missing act between *Green Hills of Africa* and *To Have and Have Not.* And fortunately, we have three short stories, originally published in the summer and fall of 1936, that do provide the missing elements in the process of reintegration. These stories, two of which are among Hemingway's best, are "The Capital of the World" (first entitled "The Horns of the Bull"), "The Snows of Kilimanjaro," and "The Short Happy Life of Francis Macomber." We have already looked in some detail at one of them, and "The

Capital of the World" is easily disposed of in terms of this discussion. The tyro hero of that story, Paco, is killed in a fight with a symbolic bull (butcher knives strapped to a kitchen chair) which in turn must be a symbolic father. He sacrifices himself with the same kind of naive idealism that Emilio, the Cuban revolutionary, entertained; and, like Emilio, he dies "as the Spanish phrase has it, full of illusions" (SS, 51). In Hemingway's writings that precede "The Capital of the World," the tyro does the killing exclusively; here sacrifice rather than destruction is emphasized, which indicates that the movement away from the separate peace has commenced.

Both "The Snows of Kilimanjaro" and "The Short Happy Life of Francis Macomber" introduce new elements into the drama. In both, the tyro is dead at the end of the story, he dies "full of illusions"; and he symbolically shucks off his past self to emerge a new man. The new radical factor introduced in these stories is the "bitch-heroine" or the "wicked-mother" figure, a character only vaguely prefigured in Hemingway's earlier fiction (specifically in several of the stories of In Our Time), and nowhere else evident after 1936 except in concealed form in the character of Pilar in For Whom the Bell Tolls. "The Short Happy Life of Francis Macomber" is a clear portrait of the dramatic changes in Hemingway's world of fantasy projection, signaling the establishment of a new perspective on which the later mergence and emergence of the tyro can be based.

The Macomber marriage, Hemingway tells us, has "a sound basis of union. Margot was too beautiful for Macomber to divorce her and Macomber had too much money for Margot ever to leave him" (SS, 22). [16] The action of the story will effect a decisive break in this unhealthy union, as it will also unmask to the tyro the identity of his real antagonist, the mother-image, and pave the way for a reconciliation with the father. The locale of the story—a safari in the African jungle—is unprecedented in Hemingway's landscapes as a fictional setting, and is highly appropriate for the tropical depths of awareness from which the story rises. The action opens with Macomber repeating Hemingway's unsuccessful attempts with the giant sable bull in Green Hills of Africa; Francis gut-shoots a lion and runs in cowardice from its retaliatory charge. He suffers the contempt of tutor-father Wilson and of wicked-mother Margot, as well as his own overwhelming self-disgust. Note, though, that this action is an exact parallel of the declaration of a separate peace in A Farewell to Arms, viewed with an entirely different system of emotional valuation. In 1929 the failure to deal masterfully with authority and the flight from it were transformed into acts of heroic nobility. Frederic Henry's final isolation at the end of the novel was treated lingeringly as a particularly poignant result of blindly malicious injustice. Now blame has been transferred from the impersonal "world" to the self-conscious tyro, signaling the first stage in a return to health and creativity.

The immediate consequences of Francis's failure with the lion are Margot's rejection and betrayal of him with father-image Wilson and the completion of Francis's self-disgust and thorough alienation. He is now in the situation of the Hemingway of *Death in the Afternoon* and *Green Hills of Africa,* but without the temporary recourse to random killing. He hates Wilson, but he cannot act on that hatred because of his own sense of fear and unworthiness. In the chase after the bull buffaloes, he dramatically loses his fear in his hatred and performs meritoriously with the buffalo—becoming a reborn man. The denouement to the drama is inevitable. In his second facing of the wounded buffalo's charge, when it is clear that he will react like a man, Margot blasts his brains out with a 6.5 Mannlicher. But here, as in "The Snows of Kilimanjaro," the true villain, the mother, has been exposed; and the separation between tyro and mother is healthily effected.

Macomber's relationship to Wilson has also been clarified. The father has been taught to respect the son, and the son can afford to feel brotherly affection for the father. Interestingly, there is no specific father image in "The Snows of Kilimanjaro." The mountain top, hitherto unapproachable because of Harry's gangrenous unworthiness, seems to fulfill Wilson's function on a more exalted plane. And the hyena, hermaphroditic and vicious, which we observed to be an extension of Helen, becomes even more closely identified with the wicked-mother figure. In sum, the self-realization of the tyro can come only when he has become man enough to tear himself free from dependence on the mother. Then, and only then, can he face his father on equal terms, symbolically becoming one with him. "The Snows of Kilimanjaro" and "The Short Happy Life of Francis Macomber" crystallize this orientation in Hemingway's fantasy life and, on a psychological level, make Harry Morgan's recantation of the separate peace understandable. It remains only to carry this discussion through Hemingway's later fiction to complete the arc of its inner struggle.

For Whom the Bell Tolls is something of an anomaly in Hemingway's fiction. Far and away his longest sustained prose narrative, it is thickly populated for a Hemingway novel, creatively agile in its handling of space and shifting of backgrounds. In terms of our argument it seems significant that the writing pace was extremely fast and regular (the book took almost exactly eighteen months to write and revise);[17] it seems fair to assume that the "inner-breakthrough" of 1936–37 had released in Hemingway prolific creative powers after a dry period of almost ten years. Further, the style of *For Whom the Bell Tolls* is much more freely flowing than the brittle staccato periods that had been characteristic of Hemingway's prose. And, most significantly, it is, with the possible exception of *The Old Man and the Sea*, Hemingway's most serene work. There are scenes of violence and horror, to be sure, but these are narrated at a distance. Pilar's description of the slaughter of the Fascists and Maria's account of her parents' murders and of her own violation are violent memories recollected in something that approaches tranquillity. Even El Sordo's stand on the mountain top is placed at a narrative distance from the reader, since it is viewed by the impersonal narrator and describes the fate of a guerrilla band only peripherally connected with the main characters of interest. It would be too much to call this novel a pastoral idyll. But the emotional center of the fiction—in sometimes jarring contrast to the action described—almost from the very beginning resonates with a harmony in perfect accord with Jordan's previously quoted speech on "communion," as well as with the Donnean echoes of the title. Indeed, it is even worth wondering whether the complete quotation from which the title derives—"No man is an *Island,* intire of it selfe; every man is a peece of the *Continent . . . .* I am involved in *Mankinde."*—is, as it is usually considered, a justification for taking part in a foreign war. More likely is Hemingway's announcement of his achieved "at-one-ment" in himself.

At any rate, such is the way the novel reads on its lower levels; it is a happy fairy tale where all the seeming evils only appear to be evil, and all the goods gain in radiance as the novel progresses. The disasters at the end are merely the inevitabilities of death, and since life has been telescoped into a seventy-hour period, death can be accepted with an almost-Whitmanesque readiness: "There is no such thing as a shortness of time, though. You should have sense enough to know that too. I have been all my life in these hills since

I have been here. Anselmo is my oldest friend. . . . Agustin, with his vile mouth, is my brother, and I never had a brother. Maria is my true love and my wife. I never had a true love. I never had a wife. She is also my sister, and I never had a sister, and my daughter, and I never will have a daughter. I hate to leave a thing that is so good" (*FW*, 381). And these statements by the tyro figure are, in terms of the symbolic inner drama, perfectly true. The good father, Anselmo, has become his oldest friend; the bad father, Pablo, has repented of his treachery and become a helper. The gypsy witch mother, Pilar, has refrained from capturing him in the domineering nets of bad incest, and has metamorphosed into the fairy godmother, bestower of all blessings. In that role she gives him an anima-mother, Maria. The inner drama achieves such a harmony of relationships that "drama," a word to denote a system of tensions, is probably inaccurate; it would be better to characterize the psychoanalytic area of action as the inner tableau.

The last two fictions can be treated much more cursorily. Ten years elapsed between the publication of *For Whom the Bell Tolls* and *Across the River and into the Trees*. It is worth remarking that in that period Hemingway began to refer to himself as "Papa." We have already noticed the effects of "the symbolic doubling" in the 1950 novel. The tyro, Richard Cantwell, becomes his own father-image, projecting his anima into the noble mother, Renata. Characteristically, this results in Cantwell's being forced to attack himself in lieu of an external antagonist, and this he does through the device of the cardiac condition. This novel, the most static of Hemingway's fiction, is largely composed of the tyro father's self-beratements and self-defenses. It does not make for good fiction, but is extremely interesting as a relatively naked exposure of the drama beneath the drama.

And finally, as we suggested earlier, *The Old Man and the Sea* (1952) completes the cycle of the arc. Santiago is father tyro, the sea is anima-mother, and the boy is a displaced remembrance of the hero as a young man. The antagonist, the male marlin, is Santiago's brother, and the parable of maturity or age is cast in fresh poetic terms. The ultimate regression of the psyche to immersion in the primordial is given an authoritative and substantive treatment. There are the scavenger sharks and the Portuguese men of war to disrupt the surfaces of unity and peace; but these are merely the last thrashings of life which, in time, will subside and submerge themselves into the great boundless all.

Two concluding items need reemphasis. As a tool for measuring the worth of a work of art, psychoanalytic criticism is of arguable value. Some critics may allow that it can be fruitful with inferior works—like *To Have and Have Not* and *Across the River and into the Trees*. But they will claim that it yields only misleading information about the personality of the creator of a work of art, that its subjective readings deal with a bundle of unassimilated material already pressed into a design for completely other purposes, and that it is ignorant of the multitude of sensations that are a part of the artist's personality and that are never made manifest in his work. Dealing with Hemingway in particular, a man whom we have seen to pride himself on his role playing, such critics will remind us that we can see only what he chooses for us to see, and that he is not beyond "hoaxing" the reader for his own sense of satisfaction. Other critics, while owning that psychoanalytic criticism can be bunglingly used, argue that it can illuminate even great works of art, can unearth hidden information about the personality of an artist, can discern unconscious and counterintended designs in a bundle of unassimilated material, can glimpse latent meanings and significance in the manifest details of an artist's work. They will claim that even with such a role-playing author as Hemingway, he too has only limited control over what he consciously chooses for us to see; indeed, his "hoaxing" is a symptom that psychoanalytic criticism can deal with.[18]

Regardless how one regards psychoanalytic criticism, its discovery of concealed meanings does not at all negate other equally valuable meanings in the interpretation of a fiction. Moreover, it can be useful as one among many tools in hypothesizing a direction or a focus of examination in which the concealed springs of the creative fountain may show themselves. The single point that seems worth the discussion is the evidence suggesting that Hemingway's fiction is consistently concerned with the metaphors of his own consciousness; that his characters are intensely felt, partial projections of his own internal war, that their conflicts are less the actions of human beings in society contending with one another, than a delicate recording of the wracking ambiguities that always verge on rending man asunder. Hemingway, in short, is a writer of romances; perhaps the most realistic writer of romances of all time, but a romancer nonetheless. And the value of his metaphors depends on his ability to make his poetic vision move his readers toward discovering truths about themselves. This point is worth retaining because it allows us to approach his fictions for what they are and not for what even he may have pretended them to be.

Chapter Four
The Structures of the Fiction

In the previous chapter we examined the standard Hemingway characters whose shifting interrelations compose the designs of the Hemingway myth. We saw that the tyro and the tutor figures, with their protean capacities to "split" or "double" themselves, were central to the typical Hemingway fiction; and that even in those cases where one existed without the other ("The Snows of Kilimanjaro," "The Undefeated"), the presence of the missing figure was strongly implied or symbolized. We shall make a new approach, then, to the tutor-tyro constellation in order to investigate more pointedly the structure of the typical Hemingway story; and we may find that this examination will enable us to see more clearly how Hemingway's life-view becomes refracted and brought to focus in his establishment of form.

There are three characteristic Hemingway stories: those in which the tyro appears more or less alone; those in which the tutor dominates the fiction; and those in which the tutor-tyro axis regulates the revolution of the story. We have already, in one context or another, dealt with fiction of all these types, so we are well prepared to look at them from a different angle. As an introductory summary we can offer the following formula: the tyro story is an exposition of severe emotional reaction, with the tension of the story dependent on the contrast between the accumulated momentum of the emotion demanding to be released and the resisting forces within the style and content that attempt to restrain that release. The tyro story thus tends to resemble an unexploded bomb in imminent danger of explosion. The tutor story has a greater degree of narrative distance and therefore depends less for its effect on the creation of an immediate emotional impact. It is a form of exemplary story with the developed tensions released along the channels of pathos. Its direction will move inevitably toward the genre of the fable and the parable. The tutor-tyro story follows the structure of the educational romance or, as it has been called, the "epistemological story," that characteristically American variation on the bildungsroman (which is too loosely termed an "initiation" or "rites of passage" story). Its direction tends to lead to a revelation of "truth," generally in the form of self-discovery or self-realization. These three forms are, of course, not that distinct and arbitrary in Hemingway's work, and there is a constant infiltration of one form into the other.[1]

The tyro stories, in their purest form, are those Nick Adams stories with no significant characters except Nick: "Big Two-Hearted River: Parts I and II," "Now I Lay Me," and "A Way You'll Never Be." "Now I Lay me" is a straight first-person narration, while the other two are presented from an impersonal third-person viewpoint so closely focused on the tyro character as to make the narrative device very similar to James's use of a "lucid reflector." In terms of Nick's biography, "Now I Lay Me" (1927) comes first; a direct recounting of his convalescence in Milan after the Fossalta wound, it deals largely with his almost Proustian inability to go to sleep and with the various ways he diverts his mind from dangerous preoccupations that might carry him over the thin edge. The last full third of the story records the banal dialogue between Nick and a wounded fellow soldier, John. The dialogue, largely John's encouragement that Nick should marry, serves as ironic contrast to the restrained terrors in Nick's mind, which John knows nothing about. The story does not quite work, however, although the straight interior memory passages are excellent; for the two sections of the story never quite engage each other. The first section is narrated with an interest that diverts the reader's attention from the state of Nick's mind to his memories themselves; and the second section is too flat to provide necessary contrast. We are meant to feel, perhaps, that Nick is in a far other country than the more prosaic, less sensitive John; this is one of Hemingway's recurrent themes, but we do not find it successfully dramatized within the texture of the prose.[2]

"A Way You'll Never Be" (1933), second in the Nick chronology, deals with this shell-shocked return to his outfit after release from the hospital. His nerves are shattered and his mind has a tendency to jump around and off, as though its flywheel were disconnected. There is some experimentation with stream-of-consciousness exposition, valuable for what it tells us about Nick; but these sections are not so selectively controlled as those in "The Snows of Kilimanjaro" and in *For Whom the Bell Tolls*. In spite of the tone of the story—more hysteria than anywhere else in Hemingway's fiction—

it fails to create a meaningful tension. There just simply is no real conflict in the plot, the structure, or the style to make this a potential bomb. The best part of the story—a part that does develop tension—is the description of Nick's ride over the war-pocked road to his meeting with Captain Paravicini.

"Big Two-Hearted River: Parts I and II" (1925), third in the sequence of Nick's adventures, describes approximately twenty-four hours of activity from the time Nick gets off a train in desolated Upper Michigan to hike to a suitable campsite until he calls the fishing over for the day on the following afternoon. Although the story has no plot of any significance, and nothing happens that is in any way untoward in such a fishing trip, it builds up an almost unbelievable tension and has justly been considered one of Hemingway's finest fictions.[3] It is a tour de force of style, since the style almost exclusively persuades the reader that Nick is in a most precarious state of nervous tension which he is desperately holding under clenched control. From having read other Nick stories, the reader may be prepared to fill in the antecedent background to this innocuous fishing trip; but even without that background the dramatic situation of the story seems obvious.

This short paragraph fairly represents the style in which the entire fiction is narrated:

Nick drove another big nail and hung up the bucket full of water. He dipped the coffee pot half full, put some more chips under the grill onto the fire and put the pot on. He could not remember which way he made coffee. He could remember an argument about it with Hopkins, but not which side he had taken. He decided to bring it to a boil. He remembered now that was Hopkins' way. He had once argued about everything with Hopkins. While he waited for the coffee to boil, he opened a small can of apricots. He liked to open cans. He emptied the can of apricots out into a tin cup. While he watched the coffee on the fire, he drank the juice syrup of the apricots, carefully at first to keep from spilling, then meditatively, sucking the apricots down. They were better than fresh apricots. (SS, 216–17)

The prose style has boned both action and reflection down to their simplest components, and it holds them inexorably there. The sentences are with one exception simple declarative ones—first the subject, then the predicate, first the subject, then the predicate—repeated monotonously with little variation. The short unobtrusive

"He liked to open cans," echoing the locution of the previous longer sentence, is a good example of the mastery with which Hemingway implies the dramatic situation. This and the last sentence of the paragraph are the only two places in which Nick is allowed to make a value judgment in this excerpt, and both value judgments are proffered with a kind of embarrassed finality that is shocking because the emphasis of their delivery is in suspicious contrast to the banality of the judgment. With no change, this paragraph, as well as the bulk of the story, could be used to describe a fishing trip by a particularly able and articulate feeble-minded fisherman. The monotonous repetition and the lack of subordination in the sentence structure give all items equal importance, suggesting that there is no principle of selectivity or discrimination in the focus of intelligence.

However, Hemingway has carefully introduced clues to reveal Nick's situation. Early in the story we are told that Nick was happy. "He felt he had left everything behind, the need for thinking, the need to write, other needs. It was all back of him" (210). When he crawls into his tent, we are told: "He had not been unhappy all day. . . . He had made his camp. He was settled. Nothing could touch him" (215). And later, "His mind was starting to work. He knew he could choke it because he was tired enough" (218). It is possible that a feeble-minded person could be happy because he believes that he has arranged things so that nothing will touch him, but we cannot believe that a feeble-minded person would have a need to write, nor that he would be concerned to choke off the activities of his mind. Hence the primitive concentration on the mechanical process of the hike, the making of camp and dinner, and the fishing on the next day can only be a superimposed restraint on an inordinately active mind that is undergoing great stress. That Hemingway is able to insinuate this desperate restraint by making his prose the stylistic equivalent of that restraint is the triumph of the story.

But the story is also something more than a very successful experiment in style. As in James's "The Jolly Corner," the things of the fictional locale compose an allegorical frame that represents the protagonist's consciousness. In James's story, the house's corridors and closed rooms make a convenient setting in which his protagonist can explore his past and under-consciousness. Similarly Nick returns to an area he had once known well. The town is now a ghost town and the stretch of countryside immediately around it has been scorched over. Nick passes through the burned-out places to "the good place," where he makes his camp and where nothing can touch him. But across the river "in the swamp, in the almost dark, he saw a mist rising" (216). He looks away from it. On the next day he fishes the stream, but he does not go into the swamp where the big trout are: "in the fast deep water, in the half light, the fishing would be tragic. . . . He did not want to go down the stream any further today" (231). And he concludes that "There were plenty of days coming when he could fish the swamp" (232).

The story operates, therefore, on two levels. On the first it describes the self-administered therapy of a badly shocked young man, deliberately slowing down his emotional metabolism in order to allow scar tissue to form over the wounds of his past experience. On another level it represents the commencement of the journey into self. But this journey is highly cautious: "He did not want to rush his sensations any" (227). He makes sure he has a good safe place from which to operate. He fishes first in the brightly lit part of his stream of consciousness. And even there he acts with slow, controlled care; precipitate action may frighten away the quarry he seeks, or it may even frighten off the seeker. He knows that the big fish are in the almost dark places, in the frightening mist-hung swamps of his awareness; he knows also that, if he is to find himself, it is there that he ultimately must look. Meanwhile he gathers his courage together and takes the first measured steps of exploration into the undiscovered country of his mind. There will be plenty of time to fish the swamp.

"Big Two-Hearted River" can be seen, then, as a tyro story that generates its power not from what it actually says, but from what it does not say. It is the latter, the unspoken volumes which shriek from beneath the pressure of the taut prose exposition, that expresses the emotional communication to the reader. This technique, which we may call "the irony of the unsaid," is one of Hemingway's favorite tricks and one of his most powerful ways of transmitting the shock of emotion in prose. This common device of the miniatures of *in our time* (his earliest tyro stories) Hemingway uses to great advantage in those tyro stories that confront Nick with situations of severe violence with which he is unable to cope. Thus, in "The Killers," in "The Battler," and in "An Alpine Idyll," situations are developed of such moral outrage as to demand a comment or an indication of appropriate reaction. The situations themselves are reported impersonally and even laconically; the presentation, as in "Big Two-Hearted River," emphasizes the disparity between what has happened and what ought to be the reaction. Hemingway's artful refusal to give an overt outlet to these reactions in the events or the style of the fiction brings the crescendo of tension to a breaking point. Hemingway, like Santiago, holds his pressure on the line until he has exacted the maximum degree of strain; if he slackens it, the reader may get away; if he pulls it too tight, the line may break (as it does in "An Alpine Idyll") and the reader will be free. But when it is just right, as in "Big Two-Hearted River," the reader is caught and forced into response.

There are fewer examples of the tutor story in the Hemingway canon than of the other types, but at least three of them—"The Undefeated," "Old Man at the Bridge," and *The Old Man and the Sea*—are among his finer achievements.[4] We have already remarked in other connections the impulses that drive these stories in the direction of the exemplar or the fable. The tutor figure has already achieved a self-containment or self-definition before he appears in the fiction; he already is, and the finality of his self-acceptance removes him from the disintegrating experiences of becoming. When Retana asks Manuel, "Why don't you get a job and go to work?" Manuel's answer defines his position in the metaphysical universe: "I don't want to work. . . . I am a bull-fighter" (*SS*, 236). Similarly, the old man in Hemingway's Spanish War sketch possesses an equal surety about who he is, even amid the chaos of a refugee evacuation: "I am without politics. . . . I am seventy-six years old. I have come twelve kilometers now and I think now I can go no further" (*SS*, 79). The tutor has thus already become himself, and his further engagement in life will not seriously affect what he is; it will only substantiate and clarify that definition; and, when his activities are figured forth in narrative, they will necessarily be saturated with a moral significance. For when the tutor is placed in a challenge situation within his scope of mastery, he will do whatever can be done in the "right" way. And "right conduct" almost always in fiction is rendered with a strong degree of ethical coercion—hence the consequent level of didacticism in all parables.

Further, the self-containment of the tutor (the is-ness, as it were) will move to minimize the particularizing individuality of the tutor character. Individuality in characterization is largely a property of a character's struggle for wholeness and his inability to achieve it. We may suggest that the more individual a literary character is, the more he tends to be a "grotesque"—a character whose idiosyncrasies establish the extent to which he is at odds with himself (Dickens's "originals" are a persuasive case in point). The exemplary tutors in Hemingway's fiction tend to transcend the fixed coordinates of their temporal lives and become types, as do Manuel and the old man caught in the flooding backwash of a civil war. As types they become representative of a limited aspect of man's condition and a model of excellence within the severe restrictions that bound the possibilities of their typicalness. However, under certain conditions, a type may be further refined of his typicality, through the process of what Hermann Broch terms "abstractism," to a point of universality where the limiting boundaries of its representativeness virtually disappear. The result is an archetype, and the actions through which an archetype communicates its epiphany are what we call myth.[5] At any rate, a process something like this has happened in the transfiguration of Manuel (1925) into the figure of Santiago (1952). The system of changes may be indicated in the following process equation: "the man of flesh and bone" (Unamuno's phrase) becomes a type (The Bullfighter—a man facing a certain kind of death) becomes the archetype Man (alone in, but not isolated from, the Universe). We will try to examine *The Old Man and the Sea* to test the accuracy of these observations.[6]

First, however, a backward glance at one of Hemingway's stories, "The Three-Day Blow" (1925), may furnish a critical frame of reference from which to pursue these investigations. In that early Nick story the two adolescents, Nick and Bill, are discussing Maurice Hewlett's romantic medieval tale, *The Forest Lovers;* Nick remembers the story in terms of its erotic interest to him:

"Yup. That's the one where they go to bed every night with the naked sword between them."

"That's a good book, Wemedge."

"It's a swell book. What I couldn't ever understand was what good the sword would do. It would have to stay edge up all the time because if it went over flat you could roll right over it and it wouldn't make any trouble."

"It's a symbol," Bill said.

"Sure," said Nick, "but it isn't practical." (*SS*, 118)

The criticism here justly describes Hemingway's conviction on the proper uses of symbolism; the symbol must be "practical" or natural. When satisfactorily employed it will blend unnoticeably into the commonsense flow of empirically observed relationships. Like the Mark Twain of "Fenimore Cooper's Literary Offenses," Hemingway demands that romances obey the practical laws of cause-and-effect behavior. But like Mark Twain also, his predilection for natural rather than artificial symbols did not forbid him their conscious use. The Hemingway who wanted to see the world clear and whole—so that any part of it would represent the whole—closely parallels Emerson's ideal poet. And his comment to George Plimpton on symbolic meanings in his fiction underscores the richness of that parallel: "I suppose there are symbols since critics keep finding them. If you do not mind I dislike talking about them. . . . It is hard enough to write books and stories without being asked to explain them as well. . . . Read anything I write for the pleasure of reading it. Whatever else you find will be the measure of what you brought to the reading."[7]

The last sentence is almost a precise equivalent of Emerson's "It is the good reader that maketh the good book." We may assume, then, that the saga of Santiago is an attempt, among other things, to represent the "whole" of man's experience through a system of symbolic correspondences.

The stripped plot of *The Old Man and the Sea* is almost as clean of clinging encumbrance as the marlin's "great long white spine with a huge tail at the end" (126). Santiago has fished the Gulf Stream for eighty-four days without landing a fish. For the first forty days he had been accompanied by the boy, Manolin; the rest of the time he had been alone in his skiff, placing his lines with practiced precision into the depths of the sea on which he floats. On the eighty-fifth day he rows farther out than usual, and at noon the hook of his hundred-fathom line is taken by a huge male marlin. The great fish pulls the skiff steadily to the northwest the rest of the day and all that night, and Santiago determinedly bends all his strength and accrued experience to the task of playing the fish well. This is what he was born to do; and in doing it, he is not just doing, but realizing his being. His action takes on symbolic reverberations when Santiago humanizes and identifies with the great fish on the end of the line: "His choice [the marlin's] had been to stay in the deep dark water far out beyond all snares and traps and treacheries. My choice was to go there to find him beyond all people. Beyond all people in the world. Now we are joined together and have been since noon. And no one to help either one of us" (50).

On the afternoon of the second day Santiago first sights the fish he has been hooked to for some twenty-seven hours when the marlin breaks the water in a long scythelike leap. The antagonists confront one another for a split second, and then the battle of skill and intelligence against brute strength continues. For a long second night the marlin pulls the skiff steadily, while Santiago holds pressure on the line in spite of a disabling cramp in his left hand. Before dawn the marlin makes a desperate run, but he is held at the expense of painful cord cuts on Santiago's back and left hand. The fish turns east to swim with the current, and it is the morning of the third day. He begins to make his circles, and Santiago, playing him with desperate care, finally works him close enough to the boat to harpoon him at noon of the third day. He lashes the over fifteen hundred pounds of fish to his boat and prepares for the homeward journey. The winning part of the drama is concluded; for in the end the winner must take nothing.

An hour passes before the arrival of a great Mako shark, which snaps a forty-pound bite of meat before Santiago is able to kill him. The bleeding marlin leaves a wide trail of attraction behind the skiff and draws the scavenger sharks to his scent. Santiago clubs at them desperately until midnight, when he loses his last weapon. The great fish is picked clean to the bone, and Santiago sails into the harbor late in the third night with the white skeleton of his catch riding high beside him. He beaches the skiff, shoulders his mast, and makes his stumbling way back to the shack. Manolin brings him coffee later in the morning, and they make plans for further fishing. The old man goes back to sleep to dream of lions playing on a beach.

This novella is probably Hemingway's most evocative construction, tense and clean on the surface, but suggesting myriad layers of meaning just out of reach in the murky levels fathoms beneath. There can be little doubt that it is meant to be a symbolic fiction, but it would be wrong to suppose that Hemingway fixed his meanings in the fable, expecting his readers to haul them up after him like so many weighted lobster traps. His remark to a reporter is revealing: "I tried to make a real old man, a real boy, a real sea and a real fish and real sharks. But if I made them good and true enough they would mean many things."[8] Nor is this remark evasive. It points out that there are meanings possible in art that evade conceptualization. For, as Emerson wrote a hundred years earlier: "the quality of the imagination is to flow, and not to freeze. . . . For all symbols are fluxional; all language is vehicular and transitive, and is good, as ferries and horses are, for conveyance, not . . . for homestead." *The Old Man and the Sea* should be approached, then, as an open-ended allegory whose ultimate meanings recede beond reach; and we must retain the critical humility to let them go. This does not rid us of the obligation to catch what we can, of course; but it reminds us that a real fable will change its shape as the needs and experience of its readers change.

Structurally, the novella follows the traditional pattern of the quest or the journey. Santiago has an unexplainable "call" or vocation to be a fisherman and to meet the marlin in the deep water. Mythically he has no choice in the matter; he has been ordained for this one encounter: "Perhaps I should not have been a fisherman, he thought. But that was the thing that I was born for" (50). And this is not a quest to be taken lightly. Santiago is not just a fisherman, he is The Fisherman—the one chosen from all the others because of his superior merits of skill and character. Manolin, who suggests the superiority of Santiago's fishing abilities, hints also that the encounter will demand something more than being merely a great fisherman: " '*Qué va,*' the boy said. 'There are many good fishermen and some great ones. But there is only you' " (23). The movement from type to archetype is prefigured. The great marlin will not come to a great fisherman; he will only be caught by a great Man. In Emersonian terms, Santiago is valuable because he is not a fisherman, but Man-Fishing; and Santiago's soliloquies in the skiff, in which he sees his profession in organic relationship to the rest of life, bequeath to his ordeal something more than exceptional competence and stamina. As he rests against the bow on the second night, he welcomes the appearance of the first stars:

He did not know the name of Rigel but he saw it and knew soon they would all be out and he would have all his distant friends.

"The fish is my friend too," he said aloud. "I have never seen or heard of such a fish. But I must kill him. I am glad we do not have to try to kill the stars."

Imagine if each day a man must try to kill the moon, he thought. The moon runs away. But imagine if a man each day should have to try to kill the sun? We were born lucky, he thought. . . .

I do not understand these things, he thought. But it is good that we do not have to try to kill the sun or the moon or the stars. It is enough to live on the sea and kill our true brothers. (75)

As he fights the fish—a solitary old man with a straw hat desolate on the great sea—he is not alone. A literal cord joins him to his "brother," the fish. Other equally strong cords bind him to the "things" of nature—the sun, the moon, and the stars; the sea life and the birds; his town, his neighbors, the boy, and his past. It is as "whole" man that he meets the fish and brings him back; and it must be as Man, not fisherman, that his experience be measured.

However, even though Santiago has been "chosen" as representative champion to go on this quest, he must be put in readiness for it. For eighty-four days his endurance to withstand failure is put to the test; he must be made "definitely and finally *salao*, which is the worst form of unlucky" (9), before his vigil is ended. And then he must go "far out," "beyond all people in the world" (50), to find what he seeks. The quest hero must be set apart from men and from their daily pursuits—the results of the baseball games and the gossip of the men of the fishing wharves—because immersion in the regularities of the commonplace will dull his spiritual readiness. He must receive his final rites of purification far out in the wilderness, beyond the glow of lights from Havana. He must be tortured with pain and hunger and thirst; he must be reduced to naked will and the capacity to reflect. And then, when he is thoroughly ready, the last barrier is stripped off. He loses for a moment—a barely perceptible but determining moment—his precious sense of individuality. His will remains through the pure momentum of his determination, but the "he" that began the voyage becomes lost:

You are killing me, fish, the old man thought. But you have a right to. Never have I seen a greater, or more beautiful, or a calmer or more noble thing than you, brother. Come on and kill me. I do not care who kills who.

Now you are getting confused in the head, he thought. You must keep your head clear. Keep your head clear and know how to suffer like a man. Or a fish, he thought. (92)

This is the final requisite for success in the quest. In this moment Santiago loses Santiago, merges into his struggle with the fish, merges into the fish and the universal struggle of life, and becomes elemental Man and quest hero.

But this successful catch, this angling vision into the heart of mysteries, cannot be brought back whole to the community of men. As they must, most men spend the greatest part of their lives enwrapped in a world where prudence and practicality are the measurements of what is. Living within the blanketing hum of everyday reality with solid earth beneath their feet, men cannot see what they have no eyes for, nor can they understand what they have not been prepared to understand. The tourists who mistake the marlin's skeleton for that of a shark are not especially culpable; there is no reason they should have known the difference, just as most men cannot discern the difference between the gleam in a maniac's eye and that in a saint's or a mystic's. The kind of experience that Santiago undergoes is incommunicable, but it is not without value to the community of men. He has been a champion of mankind for men and not for himself. He has brought back from his isolation a fragmented gift offering to his fellows, an imperfect symbol to suggest where he has been and what he found there. There are those within the community with the experience and the imagination and the necessary love to project on that skeletal symbol a feeling of the experience which it represents. For them the world has been redeemed; a shaft of knowing has pierced like a thunderbolt into their awareness of what it is to be a man, and the image of mankind has been immeasurably enhanced. And through them the experience will be filtered down to the others who are less sensitive or less prone to enflesh the mysteries. It will suffer dilution and diffusion as it is passed along, changing into legend, into folk story, into barely remembered anecdote. But the ripples of the great marlin's dive will radiate in ever-expanding circles, and each of the community of men will be the measure of what he can find there.

We have taken pains to suggest that there is no tragic quality to this myth, and that Santiago is neither saint nor martyr. He loses three hundred dollars worth of marlin, he suffers great pain and severe tribulation, but he is never shaken at his inner center by his deprivation. He is a man; he does what he is born to do; and, in doing it, he achieves being. He decides that he was beaten because he went out too far; but it is difficult to believe that he is beaten, and it was necessary for him to go out "too far" in order to catch what he had to catch. He has far too much humility to be seen as an "over-reacher," just as he has too much love for his antagonist to sit well in a Promethean role. In fact, the pervasive equanimity that is such a marked characteristic of *The Old Man and the Sea* keeps it from breaking through into the realm of great tragic poetry that rests just one layer lower beyond the reach of Santiago's harpoon.

Within the frame of the general interpretation of this story, there are many possible special readings; for Hemingway has so successfully narrated a journey and a return that almost any "incommunicable" experience may be suggested to a reader. The travail can be seen as a religious one, an introspective one, or an aesthetic one. Without at all exhausting the possibilities, we should like to investigate these three open-ended allegorical readings. The religious interpretation has certain obvious conscious referents. Santiago (St. James) was one of the Disciples of Christ; the description of the carrying of the mast from the beach to his shack is clearly meant to remind the reader of Christ under the weight of the cross; he goes to sleep after his ordeal face down "with his arms out straight and the palms of his hands up" (122). And in the most telling reference (a distinctly artificial and obtrusive one), Hemingway has him say, "*Ay,*" when he sees the school of scavenger sharks. "There is no translation for this word and perhaps it is just a noise such as a man might make, involuntarily, feeling the nail go through his hands and into the wood" (107). The Christological pattern is functional, it seems clear, if it is meant to reinforce by extended tonality the archetypicality of Man's struggle for dignified survival in a non-human universe. In other words, if the Christ brought to the reader's attention in this story is the same man-god who "was good in there" in "Today Is Friday," then it is a legitimate buttressing of meaning. But we would hesitate to ascribe more significance than that to it, for we seriously doubt that theological ideas engaged Hemingway's creative consciousness any more deeply than social or political conflicts. There is something of both Christ and Faust in Santiago, but the first has been tempered of his passion, and the second has suffered a loss in his pride; Santiago is a kind of serene and loving Ahab, and Melville's "insular Tahiti, full of peace and joy," is his true spiritual home where lions gambol like lambs on the yellow beach.

The introspective journey motif already witnessed in "Big Two-Hearted River" is likewise just barely evident in Santiago's voyage and return. In Jungian terms, every quest and confrontation is a discovery of self; and Santiago completes the fishing trip that Nick began twenty-seven years earlier. The murky swamp has descended to the cold dark waters six hundred feet deep in the Gulf Stream, but Santiago has the surety and humble confidence that will allow him to go far out because he can bring his "good place" along with him. He can fish the interior depths of himself for his "brother"-self since he is "whole" now and without fear of his own dark places. "Fish . . . I love you and respect you very much. But I will kill you dead before this day ends" (54). But if the marlin is a "secret sharer" in Santiago's interior consciousness, so must the other creatures in and above the sea also be. Remembering that this is an open-ended allegory, we would be wise to keep from making correspondences. Yet we must note that the great Mako shark is presented on the same king-sized level as the marlin and the Man-Fishing:

> But you enjoyed killing the *dentuso,* he thought. He lives on the live fish as you do. He is not a scavenger nor just a moving appetite as some sharks are. He is beautiful and noble and knows no fear of anything.
> "I killed him in self-defense," the old man said aloud. "And I killed him well." (105–6)

There is more than one buried self in the undiscovered country of the mind. The marlin is killed "for pride" and because Santiago is a fisherman and this act makes him fully realized. The Mako shark with his eight rows of teeth is also an "other" self, but a hostile one. That Santiago can recognize his beauty and nobility and kill him with respect, as well as with enjoyment, is an indication of the man's developed wholeness. For recalling our earlier discussion of the symbolic inner drama of Hemingway's fiction, the *dentuso* is clearly a symbol of the castrating mother, another figuration of Harry's hyena and Margot Macomber. But now in the clarity of age, the mother and the father can be met and accepted with mutual respect and without fear.

And finally we should like to deal briefly with the special aesthetic interpretation of *The Old Man and the Sea,* since in many ways it serves as a summary analogue of Hemingway's concept of the artist and the artistic process. We have in other places commented on the parallels between Santiago's fishing excursion and Hemingway's im-

age of himself as artist; a closer reading of *The Old Man and the Sea*
from this standpoint makes a persuasive case for placing Hemingway
firmly within the Transcendental aesthetic tradition.[9] In this reading
Santiago is the artist who must go "far out" on the seas of his
experience, plumb its depths with precise care and craft to capture
the biggest fish in his artistic world (the artistic vision and the
artistic shock), and bring what he can of it back to his readers as
an offering of fellowship and as a stimulation to human excellence.
One of the purest descriptions of the Transcendental aesthetic is
Nathaniel Hawthorne's "The Artist of the Beautiful."[10] In that story
the artist is a watchmaker who isolates himself from the community,
sacrificing his health and years of youth to create something beautiful. He is initially motivated by his love for a girl of the village,
but as his labors continue he becomes obsessed with his own search
for reality. His ultimate result is a jeweled mechanical butterfly, so
delicately wrought as to take on the appearance of actual life—to
glow and to fly—when it comes into a human contact of proper
receptivity and imagination. He delivers his symbol of beauty to
his now-married ex-sweetheart to watch with placidity the total
destruction of his labors when the symbol is crushed by brutal
indifference and cynicism.

Except for Hawthorne's predilections for the artificial rather than
the natural in his choice of plots and symbols, this story has a
striking similarity to Hemingway's fable. Like the watchmaker,
Santiago is isolated from men by his artistic pursuits; and, like him,
he knows that the community of men will judge with two-dimen-
sional eyes the gift they are not worthy to receive. The marlin will
be measured in terms of thirty cents a pound when no material scale
can possibly gauge its weight:"'Then he was sorry for the great fish
. . . and his determination to kill him never relaxed in his sorrow
for him. How many people will he feed, he thought. But are they
worthy to eat him? No, of course not. There is no one worthy of
eating him . . .'" (75). But he brings the fish home even though
it will become "garbage waiting to go out with the tide" (126),
because he is Man-Fishing and this is his contribution to mankind.
The watchmaker, Owen Warland, reacts to his great loss in words
that closely echo the triumphantly acceptant mood with which *The
Old Man and the Sea* ends: "He looked placidly at what seemed the
ruin of his life's labor, and which was yet not ruin. He had caught
a far other butterfly than this. When the artist rose high enough

to achieve the beautiful, the symbol by which he made it perceptible to mortal senses became of little value in his eyes while his spirit possessed itself in the enjoyment of the reality."

Santiago too had caught "a far other" marlin than the skeleton that is the awed talk of the fishing harbor. The bright and perfect conception and the experience of reality that are the artist's reward for his devotion and sacrifice are as far beyond the symbol that he gives to men as the shiny peak of Kilimanjaro is beyond the heat and disease of the plain. The artist's gift and his curse are to enjoy his vision in beatific fullness and to be unable to talk about it. His duty is to become one of Emerson's "liberating gods," who will cunningly practice his tricks of illusions and symbolic "suggestiveness," in order to set his readers free to create their own experiences of artistic reality. Each, as Hemingway said, is to be the measure of what he brings to the reading. "It is the good reader that maketh the good book"—and on this level the marlin's "great long white spine" becomes a symbolic referent to the novella which Hemingway fished out of the Gulf Stream of his own half century of life.

The tutor story, then, will go in the direction of the parable or the fable. Instructive as an emblem of exemplary conduct, it may even be elevating in its moral suasion. Given Hemingway's temperamental relation to the universe, its effects will move toward pathos rather than tragedy; its philosophical attitude will be one of cosmic acceptance rather than rejection. And its mode of acceptance will be framed within a mood of quiescent resignation rather than exhilaration or joy. Technically the presentation will be bound within the ironic mode; poetic evocation and suggestion will inform the prose with an overwhelming sense of surging meanings beneath the surface level of the action. In one of Hemingway's favorite aesthetic metaphors, he wrote: "The dignity of movement of an iceberg is due to only one-eighth of it being above water." Thus the device of what we termed earlier "the irony of the unsaid" is enlisted in the making of the tutor stories as well as the tyro ones; but it is subtly turned to new uses.

We must now turn to the third typical Hemingway structure—that of the tutor-tyro story. In such a story—"The Short Happy Life of Francis Macomber" and "In Another Country" are good examples—the protagonist is placed in a learning relationship to one or more characters and events that will teach him something about the nature of life; how best to live it; and also, more important, something about himself. These then tend to be stories of growth, and many critics have somewhat inaccurately dubbed them "initiation" stories or chronicles of the "rites of passage."

It will be helpful for our examination of this structure, as well as for our attempt to define the nature of Hemingway's achievement, to discriminate somewhat more closely between his employment of this structure and its more traditional use in such a fiction as Faulkner's "The Bear." The latter story can justly be called an "initiation" story because the protagonist, Ike McCaslin, is literally initiated into a comprehension of certain mysteries that had been hidden from him; through the process of initiation, he loses an old self and gains a new one. He is prepared for the ceremony by a mentor whose specific function is to play spiritual obstetrician to him and others like him; and, most conclusively, Ike's moment of illumination when he meets the bear is precisely equivalent to his cousin's earlier experience, and presumably to that of the others who have been found worthy.

"Initiation" and "passage," then, are terms taken over from anthropological studies dealing with closed tribal systems. In such systems values are considered absolute, knowable, and capable of being transmitted from one generation to another under proper conditions of incantatory sensitization. But we have found so far in our study of Hemingway that values are not absolute; that, although they are learnable, they are not teachable. In other words, the open-ended allegory, which we referred to earlier, and the carefully limited sphere of competence that Hemingway allows his professionals to be skillful within leave open the incalculable area of the unknown and the unknowable—a no-man's-land which, for Hemingway, can be dealt with only in pragmatic terms. Hence, the designation "epistemological story," which emphasizes the learning process per se, seems a more accurate description.[11]

In Hemingway's stories of this type, the protagonist is always the tyro. Sometimes, as in "In Another Country," this is difficult to see; but it is always the tyro figure who encloses and structures the story. These stories are usually narrated in the first person; but, when narrated from an impersonal viewpoint, they achieve the same effect through a variation of the Jamesian device of the "reflecting consciousness." Also, since the tyro is generally in a state of stress or imbalance, this tutor-tyro story frequently merges with the straight tyro stories or "unexploded bomb" stories. "The Killers" or "The Battler," for example, might be included in this type. The distinctive feature of the epistemological story, it seems to us, is the emphasized presence within the story of a tutor figure who serves as a model of instruction for the tyro. Such a tutor must have created for himself a specific modus vivendi that is pertinent to the tyro's immediate emotional needs. The tyro, as we have seen in an earlier discussion, cannot become as adept as the tutor. But he can learn some partial lessons, and he can, in processive pragmatic fashion, learn who and what he is at the specific time of the learning. He can also lay plans for the immediate future. These last two points should be borne in mind because they help to explain why absolute systems are incompatible with Hemingway's vision of himself and the world. Hemingway's view of man—and this will become clearer in our discussion in the next chapter—accepts and even demands the possibility of change. Thus his epistemological stories are "growth" stories in which the new shapes of growth are unpredictable beforehand.

We will look briefly once more at "In Another Country" to get a short view of how this structure operates. And then we will take a longer view of *A Farewell to Arms* for a fuller perspective. "In Another Country" seems at first to be more of a sketch than a story. Narrated in first person by Nick Adams, it describes in seemingly random fashion his experiences undergoing rehabilitation treatment for his knee wound in Milan. He, along with other wounded, reports to the hospital every afternoon to work on the therapeutic machines. He becomes friendly with three wounded officers, all of them deservedly decorated for valor in combat; and they make it a custom to walk home from the hospital together: "we felt held together by there being something that had happened that they, the people who disliked us, did not understand" (*SS*, 269). It is clear that the experiences of battle and of being wounded have set the four of them off "in another country" from the people who jostle them on the streets. Similarly, the hospital is separated from the main part of the city by a network of canals; and, from whatever direction it is approached, it can only be entered by crossing a bridge. However, Nick's three friends, "the hunting hawks" who have proved their bravery, read the papers on his decorations and realize that he is not really one of them; his decorations have been given him because he is an American. They are not friendly with him after that because they have already crossed a bridge that is at the moment beyond his approach. Nick does stay friendly with a boy who was wounded on his first day at the front, because he also is not a "hawk."

At this point Nick meets the Major, and the events occur that we have described in chapter 3; and from this point on in the story, Nick appears to become merely a spectator-recorder of the Major's travail. But to read the story in this way is to miss Hemingway's careful construction of background in the first section. Nick knows that he would not have performed as bravely as the "hunting hawks," and he worries about his real or potential lack of bravery. Set apart by an unrecrossable bridge from the people who have not suffered the immediate violence of war, he is also set apart from those who have fought bravely and without fear: "I was very much afraid to die, and often lay in bed at night by myself, afraid to die and wondering how I would be when I went back to the front again" (270). The Major's agony and his heroic hold on dignity under the burden of his wife's sudden death—a dignity that does not place itself above showing emotion in basic physical ways—become an object lesson to Nick that is directly relevant to his concern with bravery. The "hunting hawks" believe in bravery; it is because they do that they can reject Nick. The Major "did not believe in bravery"; he also had no confidence in the machines that were to restore his hand. He does believe in grammar, in punctuality, in courtesy, and in following the line of duty. And in the story he becomes an exemplar of courage and of dignified resolution in meeting disaster. His actions point out to Nick that a man should find things he cannot lose; that is, a man should slice away from his thoughts and convictions all the illusions that he can live without. And to Nick's immediate concern, he demonstrates that bravery is merely another illusion. He teaches Nick of "another country" that he can enter, one open to him even with his fear. And in this country unillusioned courage is a more valuable human quality than bravery.

One of Hemingway's masterful achievements in modern short-story technique is exhibited in the structure of this story. His device of "the irony of the unsaid" takes on another employment in his handling of the educational climax of Nick's studies. Nowhere does he indicate that Nick learned anything from the Major's example. Reading the story swiftly, it appears that Nick is not even present at the denouement. But from the first magnificent paragraph describing the cold autumn in Milan to the last description of the

Major looking emptily out the window, the selection of every detail is controlled by Nick's mind and by his urgent concern with his fear. The power of the Major's resolution is communicated because it makes a powerful impression on Nick. Nick does not state its impression on him, probably because he has not yet synthesized his impressions into a conceptual form. But they have been synthesized in the narrative structure through juxtaposition and a repetition of the bravery theme. Hemingway once wrote proudly that he chose not to put a "Wow" at the ends of his stories: he preferred to let them end and hang fire, as it were. In a story like "In Another Country," we can see the device handled with consummate artistry. The reader is forced into a participative position; he dots the *I*'s and crosses the *T*'s and learns Nick's lesson simultaneously with him. At times Hemingway's use of this structure becomes so over subtle as to be entirely lost to a reader, and the story drifts away into vignette or sketch ("The Light of the World," "Wine of Wyoming"); less frequently, the lesson is too well learned and overly articulated at the end, and the story becomes the text for a moralizing sermon ("The Gambler, The Nun, and the Radio"). But in those cases where the "wow" is deliberately withheld to create a cogent, meaningful ambiguity at the end, the tutor-tyro stories can be extremely effective.

A Farewell to Arms is not generally regarded as an "epistemological story." It has been called among other things a "tragedy," an unconvincing romance, a masterful depiction of the impersonal cruelty of war.[12] It may be some of these other things as well (although not, we think, a tragedy); but the key to its structure must lie in the lesson that the total experience has taught to Frederic Henry. It is his story that he tells in his own voice; the meanings sunk in the texture of the story can only be the meanings that he has recognized as salient in his experience because they offer him pragmatic hypotheses on what life is and, more important, who he is. The total effect of the story depends on the degree of Frederic's self-realization or acceptance of the implicit meanings in his experience; for, as we have seen with Hemingway, the identity of a man is measured by the processive recognitions of his meaningful experience. *A Farewell to Arms* departs slightly from the rigid format of the tutor-type structure in that there is no single tutor whom the tyro, Henry, will accept. There are, however, several tutors; and, in a sense, his entire series of episodic adventures is a composite tutorial stimulation.

The key to the motif of self-discovery occurs early in the novel when Frederic Henry attempts to explain to the priest and to himself why he had spent his furlough in the opiate-inducing carnival atmosphere of the cities rather than in the priest's home area, the Abruzzi:

> I myself felt as badly as he did and could not understand why I had not gone. It was what I had wanted to do and I tried to explain . . . winefully, how we did not do the things we wanted to do; we never did such things. . . . I had wanted to go to Abruzzi. I had gone to no place where the roads were frozen and hard as iron, where it was clear cold and dry and the snow was dry and powdery and hare-tracks in the snow and the peasants took off their hats and called you Lord and there was good hunting. I had gone to no such place but to the smoke of cafés and nights when the room whirled . . . nights in bed, drunk, when you knew that that was all there was, and the strange excitement of waking . . . and the world all unreal in the dark and so exciting that you must resume again unknowing and not caring in the night, sure that this was all and all and all and not caring. Suddenly to care very much and to sleep to wake with it sometimes morning and all that had been there gone and everything sharp and hard and clear. . . . I tried to tell about the night and the difference between the night and the day and how the night was better unless the day was very clean and cold and I could not tell it; as I cannot tell it now. But if you have had it you know. He had not had it but he understood that I had really wanted to go to the Abruzzi but had not gone and we were still friends, with many tastes alike, but with the difference between us. *He had always known what I did not know and what, when I learned it, I was always able to forget. But I did not know that then, although I learned it later.* (13–14; italics added)

This lengthy excerpt is crucial, we believe, in outlining the frame of reference in which Frederic's experiences coalesce into a significant shape. We must first know, of course, what he is before his experiences begin; for only through measuring the distance between what he had been and what he becomes can we know what he is at the end of the novel after he has finally learned what the priest had always known. We must also remember that the complete novel is told in one long memory-flashback; that there is a qualitative difference between Henry the narrator-protagonist and Henry the actor-protagonist in the novel; and that this difference—one in both time and knowledge—will necessarily impart a dynamic irony to the narrative perspective.

Frederic Henry's character at the beginning of the novel can be readily summarized. He is rootless; he has a stepfather somewhere in America, but he has quarreled so much with his family that the only communication between them is in their honoring of his sight drafts. His general attitude toward life can be almost entirely abstracted from the previously quoted excerpt. Most of the time he does not care about anything at all: "the world all unreal in the dark . . . and not caring in the night, sure that this was all and all and all and not caring." He has been a student of architecture, but there is no indication that this represents anything more than a casual, easily dissolvable interest. He has volunteered to serve in the Italian Ambulance Corps for reasons never made clear. He has neither patriotism nor hatred of the Austrians. In fact, the war and his involvement in it are as unreal experiences to him as anything else in his thoroughly meaningless and unconnected life. "Well, I knew I would not be killed. Not in this war. It did not have anything to do with me. It seemed no more dangerous to me myself than war in the movies" (37). Although he has had sexual experiences with many women, none of them has lodged in any meaningful way in the designing of his person. Or, to put it in other terms, the character or selfness of Frederic Henry that we meet at the beginning of the novel is practically nonexistent. He is his manners and his intermittent drive to satisfy his creature-instincts in drinking, sex, and the sporadic excitement of the sensations that the violence of war provides. And this central emptiness is brilliantly symbolized in the persistent image of the masquerade; he is an unrooted American disguised in an Italian uniform. Or, as Ferguson perceives when she calls him a "dirty sneaking American Italian," he is "a snake with an Italian uniform: with a cape around [his] neck" (246).[13]

There is, however, another aspect to his character to which the priest responds. Although Henry represses and ignores it for the most part, he does possess a strong potential "caringness." There are times, as we see in the excerpt, when he cares a good deal; and everything becomes "sharp and hard and clear." It is this aspect of his character that grows during the novel and that serves as a force field for the development of his personality. In the beginning of the novel, however, and up to the time of the wound, this aspect is consistently and consciously smothered. "It was what I had wanted to do and I tried to explain . . . winefully, how we did not do the things we wanted to do; we never did such things. . . ." The careful adverb, "winefully," is the exposing clue to the masquerade lie of Henry's protestations. It was not what he had wanted to do at all. He wanted to go to the cities where he could merge his excited emptiness into the empty carousings of a soldier's leave in wartime. For one of the lessons Henry learns in the course of the novel is that people always do the things they want to do; and when their capacity for "caring" is limited or negligible, their wants are most easily assuaged by passive activities of an instinctual nature. Somewhat later in the novel when the characterization is no longer completely true, Rinaldi acutely describes the Henry of emptiness: "You are really an Italian," he says. "All fire and smoke and nothing inside. You only pretend to be an American" (66).

Thus Henry is, in a sense, playing a double masquerade. He is to Ferguson a sneaking American hiding in an Italian uniform; to Rinaldi he is an Italian pretending to be an American. The ironies of ambiguous identity will multiply at the bridge over the Tagliamento when Henry will realize that to the battle police he will be "obviously a German in Italian uniform." But at his second meeting with Catherine Barkley he is merely "not-caringness" willing to play the game of caring if there is any prospect of an exciting reward; in other words, his attitude toward her is precisely similar to his attitude toward the war in general. We see this fact when she slaps him at the beginning of their courtship: "I was angry and yet certain, seeing it all ahead like the moves in a chess game" (26). And then later he extends the game-playing metaphor, adding the disguise-motif: "I knew I did not love Catherine Barkley nor had any idea of loving her. This was a game, like bridge, in which you said things instead of playing cards. Like bridge you had to pretend you were playing for money or playing for some stakes. Nobody had mentioned what the stakes were. It was all right with me" (30–31).

In his incapacity to care he can, of course, play for any amount of stakes because he has nothing to lose. The wound is the first lesson to him of what he stands to lose. He realizes in the explosion of the trench-mortar shell that he does have a me that the war has something to do with: "I tried to breathe but my breath would not come and I felt myself rush bodily out of myself and out and out and out and all the time bodily in the wind. I went out swiftly, all myself, *and I knew I was dead and it had all been a mistake to think you just died.* Then I floated, and instead of going on I felt myself slide back. I breathed and I was back" (54, italics added). The italicized segment is curious; it seems to say that, in this moment of extreme shock, Henry realizes that he is dead and has been dead for a long time; and that the mistake is in thinking that he has just died. Such a reading would substantiate the thesis that Henry has lacked a self up to the time of the wound, because, in these terms, "not-caringness" is equivalent to death. But even if the italicized section is an awkward construction, the effect of the nearness of death and the horror of the wound (the pain and the drip of the hemorrhaging corpse above him in the ambulance) is enough to indoctrinate that value of life which the fear of death must inevitably cause.

In the field hospital the issue is dramatically externalized in the successive visits of Rinaldi and the priest. Rinaldi, as he later describes himself, is "the snake of reason," or the rationalization of not-caringness; the priest is his opposite number, the dove of faith, the consecration of *caritas*. Rinaldi warns Frederic that love is an illusion when he perceives his friend's encroaching involvement with Catherine. He insists that he and Henry are similar inside; that neither of them entertains illusions (or "care"); hence, both are invulnerable: "I just tell you, baby, for your own good. To save you trouble" (66). Henry does not accept the advice of his reason, but he does not reject it either.

With the arrival of the priest, the counterargument is delivered. The priest, filled with shame and disgust at the war, observes correctly that Frederic really doesn't mind the war. "You do not see it. . . . even wounded you do not see it. I can tell" (70). In the ensuing conversation the priest diagnoses Henry's deficiency and gives the definition of care which Henry will later come to embrace with qualifications:

He looked at me and smiled.
"You understand but you do not love God."
"No."
"You do not love Him at all?" he asked.
"I am afraid of Him in the night sometimes."
"You should love Him."

"I don't love much."

"Yes," he said. "You do. What you tell me about in the nights. That is not love. That is only passion and lust. When you love you wish to do things for. You wish to sacrifice for. You wish to serve."

"I don't love." (72)

The issue has been drawn; and, although Frederic will come to a balance somewhere between Rinaldi and the priest, the rest of the novel will be an uninterrupted progress away from Rinaldi.

Book 2 records the consummation of the affair with Catherine and the idyllic union they share in the four or so months of Henry's convalescence. According to the priest's definition of love, there is little doubt that Catherine achieves it: "I want just what you want. There isn't any me any more. Just what you want" (106). But Henry's position is more difficult to determine. He "loves" Catherine, worries about not having married her when he learns that she is pregnant, and certainly enjoys her serviceable company. During his stay in the hospital, he centers on the island of pleasure and fulfillment that she fashions for him in the midst of the war. But his role is consistently that of the accepter of services; nowhere is there any indication that he is moved to become servitor as well as master. She creates the various "homes" they occupy, and at the termination of his treatment she remains outside the railway station, while he entrains to return to the front.

Book 3 returns Frederic to the front and to the persuasive ministrations of his two friends, both of whom have fared badly under the strain of the summer offensives. Rinaldi fears he has contracted syphilis (a traditional disease of lust); and, incapable of believing in anything not measurable by the empirical reason, he has buried himself in his work to avoid seeing the carnage and degradation that he works within. Henry is offered an insight into the inner life of his friend without illusions when Rinaldi, drunk, bitter, and a little hysterical, tries to goad the priest into an argument: " 'No, no,' said Rinaldi. 'You can't do it. You can't do it. I say you can't do it. You're dry and you're empty and there's nothing else. There's nothing else I tell you. Not a damned thing. I know, when I stop working' " (174).

The priest, on the other hand, has also become depressed in his faith by the action of the war. He had believed in some kind of miracle that would intercede and cause men to lay down their arms, but now he has begun to doubt his belief. When he asks Frederic what he believes in, Frederic tells him, "In sleep." The answer receives an ironic doubling when Frederic apologizes: "I said that about sleeping, meaning nothing" (179). The ironic slip may have been unconscious on Frederic's part, but it suggests that his capacity to care has not yet moved into the domain of the priest's definition.

The rest of book 3 takes Frederic into the Caporetto retreat, his vain attempt to save his ambulance crew and follow out his orders, and his climactic jump from the bridge into the Tagliamento. Yet his actions throughout this book still maintain the passive, moved-about quality that we observed in his character before his meeting with Catherine. He deserts at last, but only because he has been pushed to the wall. And, as he rides the flatcar to Mestre, he reflects: "I was not made to think. I was made to eat. My God, yes. Eat and drink and sleep with Catherine. . . . and never going away again except together. Probably have to go damned quickly. She would go" (233). There is probably a fractional move closer to a commitment to a mutual love relationship here, but it should be noted that "the separate peace" is filed byHenry neither as an action through which he can rejoin his beloved, nor as an act of disillusionment with the ideals of war. As we saw earlier, he had none of these ideals to start with; and we can suppose that, had there been no battle police on the bridge, he would not have left his unit at this time.

In book 4, Frederic's course is confirmed. Moved by circumstances beyond his control, he accepts the consequences of his forced actions, among them the obligations of caring for Catherine in the priest's sense. On the train for Stresa, he feels like a "masquerader" in his civilian clothes, which is an ironic turnabout, because he is now going to Catherine wholly as himself for the first time. The extent to which he has allowed himself to be penetrated by his openness for her can be seen in the following reflection:

Often a man wishes to be alone and a girl wishes to be alone too and if they love each other they are jealous of that in each other, but I can truly say we never felt that. We could feel alone when we were together, alone against the others. It has only happened to me like that once. I have been alone while I was with many girls and that is the way that you can be most lonely. But we were never lonely and never afraid when we were together. I know that the night is not the same as the day: that all things are different, that the things of the night cannot be explained in the day, because they do not then exist, and the night can be a dreadful time for lonely people once their loneliness has started. But with Catherine there was almost no difference in the night except that it was an even better time. (249)

In terms of the earlier discussion, the Frederic who meets Catherine at Stresa has gone to Abruzzi; and, in his caring, things have become "sharp and hard and clear" to him. Later in his conversation with the aged Count Greffi, he answers the latter's question as to what he values most by saying "Some one I love" (262). And the Count, worried because he has not become devout in his old age, brings the priest's definition to bear on Frederic's new feeling when he tells him that his being in love is "a religious feeling." The game that Frederic had entered so blithely some six months before has become a game that he cannot back out of, and the stakes are high. In the escape across the lake to Switzerland, the "separate peace" has become a separate "union," and the way is prepared for the fulfillment of Rinaldi's earlier prophecy that the "caring"-Henry would have a better time than he, but would also suffer more remorse (F, 181).

Book 5 moves swiftly to its inevitable catastrophe. The interlude of waiting outside Montreux brings the separate "union" to its apotheosis; the move to Lausanne and the brilliantly handled hospital scenes leave Frederic Henry "saying good-by to a statue," which is all he has left of his gamble with love. In the rain, the persistent symbol of foreboding in the novel, he returns alone to his hotel, a winner who is taking nothing away from the gaming table but a self vulnerable to the hurts of the world. For we must realize that there are two opposite movements in the novel, and to neglect one of them is to throw the delicate ambiguity of the novel's balance awry. One movement is the current of doom—the inexorable march of tragic warning that is echoed in the imagery, the rain, and the narrator's prescient comments. It is this movement, presumably, that Hemingway must have been referring to when he termed *A Farewell to Arms* his *Romeo and Juliet*.[14] It may be his *Romeo and Juliet*, although it bears little resemblance to Shakespeare's. Frederic and Catherine do not fall in love at first sight; it is only very gradually that Frederic allows himself to be exposed to a real love; Catherine's death may be "a dirty trick," but it is not accidental; it is eminently natural. To compare Hemingway's lovers to those other "star-crossed" ones tells us little about Shakespeare and forces an unjust criticism of Hemingway's more limited success.

For the other movement in the novel has no precedent in Shakespeare's tragedy. Frederic Henry establishes a connection with the world in his love affair with Catherine and, in so doing, becomes humanly alive. That she dies does not negate his experience; it pushes him into the position of the Major who also had trouble in resigning himself. Frederic moves from the safety of the half-man who has found things he cannot lose, to the precarious and highly vulnerable position of the man who has made an investment in life and must learn to back his play. And that he does learn to resign himself is obvious in that he, not an impersonal narrator, tells the story. As in "In Another Country," Hemingway does not spell out the process of adjustment that Frederic goes through in order to learn to endure his loss. He leaves the significant facts in the narrative structure; they are there because the narrator Frederic has abstracted them from the actor Frederic's experience. And these tell us that Frederic does not return to the Rinaldi position where there is nothing but emptiness and dryness underneath; nor does he embrace the faith of the priest. He accepts the reality of the naturalistic world in which death is a fact every bit as real as sex; but he also accepts the reality of a love he helped to create, and this fact is also as real as death. And, as a final gloss on the novel, we may find a small substantiation in the title. *A Farewell to Arms* is beautifully ambiguous in two obvious realms: the farewell to war in the separate peace, the farewell to the beloved in death. But it also may suggest a farewell to those arms that the early Frederic Henry had opposed to the world: a farewell to "not-caringness" that gives a death-in-life to which no one can resign himself.

Chapter Five
The Code: A Revaluation

Our discussion of *A Farewell to Arms* raises several interesting questions concerning the Hemingway "code" and suggests that the code is more complicated than it at first appears to be. We noticed that although Frederic Henry learns a good deal from his experience, he embraces no single code from one of his professional tutors. He rejects both Rinaldi's stance toward life and that of the priest. Similarly, Mr. Frazer in "The Gambler, the Nun, and the Radio" does not embrace the way of life represented by the Mexican gambler, Cayetano Ruiz, although he respects and admires Cayetano's capacity to restrain and control his responses in a painful situation. Even Francis Macomber, the most famous code learner in Hemingway's fiction, cannot be described as a disciple of Wilson in the usual sense; certainly there is no likelihood that, had Francis survived his safari, he might have become a white hunter. And yet these protagonists do learn something from their fictional experiences and are able to apply their knowledge in a practical manner to the way they live their lives. They become recipients of something usually called "the Hemingway code." To understand the implications of this code, we retrace our steps slightly to revaluate its significance in relation to the whole focus of Hemingway's work.

At the start, it may be helpful to think of two Hemingway codes. One is the notorious sportsman's code of so much hostile Hemingway criticism: the ethic of the professional that applies to the areas in which he operates: soldiery, prostitution, gambling, or deep-sea fishing. This code, in whatever area of violent or nonviolent sport it covers, can be easily understood. It is a system of arbitrary "thou shalt not's" that comprises the rules governing professional activity within the particular sport. The hunter does not shoot at game from moving vehicles; the bullfighter does not win glory in killing unless he goes in with his sword over the horns; the gambler does not tell the police who shot him; the soldier does not disobey orders even when convinced of his superior officers' stupidity.

First, as is frequently pointed out, these various systems that make up the professional code are extensions of juvenile and adolescent game playing, in which the imposition of "rules" makes a game more interesting ("fun") to play since there will be a designed "order" to constitute a challenge for the player. Second, the rules provide a hierarchy of valuation ("morality") by which the achievement of the individual player may be measured. The best fisherman is not the man who brings in the biggest or the most fish; a hand grenade exploded in a small pond will do that. The best fisherman is the one who plays the fish according to the rules that impose the highest degree of challenge on the fisherman without canceling out his chances for success. And since most sports are followed for the pleasure of the challenge rather than for the material success (the dead fish, birds, etc.), the rewards of victory are measured in terms of sports-code morality. Skill, endurance, courage, and honor are some of the characteristics that this code is equipped to evaluate.

The sports code also functions as a pragmatic program for prediction within the area defined by the rules. The player knows in advance what is expected of him in the game he is to play; he does not know what combination of challenges are likely to converge on him at any single time. Through training and experience in his sport, he can learn a set of automatic (almost reflex) responses to a broad variety of differing challenges, although he must always bear in mind the uniqueness of every individual challenge. When a player's skill is developed to a high degree and when his accumulated experience in the game is wide enough to give him a substantial backlog of unique challenges from which to generalize, he can be called a "professional." When, on top of that, he possesses enough confidence in his ability to predict quickly and to act resolutely in the face of the challenge, he is likely to be a good professional.

Finally, if the particular sport he engages in includes the physical risk of his own life, reputation, or property when he is clumsy or inept in his judgment, and if he possesses all of the above-listed qualifications and the courage to control his natural fear at the thought of the possible consequences, then for Hemingway he is a great and enviable professional. And his rewards will consist of his satisfaction in being able to do a difficult thing well, his transferred confidence to areas outside his field of mastery, and the emotional thrill that accompanies the act of meeting a demanding challenge with grace and adequacy.

But this sportsman's code is not the Hemingway code. We noticed earlier that Hemingway's professionals do not act well within and outside their areas of supposed competence. Pablo in *For Whom the Bell Tolls* is disgusted to discover that the Fascist priest does not die well; the *Gran Maestro* is incompetent in those discussions with Colonel Cantwell that move into the areas of higher strategy; and the successful bullfighter in "The Mother of a Queen" is less than adequate in his responses to normal sexual demands and to his obligations to his dead mother. Neither Hemingway nor his characteristic tyro protagonists are really concerned with the sportsman's code, although it provides useful metaphors and dramatic illustrations for the workings of the real code.

For Hemingway, life is consistently imaged as a game, but the game is like none that was ever played for sport. The rules are simple: man the player is born; life the game will kill him. The code that does concern Hemingway and his tyros is the process of learning how to make one's passive vulnerability (to the dangers and unpredictabilities of life) into a strong rather than a weak position, and how to exact the maximum amount of reward (honor, dignity) out of these encounters.

In a famous comment in *Death in the Afternoon,* Hemingway wrote: "all stories, if continued far enough, end in death, and he is no true story-teller who would keep that from you" (122). The Hemingway code is the ethic, or philosophic perspective, through which Hemingway tries to impart meaning and value to the seeming futility of man's headlong rush toward death. And as we shall attempt to demonstrate, the Hemingway code does more than erect a barrier of resignation, or stoicism, between man's struggles and ultimate failures. It also provides a significant measure of freedom for human actions within which morality can operate and human responsibility can be judged in terms of active rather than passive responses. This final point should be carefully examined because its neglect will inevitably distort Hemingway's considered stance toward life into either an ephebic code of primitive bravery or a desperate style of abject surrender.[1]

In its simplest terms, the Hemingway code—what his tyro figures painfully learn and relearn—consists of two lessons: the ability to make realistic promises to oneself, and the ability to forgive oneself one's past. Both of these capacities can be found analogically within the sportsman's code, but their transference into a life-attitude removes them far beyond the juvenile restrictions of "playing the game" and "being a good sport." It makes them, in fact, as viable an attitude to bring toward life in any of its aspects—domestic, social, and philosophical—as any other religiously or humanistically oriented twentieth-century life philosophy. That Hemingway frequently dramatized this perspective in the activity of violent games should not conceal the fact that the perspective was created to operate meaningfully in just one violent game—the game of life. More misunderstanding and conscious or unconscious distortion of Hemingway's position has accrued about this single point in Hemingway's philosophic perspective than around any other aspect of his fiction. It is, therefore, crucial to a just appreciation of his achievements that we apprise ourselves of what the code actually is and how and why it is designed to function.

The creation of the code is such a persistent preoccupation in Hemingway's fiction that no single work fully illustrates it. A good introduction into its form and subtleties, however, may be found in that magnificent story that Edmund Wilson called "a five-page masterpiece"—"A Clean Well-Lighted Place" (1933). This story is unusual in the Hemingway canon since it departs from the typical structures discussed in the last chapter; there is no clear tyro figure (unless it is the older waiter) and no clear tutor figure (unless it is the old man). In this one instance Hemingway seems to have given rein to his poetic vision and to have contented himself with casting an indelible image in which placement and chiaroscuro function as dramatic entities (Sean O'Faolain calls this "an almost-silent movie").[2] The story has the symbolic resonance of a fable; but unlike *The Old Man and the Sea,* it is a fable without a fixed referential base. To continue the terms earlier employed, "A Clean Well-Lighted Place" is an open allegory.

Nothing dramatic occurs in the story; the setting is almost all there is. It is late at night in a simple Spanish café; the only customer is an old man who had unsuccessfully attempted suicide a week before. The two waiters in the café—one young, the other older—discuss the old man; and the younger waiter, eager to get home, closes up the place despite the older waiter's objections.[3] The older waiter muses on such matters as the difference between a well-lighted café and an all-night *bodega,* the problems of age, and the difficulties of getting to sleep when one has nothing to attach oneself to: "What did he fear? It was not fear or dread. It was a nothing that he knew too well. It was all a nothing and a man was nothing too. It was only that and light was all it needed and a certain cleanness and order. Some lived in it and never felt it but he knew it was all nada" (SS, 382–83). Then the old waiter recites the Lord's Prayer, substituting the word *nada* for all the important verbs and nouns; has a cup of coffee at a *bodega;* and prepares to return to his room to toss wakefully until dawn comes.

The story radiates its meaning around Hemingway's ability to make the experience of *nada* (nothingness) palpable and convincing to the reader. The nothingness of the fable would include everything that exists outside of the "clean well-lighted place." The nothing is everywhere, "so huge, terrible, overbearing, inevitable, and omnipresent that, once experienced, it can never be forgotten."[4] It is characterized by an absence of order, an absence of light, an absence of meaning. It is, in pure and ominous terms, the chaos of nonmeaning—primordial and ineffaceable—which, for Hemingway, exists in its most concentrated and terrifying form at the point of the still moment of time in which the human will is challenged to respond. T. S. Eliot graphically describes that moment in "The Hollow Men" (1925):

> Between the idea
> And the reality
> Between the motion
> And the act
> Falls the Shadow
>
> *For Thine is the Kingdom*
>
> Between the conception
> And the creation
> Between the emotion
> And the response
> Falls the Shadow
>
> *Life is very long*
>
> Between the desire
> And the spasm
> Between the potency

> And the existence
> Between the essence
> And the descent
> Falls the Shadow
>
> *For Thine is the Kingdom*

But there is a distinctive difference between Eliot's presentation and Hemingway's. The "shadow" that falls on the still moment of time in Hemingway's description is not a presage, even connotatively, of theological existence. Hemingway's fiction, at least, does not take place "in His Kingdom," and the pragmatic code he erected and clung to is without spiritual sanctions or sanctifications. A successful passage across the "shadow" is the test of all ethical and moral codes. In fact, moral codes exist largely to function as guides of the passage. A comparison of Hemingway's mode of passage with that of traditional religious philosophy ought to highlight the differences between Hemingway's faith in a clean well-lighted place and Eliot's.

The still moment of time—the moment in which human beings make decisions—exists, in terms of morality, sui generis, outside of time, within the space of its own creation. On the other hand, it is the product of all past time that ever was; and it is the genesis of all future time that ever will be. Any code of morality that attributes the freedom of responsible choice to human behavior will reject the notion of a completely deterministic past, for such a notion would make morality irrelevant and human beings not responsible for their acts and failures to act. But our empirical sense (whether the commonsensical variety or the scientific code of philosophical naturalism) is a persuasive agent in demonstrating to us that the past in its inexorable continuum does determine the future and does control the passage across the shadow.

From a human viewpoint this suggests that the shadow is meaningful only as a manifestation of physical principles at work; that man's dearly held values (love, justice, courage, etc.) are sheer illusions and that his attempt to act with dignity (he who is but a bundle of externally motivated responses) is a rather pitiful joke. This is the great dilemma for the modern artist: are values jokes or are they worthy of belief? Is there meaning in this chaos of seeming nonmeaning *(nada)?* And with the failure of modern religion to supply a deeply convincing rationale in which man can trust to a

Providence beyond his understanding to make a supersense out of what appears to be nonsense, modern man's attempts to effect a passage across the shadow have stimulated some of his most unnerving reflections and, peripherally, some of his most intense creations of art. As we can guess from the excerpt from Eliot's poem, Eliot will move out of the shadow by embracing a theological sanction for the passage that removes it to a nonempirical dimension of grace. Hemingway's code is an attempt to cross the passage by creating a dimension of meaning within the naturalistic flow of physical events, but without invoking a realm of supernatural focus. Both resolutions of the problem contain "mysteries," but Hemingway's mysteries are humanistic rather than theological.

Hemingway's consistent belief in the freedom of the individual to make responsible choices was paid for at the painful expense of having constantly to wage battle with the fearful unpredictability of the future. If man is really free in the isolated moment of time, the importance of what he does and does not do in that moment are staggering. He has in effect elected to create the universe all by himself, and he has made himself answerable for the worth of his creation. Standing apart from the flux of eternally succeeding sensations, he becomes the sole maker of time and meaning. He asserts his freedom not only from the guides of tradition, but also from his total experience of the past—from all the selves he was in other existences. For to create the new moment of time, he must create himself whole and unique in that moment; and this means he must destroy what he was before that moment.

A constant act of creative will and a constant sense of universal responsibility conjoin in the awareness of the Hemingway hero. And the omnipresent threat that hangs over his head is *nada*—a total whimsical destruction to his will, his responsibility, and the meaning he has paid so highly for. The code is the tentative bridge he erects into the future to effect a passage over the shadow; it is a network of promises to himself of future challenges and how he will respond to them. It is tentative, flexible, and subject to swift changes; but, according to his capacity to redeem those promises to himself that can be kept, it gives the Hemingway hero minimum surety and rest in a quixotic world that is his only guide to the future.

To continue the bridge metaphor, if one support for the bridge is flung into the future, the other goes back into the past. One end of the bridge's span depends on the capacity of man to make promises to himself; the other, on his capacity to forgive himself his mistakes and inadequacies. The importance of this rear support, forgiveness, is too easily underestimated. A man unable to forgive his past actions becomes insidiously but irrevocably determined by them; and he loses his freedom to begin anew. He loses contact with the immediate moment of time because he must forever be caught up in that old played-out moment of time. His forgiveness frees him from the past and makes it possible for him to project new promises into the future, but it does not allow him to wipe out the past: "No, himself said. You have no right to forget anything. You have no right to shut your eyes to any of it nor any right to forget any of it nor to soften it nor to change it" (*FW*, 304). Forgiving without forgetting is a large order for humans, but projected promises without a tough fibrous memory to give them substance would mean an inevitable descent into the chaos of the shadow.

"A Clean Well-Lighted Place" corroborates some of these notions about the code. The story can be read as a metaphor of the code. The clean and pleasant café is a lighted island within the darkness and confusion of the city. It is a place where those without the illusions of belief (religion, youth, confidence, family ties, insensitive indifference) can come, can sit, can drink with dignity; can find a small surcease or point of rest from their constant awareness of the meaninglessness of life and their struggles to oppose that meaninglessness. The story makes a spatial image for the code, which is, of course, a temporal metaphor, not a spatial one; but its quick focus on the old man suggests a temporal dimension as well. He had attempted to commit suicide the week before because "he was in despair" (*SS*, 379). When asked what he was in despair about, one of the waiters answers "Nothing." We have already noticed how many of Hemingway's tyro figures are in constant fear of this same "nothing," which keeps them from going to bed at night without a light on, which makes them eager to find the opiates of the radio, whiskey, or immersion in work or sex, as Mr. Frazer chronicles in "The Gambler, the Nun, and the Radio."

But having tried to kill himself out of despair, the old man comes to the café to rest momentarily from his fight. Hemingway takes special care to point up his dignity. The older waiter defends the old man to the younger waiter: "This old man is clean. He drinks without spilling. Even now, drunk. Look at him" (381). And when he leaves the café he is described as "walking unsteadily but with dignity" (378). The word "dignity" is the key to the operation of the code. In the creative act of imposing meaning on a senseless universe, in making the passage across the shadow, the Hemingway hero who works within the code may achieve dignity as the sole value for the game he has played. We have seen that the Major in "In Another Country" possessed it; that Santiago possessed it; that even Harry ("The Snows of Kilimanjaro") and Francis Macomber gained it in their deaths. We saw that almost the total lesson of Frederic Henry's experiences in *A Farewell to Arms* was directed toward making him responsible for his self in order that he could achieve dignity and some somber meaning out of Catherine's death. The clean well-lighted place is the structure that man imposes on the chaos to wrest order and temporal regularity out of a meaningless flux of sensations. But this structure is not equal to the chaos it opposes. The café must close eventually, and its customers must leave again to face the nothingness that leads to despair. And even when it is open, the leaves of the trees throw shadows into the café; the nothingness can invade and disrupt the imposed order at any time.

It is interesting to notice how frequently Hemingway has explicitly and implicitly used the image of "the clean well-lighted place" as the arena of conflict, the dramatic locus of an onslaught or a challenge. The lighted lunchroom into which the two gunmen enter, bringing machined and absurd terror in "The Killers," is such a place. The fire in the hobo jungle near the railway embankment in "The Battler" where Nick meets the punchdrunk fighter and his black friend is such a place. The cone of light that floods the prize ring in "Fifty Grand" is the same place. And the lighted sands in the middle of the darkened plaza where Manuel receives his *cogida* in "The Undefeated" is that same place. We could add the bull rings of *Death in the Afternoon,* the glow of the campfire in "The Snows of Kilimanjaro" into which the hyena and death will creep, or the operating table under the white lights of *A Farewell to Arms.* In each case, the clean well-lighted place is a temporary stay against confusion and terror. But when the terror remains on the outside, it is "the good place" of "Big Two-Hearted River," or the unbelievably white crown of Kilimanjaro, or the shining sands where the yellow lions play in Santiago's dreams. The clean well-lighted place is thus both an image of the code and a hopeful dream of its transcendent reality.

In this context the apparent hedonism of Hemingway's professed morality takes on a different coloration. In *Death in the Afternoon* he wrote: "So far, about morals, I know only that what is moral is what you feel good after and what is immoral is what you feel bad after and judged by these moral standards, which I do not defend, the bullfight is very moral to me because I feel very fine while it is going on . . . and after it is over I feel very sad but very fine" (4).

His characters—amazingly guiltless for twentieth-century literary characters—have similar emotional standards of morality. Catherine Barkley wishes she could do something that was really sinful; Harry Morgan is described thus after he machine-guns the four Cubans: "All the cold was gone from around his heart now and he had the old hollow, singing feeling and he crouched low down and felt under the square, wood-crated gas tank for another clip to put in the gun" (*TH*, 171).

Jake Barnes feels rotten after he arranges Brett's liaison with Pedro Romero, and Brett gives the classic formulation of the moral code: "You know it makes one feel rather good deciding not to be a bitch" (*TS*, 245). We must investigate the relation of this emotional test of morality to the code which is its justification. But we will find that it is neither so haphazard nor so untraditional a system of determining "rights" and "wrongs" as it originally appeared to readers and critics of the early 1930s.

Since the code is designed to function in the place of absolute and externally imposed guides on human conduct, the delegation of the judgment of behavior will inevitably be given to the involuntary emotions. We have already noticed the consistent anti-intellectualistic bias of Hemingway's perspective (a bias that in this, as well as in other aspects of his work, makes him a twentieth-century heir to his Transcendental granduncles), and it would be strange for him to deny the primacy of the feelings in this most subjective area. Hemingway has persistently argued that values are a product and not a determinant of experience: "when they have learned to appreciate values through experience, what they seek is honesty and true, not tricked, emotion . . ." (*D*, 12). Hence, it would follow—as in any other variation of a pragmatic code—that good and bad can be ascertained only after the process has come to some sort of completion. The good is not, in Hemingway, what man wants to do; it is what gives man a feeling of self-completion ("wholeness") after he has done it; and this sense of pleasure may be achieved through indulging one's whims or sometimes through sacrificing immediate desires.

Further, Hemingway makes a distinction between the people who can and cannot be trusted in their self-trust. One of his constant and frequently irritating strategies is to divide the human race into those qualified to live by the rigors of the code (those who are "one of us") and those who are too flabby in their self-indulgence, too susceptible to a variety of illusions concerning themselves and life to be allowed to take over the responsibilities of creating their own lives. We will examine this as a dramatic theme in *The Sun Also Rises* in a later chapter, but most Hemingway fictions arbitrarily divide those possessing what Emerson called "an active soul" from those who are mere "formalists" in living. The fictitious organization of *Across the River and into the Trees*, El Ordine Militar, Nobile y Espirituoso de los Caballeros de Brusadelli, is perhaps the most notorious example in his fiction of the willful line that Hemingway frequently drew between the "in's" and the "out's" (the professionals and the tourists). And his basis of inclusion is perhaps overly arrogant, but it is not without a guiding principle:

> I wish he did not have to have that glass eye, the Colonel thought. He only loved people, he thought, who had fought or been mutilated.
> Other people were fine and you liked them and were good friends; but you only felt true tenderness and love for those who had been there and received the castigation that everyone receives who goes there long enough.
> So I'm a sucker for crips, he thought. . . . And any son of a bitch who has been hit solidly, as every man will be if he stays, then I love him. (A, 71)

The same distinction is arbitrarily made in *To Have and Have Not* where the title—ambiguous as most of Hemingway's titles are— underscores the distinction. Those who "have" wealth, security, position, and the protective comforts that these possessions erect as a barrier against the elemental struggle of life, are also those who "have not" been there; hence they have no basic experience from which to create meaningful values. That Hemingway consistently ignored or underrated the equally real struggle taking place under the camouflage of "respectability" and social forms is perhaps a regrettable indication of his lack of empathy and the narrowness of his fictional range; but it should not keep us from seeing that his test of inclusion rests on a solid pragmatic base. Those "who had been there" and had survived had been taught the implacable rules of the game on their heart and pulse beats; they cannot countenance the illusions of the "out's," because their knowledge of the stakes involved forces them to accept the reality of life as a grim, relentless struggle. "Only so much do I know, as I have lived," said Emerson; and, if he was more optimistic than Hemingway in his hope that all men could learn to become defiant and self-reliant, still the intuitive bases of their faiths are similar and equally responsible.

From this viewpoint Hemingway's concern with the "techniques" of professionalism may also take on a different cast.[5] "Only so much do I know, as I have lived," makes a constant active quest for experience a fundamental prerequisite for knowledge. The soul that would become alive must be as fully exposed or receptive to life as possible; the preferential emphasis on doing proceeds from the pre-Deweyan faith that doing leads to being and not the reverse. Hemingway's passion for knowing how things are done and what it feels like to do them—manifested in his private life as well as in his fictions—need not be labored here. From the mechanisms of making love in a Venetian gondola to the experience of walking through the working-class district of Milan to a hospital, Hemingway has taken on the gargantuan task of recording in his fiction almost everything he has patiently and obsessively learned.

Characteristically, as we saw in "Big Two-Hearted River," he will mercilessly analyze a process of action into its slowmotion components. At times the effect is merely silly or exclusively "knowing," as when Colonel Cantwell "reaches accurately and well" for a fresh bottle of Valpolicella. This insatiable desire to be expert in all areas of life can lead to a grotesque over-concern with and over-valuation of the trivial (as when we are meant to admire Robert Jordan's professional knowledge of horses or Professor MacWalsey's expert knowledge in handling himself in tough saloons); but it also maintains vigilance and receptivity to the challenges of every moment. It insures a kind of "activity" of the soul, or at least a forced physical awareness to the offerings of the "Daughters of Time, the hypocritic Days," which may decrease the threshold degree of resistance to new experience. And finally, the concern with the techniques of action gives the hero a program of behavior for positively confronting the new moment in which the mechanisms of his learned responses may aid him in successfully bridging the shadow of the passage and creating an order where none existed before.

We may not leave this discussion of the Hemingway code, however, without making a provisional attempt to deal with two strong criticisms frequently levied against it. One persistent attack denies the code any philosophic substance on the grounds that Hemingway's heroes are either adolescents or mindless automata; hence their behavior is of the passing interest to a reader that a traveling freak show may engender. The other line of attack, closely related to the first, takes various forms and is rarely as explicit as in our descriptions; however, it can be summed up as a simple denial of Hemingway's relevance because of the inadequacy of his world view. He just does not possess a mature enough vision of evil to come to serious grips with the problems of the modern human condition.

The simplest way of defending Hemingway, or any other artist, against attacks of such a nature is to deny the pertinence of the criticism. The artist is under obligation only to create mimetic worlds that may engage the imaginations of his audience; his psychological or philosophical competence is immaterial unless it seriously detracts from the successful workings of his art. "Let those who want to save the world. . . ." said Hemingway; and the creation of a philosophical formula to resolve the agonizing ambiguities of our modern uncertainties is surely a strategy for saving the world. Inasmuch as these criticisms are directed ostensibly at the successful workings of Hemingway's art, however, it would be dishonest criticism on our part to ignore their existence.

And since the two attacks are extensions of one another, we Procrusteanly combine them for economy's sake in three excerpts from D. S. Savage's withering analysis of Hemingway's works:

His typical central character, his "I," may be described generally as a bare consciousness stripped to the human minimum, impassively recording the objective data of experience. He has no contact with ideas, no visible emotions, no hopes for the future, and no memory. He is, as far as it is possible to be so, a *de-personalized* being.

The Hemingway character is a creature without religion, morality, politics, culture or history—without any of those aspects, that is to say, of the distinctively human existence.

The characters of Hemingway reflect accurately the consciousness of the depersonalized modern man of the totalitarian era, from whom all inward sources have been withdrawn, who has become alienated from his experience and objectivized into his environment.[7]

Some of Mr. Savage's strictures we have already dealt with; the more important ones we can try to counter. We saw that the operation of the code depends on precisely those "inward sources" that are denied existence. The code is created largely because the Hemingway hero is unwilling to accept the fatality of the coming moment; it is his unillusioned hopes for the future that cause him to act at all, rather than to take the much easier way of reacting passively to circumstances: "It is silly not to hope, he [Santiago] thought. Besides I believe it is a sin" (*OM*, 104–5). And we also saw that the Hemingway heroes are not "men without memories," but men determined not to become slaves to their pasts (memories); they are men who have made signal attempts to become masters of the present; and they know they can strive to do this only through disengaging the present moment from all past moments. It is this, as we saw, that makes the act of self-forgiveness so important in the code.

Evidence for this is the discussion in *For Whom the Bell Tolls* between Anselmo and Jordan about the need of killing in war. Anselmo says:

"I am against all killing of men."
"Yet you have killed."
"Yes. And will again. But if I live later, I will try to live in such a way, doing no harm to anyone, that it will be forgiven."
"By whom?"
"Who knows? Since we do not have God here any more, neither His Son nor the Holy Ghost, who forgives? I do not know."
"You have not God any more?"
"No. Man. Certainly not. If there were God, never would He have permitted what I have seen with my eyes. . . . I miss Him, having been brought up in religion. But now a man must be responsible to himself."
"Then it is thyself who will forgive thee for killing."
"I believe so," Anselmo said. "Since you put it clearly in that way I believe that must be it. But with or without God, I think it is a sin to kill." (41)

It is anything but a depersonalized man who is willing to take on his own conscience the sole responsibility for his acts; and it is anything but "a bare consciousness stripped to the human minimum" that would have the odd combination of humility and pride to enable him to forgive himself his sins. It may be, from a philosophical point of view, that Hemingway's image of man gives entirely too much credit for the workings of a principle of divinity within that man; but this is precisely opposite to Mr. Savage's denunciation. His other claims—that the Hemingway hero has "no visible emotions" and "has become alienated from his experience"— we have already dealt with. This general argument is based on the fallacy of construing the sportsman's code to be the Hemingway code.

It is probably true, however, that Hemingway does lack a fashionable sense of evil, often considered today to be a "mature" world view. Offhand we can think of no Hemingway character who is an animation of Original Sin; we can think of no Hemingway plot that could aptly be described as one of motiveless malignity. There are many instances of evil, or certainly unpleasant, happenings in Hemingway's fiction, and most of his characters would patently fail to qualify for sainthood; but evil as such does not play an important role in his work. And because there is this uncommon deficiency, there is also a lack of concern with a torturing sense of guilt or a crazed need for redemption. This may explain why attempts to explicate his work in terms of Christological symbolism rarely prove illuminating in any way. And here, too, we may find a precedent in Emerson—himself very unfashionable in his indifference to evil. His famous exhortative approach to evil could almost be synonymous with what seems to have been Hemingway's: "Good is positive. Evil is merely privative, not absolute: it is like cold, which is the privation of heat. All evil is so much death or nonentity."

This citation returns us to one of Hemingway's major concerns: the emotional paralysis of man faced with the overwhelming envelopment of *nada*, of nonentity, and his resolute determination to impose meaning on that which is without meaning. Had he come to believe this struggle fruitless, he might have converted his vision of privative emptiness into positive evil. His faith in man (and, we suppose, in himself) would not allow him to do this. It may be that this faith was inordinate, but such a question is surely beyond the jurisdiction of literary criticism. It is certain that his faith allowed him to project an image of man-as-hero that is unparalleled in twentieth-century writing. This, it would seem to us, indicates a strength and not a deficiency.

Jean-Paul Sartre, in a passage that has the dubious distinction of being unfair to both Hemingway and Albert Camus, writes: "When Hemingway writes his short, disjointed sentences, he is only obeying his temperament. He writes what he sees. But when Camus uses Hemingway's technique, he is conscious and deliberate, because it seems to him upon reflection the best way to express his philosophical experience of the absurdity of the world."[7] Leaving the question of Sartre's judgment of Camus's purposes aside, we find it strange that the distinguished French existentialist should decide out-of-hand that the one novelist writes on the basis of deliberate reflection and the other, seemingly, without thinking at all.

It makes an interesting hypothesis to think of Hemingway as a compulsive, automatic writer, "obeying his temperament" like a lemming racing to the sea; but it is less an act of responsible literary criticism than another instance of the deeply rooted European tradition that is determined to regard American literature as the casual off-droppings of noble or ignoble savages. The difficulty, as has so frequently been the case in the judgments of other major American writers by both native and foreign critics, is the stubborn refusal to recognize that American literature has always been marked by a powerful commitment to an overriding moral purpose. Literature in an open democratic society must do more than entertain and instruct; it must also function as a potential instrument for the creation of identity and of culture definition. Emerson's "liberating god" offers the metaphors of his vision to his society in order that its individuals may become themselves in their creative participation in those metaphors. The tropes of the "god" are fluid incitements toward becoming, not dogmatic pronouncements of being. It would not be too much to say, in Whitman's phrase, that the function of the American writer is "to be commensurate with a people"; and a people, at that, characterized throughout its history by metamorphosis, not stasis.

Because of this overriding function, consciously or unconsciously accepted by every major American writer, the individual works of American literature are curiously "open" on at least one end. Through a variety of experimental devices in style, structure, symbolism, and through the use of personae, the reader is invited—sometimes forced—to "live into" the work, to create his own values out of the collision of his experience and that which the successful work plunges him into. We have noticed that Hemingway's style, his use of the tyro protagonist, and his characteristic structures are shaped to this end of implicating a reader in the rhythms of growth that inform his fiction; and we noticed as well that the climax of the implication (in his best fiction) occurs with an act of self-discovery or self-revelation. Melville's "shock of recognition" or James's "suddenly determined absolute of perception" are examples of the same immediacy that is the bardic aim of American literature.

No writer can possibly be "commensurate with a people," particularly with a people as heterogeneous and purposely committed to change as has been the American people. The writer is consequently led to a kind of personal "invisibility," so that his actual personality will not impede the process of reader participation. The reader will be presented with narrator-protagonists (frequently unformed adolescents like Nick Adams) or with abstracted personages devoid of social reality but charged with mythic or symbolic attraction. There will thus be a strong ironic distance between the actual flesh-and-blood writer (in almost no case in American literature do we really know who he is) and the pose or series of poses that the writer projects into his fiction and sometimes into public life.

To overlook this ironic distance is to fall into the trap of equating the man with the writer's mask—to assume, as Sartre does, that Hemingway lacks some essential intelligence or minimal self-consciousness, and that he cannot possibly be standing apart from his creations paring his fingernails or oiling his shotgun with casual insouciance. We would suggest that Hemingway's writing-mask can be sketchily characterized as a curious synthesis of some of the elements of Mark Twain's mask and Walt Whitman's mask, with certain added embellishments of his own. All three writers seemed to enjoy the role of the knowing innocent abroad, and all three seemed to enjoy "playing the fool" on occasion, as well as being the butt of their own jokes. None of them considered himself above that kind of sly defensive humor that allowed two modern American Nobel Prize winners to describe themselves as "just a country boy" and Ole Possum. But to equate Mark Twain with Huck Finn and to forget the shrewd man standing ironically behind Huck Finn, or to dispose of Whitman as the sounder of "the barbaric yawp" would be a strange aberration for a literary critic to indulge in. And yet this aberration has been literally endemic among Hemingway critics. We have tried to demonstrate not the validity but the presence of a sound philosophical base for the Hemingway code. If we can assume that Albert Camus's attempt to present an expression of, and an artistic resolution to, "the philosophical experience of the absurdity of the world" is a product of removed reflection and considered design—then we must grace Hemingway with the same prerogatives of the non-automatic writer. To do otherwise would surely lead us into non-Sartrean effusions on divine inspiration and shamanism.

Chapter Six
Of Time and Style

During the Caporetto retreat in *A Farewell to Arms,* one of the engineering sergeants steals a clock from an abandoned house, and Frederic Henry forces him to return it. The incident is trivial except as it makes a small preparation for Henry's later antagonism to the sergeant, but a further significance was probably not intended. The idea of hauling a clock along in the chaotic confusion of a mass retreat is deliciously grotesque enough to characterize the sergeant, but it also indicates Hemingway's contemptuous unconcern with the conventions of horological time. Nor should this be surprising in terms of our discussion in the last chapter of the operation of the Hemingway code. Only two kinds of time enter into Hemingway's fiction in any significant way: geological—the time used to measure the erosion of continents and the shrinking of mountains; and the now—that time variously described as "the moment of truth," "the captive now," or "the perpetual now."[1] In different ways these two concepts of time conspire to aid in the formation of Hemingway's style, his aesthetic, and the characteristic concerns and directions of his fiction. Although we have implicitly alluded to this aspect of his work in other places, we may now try to discover its inner workings and to estimate the importance of its function in terms of Hemingway's over-all fictional approach. Having done this, we will then examine *For Whom the Bell Tolls* to test and illustrate our findings.

Green Hills of Africa has what must be the longest and most rhythmically flowing sentence in all of Hemingway's work. We only quote it in part, but it is even a good deal longer than the following:

That something I cannot yet define completely but the feeling comes when you write well and truly of something and know impersonally you have written in that way . . . and when, on the sea, you are alone with it and know that this Gulf Stream you are living with, knowing, learning about, and loving, has moved, as it moves, since before man, and that it has gone by the shoreline of that long, beautiful, unhappy island since before

Columbus sighted it and that the things you find out about it, and those that have always lived in it are permanent and of value because that stream will flow, as it has flowed, after the Indians, after the Spaniards, after the British, after the Americans and after all the Cubans . . . are all gone as the high-piled scow of garbage, bright-colored, white-flecked, ill-smelling, now tilted on its side, spills off its load into the blue water, turning it a pale green to a depth of four or five fathoms as the load spreads across the surface, the sinkable part going down . . . ; the stream, with no visible flow, takes five loads of this a day . . . and in ten miles along the coast it is as clear and blue and unimpressed as it was ever before the tug hauled out the scow; and the palm fronds of our victories, the worn light bulbs of our discoveries and the empty condoms of our great loves float with no significance against one single, lasting thing—the stream. (148–50)

This passage illustrates imperceptibly flowing geological time with a romantic vengeance; and although Hemingway's thinking is not usually so explicitly directed to the view, *sub specie aeternitatis,* as we see here, rarely is this concept of time completely absent from his notions of life and art. He chose the title for *The Sun Also Rises,* his first major novel, from those passages in chapter one of Ecclesiastes that closely parallel the above, and these same passages were read at his burial service. In his fiction he used images of mountains and the sea and natural countryscapes (as well as the rain in *A Farewell to Arms*) to reflect this long view of time that comments ironically on the vanity of human intercourse played against a sonorous background: "One generation passeth away, and another generation cometh: but the earth abideth for ever." Santiago's battle with the fish takes place on that same inexorably moving stream, and Harry Morgan bleeds his life into it. Richard Cantwell moves among the well-worn stones of a city notorious for its long tradition of vanities, and he dies fittingly across the river and almost into the trees. And Robert Jordan's love and death are framed by the rugged Spanish mountains that are not unlike the towering peak of Kilimanjaro.

"What profit hath a man of all his labour which he taketh under the sun?" To this unanswerable question Hemingway seemed to find a meaningful response in the fact that "the earth abideth for ever," and "the things you find out about it . . . are permanent and of value," even though knowledge and all the records that men leave will also succumb to extinction in the slow erosion of time.

We noticed in the last chapter that the image of "a clean well-lighted place" could sometimes become an image of a transcendent reality in which the transiency and ephemerality of human existence were suddenly locked in another dimension of time; that feeling, in other words, which Hemingway could not yet define completely, arcs itself out of human time and becomes one and immortal with the earth that abides forever.

Hemingway's metaphysic of time attempts to squeeze the moment into that distilled, charged essence of felt emotion that, as we have seen, gave him a feeling of immortality. And to portray this essentially mystical experience in a prose narrative (which takes place in terms of straight sequential time), Hemingway experiments with language and portrayal of action to simulate contraction and expansion of events simultaneously. An early indication of the direction that his prose seeks may be seen in the description of the bullfighter Maera's death in one of the miniatures of *in our time:* "There was a great shouting going on in the grandstand overhead. Maera felt everything getting larger and larger and then smaller and smaller. Then it got larger and larger and larger and then smaller and smaller. Then everything commenced to run faster and faster as when they speed up a cinematograph film. Then he was dead" (*SS,* 207).

The device, crude here, is effective only because of the movement of the narrator into Maera's point of view, and then his shockingly abrupt removal in the final sentence. But the careful regulation of tempo in the passage—the accelerating pace of the words themselves (short simple words connected by temporal conjunctions forced into motion through the rhythmic repetition)—presages the much more sophisticated uses of this device that Hemingway later employs. The ironic contrasting staccato of the last sentence—now a commonplace technique in modern prose—stops the action like a bullet and shifts the narrative point of view outside of the human context to something almost like the long impersonal view of the ever-abiding earth.

Some three years later (1927), Hemingway's mastery of this stylistic device had developed immeasurably, as we can see in the opening paragraph of "In Another Country"; no residuum of dramatic action forces the alternate closings and openings of time: "In the fall the war was always there, but we did not go to it any more. It was cold in the fall in Milan and the dark came very early. Then the electric lights came on, and it was pleasant along the streets looking in the windows. There was much game hanging outside the shops, and the snow powdered in the fur of the foxes and the wind blew their tails. The deer hung stiff and heavy and empty, and small birds blew in the wind and the wind turned their feathers. It was a cold fall and the wind came down from the mountains" (*SS*, 267).

This is a passage of extraordinary stylistic subtlety that analysis can hardly plumb, but perhaps we can indicate some superficial procedures that have a bearing on this problem of time. The time sense of the passage could be described as "suspended present," even though the narrator is recounting the events from a point in the future looking back into the past. Throughout the story we are aware that this has already happened, that this is being told to us through the processes of selective remembrance. Yet the descriptions are rendered with an overpowering sense of immediacy as though they had happened, but had not yet ceased to happen. The effect is to isolate this segment of artificially circumscribed time in its natural momentum and to pluck it out of the meaningless ticking of sequential time. In effect Hemingway has returned the clock to the abandoned house and imposed his own time sense on the events he has chosen to chronicle.

A closer examination of the passage indicates the control that Hemingway has achieved in manipulating his effects. The speech rhythms in the excerpt clearly echo the rhythms of the King James Version in their sonority and finality of phrasing. This effect is largely a result of the deliberate repetition of words and sentence structure; the poetic connotations of the recurrent "and's" and the auxiliary "was," which becomes almost an active verb of existence instead of a mere connective; and the pervasive hint of Elizabethan formality in the locutions ("but we did not go to it," "and the dark came very early," "and the wind blew their tails," etc.). This effect is given additional support by the diction (short simple words, minimal use of adverbs, an almost ponderous emphasis on adjectives used not to modify but to bring into being as it were).

The imagery demonstrates how well Hemingway had learned the lesson of the unnoticed detail that stimulates emotion: "and the snow powdered in the fur of the foxes and the wind blew their tails. The deer hung stiff and heavy and empty, and small birds blew in the wind and the wind turned their feathers." This is highly impressionistic description; everything is seen in a very abstracted, non-concrete selection of detail, and yet it gives the illusion of being extremely realistic. As we noticed in our discussion in chapter 2 of one of the miniatures, the realism is not in what is seen, but in the fact that someone is intensely seeing; and in line with this discussion on the uses of time, that act of seeing is so intense as to become identified in its abstractness with the way the mountains themselves might see such a scene. The cumulative roll of the passage persuades the reader that this is the way it was, and thus has it always been, and thus will it ever be. The small birds will always blow in the wind, and the wind will always turn their feathers.

And the references to the stability of the seasons, the weather, the wind, and the mountains suggest an implicit awareness of the long Ecclesiastes view of time. Although Hemingway introduces the word "always" only in the first sentence, and there ironically to describe a temporal, not an eternal event, the eternality of the "always" carries through the whole paragraph. And finally we must at least call attention to the hinted appearance of the "clean well-lighted place" image (". . . the electric lights came on, and it was pleasant along the streets. . . .") that contrasts with the cold fall and the sharp wind coming down from the mountains to suggest a temporary stasis of fixed illumination within the unimaginable eternality of relentless geological time.

Stylistically the passage fuses the now and the always in the moment of illumination (of the electric lights and the intense act of abstracted perception that the narrator expresses) when both become synonymous. Action, which occurs in the temporal onrush of flux, becomes so intensive in the act of seeing that it becomes a distillation of itself and merges with the monumental passivity of eternal time. Conversely, the passivity of eternality is made active in the motion of the wind and, by association, with the motion of the weather, and with the mountains. The suspended moment of vision (the now) is surrounded by time, which will move forever, but, because everything in the description of "the forever" is frozen in motion (the snow is powdering, the wind is blowing, the deer are hanging, etc.), the total effect gives the moment of seized time the immortality of always time.

Harry Levin has pointed out one of the effects of Hemingway's style that, in this context, functions to aid in this time-seizure: "Hemingway keeps his writing on a linear plane. He holds the purity of his line by moving in one direction, ignoring sidetracks and avoiding structural complications. By presenting a succession of images, each of which has its brief moment when it commands the reader's undivided attention, he achieves his special vividness and fluidity."[2] But this succession of individual images, like the frames on a reel of motion-picture film, do more than create an effect of "vividness and fluidity." They also force the illusion of "time suspended," caught and held and merged into that greater time which is timelessness. And to experience that feeling of fusion between the now and the always is to have something "permanent and of value" for Hemingway, and of sufficient "profit" for all the seemingly vain labor that man must do under the sun.

Because the handling of time in fiction is as much a structural as a stylistic problem, we must reinvestigate Hemingway's employment of structure in terms of this aspect of his aesthetic ideals. But instead of analyzing one of his fictions as an illustrative test, we turn again to that handy primer of composition, *Death in the Afternoon*. One obvious reason the bullfight so fascinated Hemingway was the congenial metaphysic of time inherent in its formal structure. The *corrida* takes place in time, within sequential horological time; as a matter of fact, quite punctually and precisely so—as García Lorca pointed out in his great elegy for Ignacio Sanchez Mejias, *a las cinco de la tarde*—at five o'clock in the afternoon. But although it takes place in sequential clock time, a more important designed time is imposed upon it that has the effect of enclosing the actual clock time in a formal net of suspension. Hemingway describes the formal structure of the bullfight as follows: "There are three acts to the fighting of each bull and they are called in Spanish *los tres tercios de la lidia,* or the three thirds of the combat. The first act, where the bull charges the picadors, is . . . the trial of the lances. . . . Act two is that of the banderillas. . . . and the third and final division is the death" (96–97).

As formally organized as a classical tragedy, and yet as open to improvisation as the commedia dell'arte because of the unpredictable behavior of both man and bull, the *corrida* makes a perfect symbolic stage for the enactment of Hemingway's code within the specific compression and expansion of time that his metaphysic demanded. That he felt that there could be this fusion of the now and the always in a great bullfight we have already seen, but it bears reillustrating:

If the spectators know the matador is capable of executing a complete, consecutive series of passes with the muleta in which there will be valor, art, understanding and, above all, beauty and great emotion . . . they have the hope sooner or later of seeing the complete faena; the faena that takes a man out of himself and makes him feel immortal while it is proceeding, that gives him an ecstasy, that is, *while momentary, as profound as any religious ecstasy;* moving all the people in the ring together and increasing in emotional intensity as it proceeds, carrying the bullfighter with it, he playing on the crowd through the bull and being moved as it responds in *a growing ecstasy of ordered, formal, passionate, increasing disregard for death* that leaves you, when it is over . . . as empty, as changed and as sad as any major emotion will leave you. (206–7; italics added)

Within a structure of artificially suspended time, the bullfight (under its ideal conditions) may further compress the suspended time (the now) to a point of excruciating ecstasy that results in a feeling of immortality (always-time). The structures of Hemingway's fiction move toward the formal closed design of the bullfight but with opportunity within the internal context for that fusion of now and always so important to him. We find, in other words, that the structures of Hemingway's fiction are in some special way conducive to an establishment of that formal confrontation we found imaged in the metaphor of "a clean well-lighted place."

In our discussion of Hemingway's typical structures in chapter 4, we divided Hemingway's stories into tyro stories (unexploded bombs), tutor stories (exemplary fables), and tutor-tyro stories (epistemological romances). Remembering that these arbitrary categories are far from exclusive, we discovered two characteristics common to all three structures, although varied in their uses and effects. These were a distinctive use of irony as a narrative technique, and a common development to a climax that would conclude in an act of self-discovery or self-realization. In the tyro story the "irony of the unsaid" worked through a measured withholding of shock and through a cumulative build-up of tension, resulting ideally in the release of emotion that the reader receives in the revelation of the true concealed drama in the fiction. In the tutor story, the irony resided in the symbolic suggestiveness of the parable, generating a stronger and stronger suspicion that the fiction meant more than it actually said, which tension is also ideally released in the reader's discovery of hitherto hidden "truths." And in the tutor-tyro story, the irony was inherent in the dramatic distance between the knowledge of the narrator-protagonist and that of the actor-protagonist, the released emotion again coming ideally in the reader's perception of the knowledge that is never explicitly detailed in the narrative action. In the light of our discussion on Hemingway's metaphysic of time, these two characteristics of Hemingway's fiction—irony and revelation—function to control his structures and make them susceptible to that fusion of now-time and always-time which was the aim of his aesthetic.

We would argue that this is exactly what happens. The first effect of the irony is distancing; this effect can work in many different ways, but the result is a radical displacement of the fictional experience away from the reader and away from the fictional equivalent of horological time, the realistic portrayal of human behavior within a convincing socio-historical dimension. The complex images of the fiction are "struck from the float forever held in solution" (Whitman) and detached from objective reality to become an experience for reflection rather than for empirical perception. Such an effect is inevitable in the contemplation of any artistic object, of course, but Hemingway's employment of irony tends to magnify the process of distancing to a greater extent than possible in nonironic narration. Further, his characteristic concern with the presentation of internal rather than external images (the fantasy-projections of his own consciousness) is an additional contributing element to this process of artistic detachment. The net effect gives individual stories the semblance of closed pockets; that is, they are defined and delimited by their own internal activity. Or, to return to the immediate problem, their artistic isolation and self-enclosure provide a structural equivalent for suspended temporality. What the style effects in giving an illusion of stoppage to the narrational flow of language, the ironic structures parallel in suspending and in closing in the simulation of human behavior in time.

The characteristic of developing a climax in the structure through the device of discovery or revelation operates to allow a passage from the now-time of the suspended and enclosed moment to the always-time of eternality. Revelation or illumination can be understood as an experience of Gestalt perception in which all the disconnected fragments of experience (conscious and subliminal) cohere with a suddenness and completeness that is involuntary, compelling, and frequently termed "ecstatic." The experience has often been described in terms of mystical transport and transcendental elevation.

Without arguing its psychological validity, this experience has traditionally been associated with the intense emotion that aesthetic
contemplation is able to offer under unique and rare circumstances,
and it is a fact of human experience that what people call "the
moment of truth" (the "light bulbs of our discoveries") is felt to be
out of space and out of time—and hence immortal. At any rate,
the structural devices that lead a narrator-protagonist to self-discovery, while insidiously drawing the reader into a participative self-
discovery of his own, facilitate the possibilities of rendering Hemingway's full metaphysic of time in his fictional forms. The irony
surrounds and suspends the action similar to the way the *barrera*
and the traditional stylized design of the *faena* suspend horological
time; and the moments of revelation in the fictions transcend the
action in the same way that the great series of *suertes* creates the
ecstasy of deliverance. We may conclude, therefore, that Hemingway's characteristic style and structure both function to make that
illusion of mergence between now and always that is of cardinal
importance to his aesthetic.

An additional note should be added, however. Hemingway has
no monopoly on an ironic narrative perspective or on a passionate
interest in achieving moments of illumination in his fiction. Many
other writers, especially Americans, have been similarly concerned
and rather equally successful. James's fiction, particularly that of
his later period, uses a similar and more sophisticated kind of irony,
and his prose structures are very consciously built to lead to the
moment of self-confrontation—the moment of "the suddenly determined absolute of perception." Hence in characterizing Hemingway's treatment of time, we must add to the function of style
and structure the typical violent action of his subject matter. As in
the *corrida,* there is almost always in Hemingway's fiction a manifest
physical conflict between the protagonist and a brutal animation of
physical nature. It is not always an animal or another violence-
bearing human being; it can be a heart attack or the death of a
beloved. But it is the invasion of *nada* in physical form, and therefore
it can be opposed by the code only through some sort of physical
activity. Hemingway's moment of fused time will generally be symbolized in a physical act—an act of killing or being killed, an act
of sexual union, or a reaction of extreme physical shock that leads
indirectly to the discovery of a truth. This temperamental emphasis

on the physical will inescapably impart the distinctive Hemingway signature to his emotional communication of timelessness.

Finally, although the exigencies of literary criticism require us to deal with such categories as style, structure, subject matter, and theme as though they were separate and different strategies or modes of attack for dealing with a common problem, such analytical divisions are mechanical. From our discussions of the code and of Hemingway's metaphysic of time, we realize that on the level of engaged fictional experience, the abstractions with which we clumsily approach the thing in itself dissolve and coalesce in our moments of real artistic perception. For us such a moment occurs in the composite radical metaphor of "A Clean Well-Lighted Place"—a moment in which the temporal image of the code and the spatial image of fused time become one. "It was all a nothing and a man was nothing too. It was only that and light was all it needed and a certain cleanness and order" (*SS*, 383). Here the "place" becomes the encloser and suspender of time and action, tenuous and removed; the "cleanness" and the "order" become the deliberate regularities with which man attempts to confront the "nothingness" with dignity and resolution; and the "light" is the measure of his success in illuminating the shadow and finding those truths about himself and life that are permanent and of value, and that make him in that seized moment know as much of immortality as he can ever know.

For Whom the Bell Tolls is, as we noted earlier, Hemingway's most ambitious novel. It is almost two hundred thousand words long; it is set in the foreground of an international civil war rather more complicated in its alliances and divisions than most; and it attempts to suggest all those experiences Hemingway had felt with Spain (perhaps his favorite country) that, as he notes in the last chapter of *Death in the Afternoon*, he had been unable to include in that book. Hence the novel is many things: an attempt to present in depth a country and a people that he loved very much; an effort to deal honestly with a highly complex war made even more complex by the passionate ideologies that it inspired; and, beyond these, a struggle to cast a personal metaphor of his unique vision of life. Given Hemingway's peculiar strengths and weaknesses as a novelist, it is inevitable that the novel should fall short of his ideals; the remarkable thing, however, is the extent of its success even in its areas of failure. Although our examination of the novel will be occupied largely with its attempts to render the metaphysic of time, we acknowledge that this is only one of many ways of approaching *For Whom the Bell Tolls*.[3]

As many critics have pointed out, the structure of *For Whom the Bell Tolls* is circular; its center, which we are never allowed to be unaware of, is the steel bridge that spans the gorge "in solid-flung metal grace." From that center all the actions of the novel, dramatic and symbolic, radiate in widening concentric circles of meaning. The Loyalist offensive depends on the certainty that the bridge be exploded so that the road will be closed to the movement of Fascist reinforcements. Robert Jordan's sole reason for going behind the enemy lines is to blow up the bridge; like Santiago, his mission is what he was born for. The disruption of Pablo's guerrilla band directly relates to the significance of the bridge, as does the extermination of El Sordo's band on the hilltop. By extension, the bridge becomes symbolically a pivotal center for the destiny of mankind: ". . . there is a bridge and that bridge can be the point on which the future of the human race can turn" (43). The bridge then is the absolute point of confrontation, the proper meeting of which ought to justify the code and provide that contact with immortality that the metaphysic of fused time demands. For this fusion to succeed, the novel must create the illusion that time has been suspended, contracted down to an explosive point of now, and expanded endlessly into a communicated sense of always.

The technical problems facing Hemingway in this attempt were enormous. He had chosen to depict a group action rather than the struggle of one man; and, although the novel ultimately concerns itself with Robert Jordan, more than a dozen other characters must be fit into the dramatic organization and be suitably disposed of. Further, since Hemingway consciously wanted Robert Jordan's action to be representative, he had to find means of relating both Jordan and his action to situations and events outside the immediate dramatic compass of the novel. This aim makes for additional problems; for every time Hemingway departs from the immediate "thing of the bridge," in order to expand the meaning of the action, he runs into the danger of opening up his closed stage and destroying the suspension of time. Yet if he does not do this, Jordan's adventures with the bridge may appear simply eccentric—the isolated maneuvers of a super-hero behind the Fascist lines.

Thus, on the one hand, if the suspension of time is lost, the novel will be judged according to its realistic depiction of an actual historical event, and the actions of its characters may justly be expected to reflect sociological and political realities. If, on the other hand, the action is not in some way universalized, it can be justly categorized as a romantic adventure story bearing no significant relationship to the setting that is its locale. We have already seen that Hemingway's powers were not those ordinarily associated with the doctrines of realism, and we have also seen that the abstractions of ideology were not the materials that engaged his creativity. The obvious solution to his problems he chose—for whatever reason— to ignore; namely, to write a fable, an exemplary story like *The Old Man and the Sea* that would be both suspended in time and universalized. It is probable that he wanted too much to record the Spanish war directly, or that he was committed still to the use of a tyro rather than a tutor character; at any rate, his resolution of these problems was not completely successful (as we may judge by the criticism levied against the novel) since justifications for both criticisms do exist in the novel's structure. But the novel is astonishingly successful even with its failures, and it is useful to investigate how Hemingway dealt with these technical problems in the pursuit of his aesthetic fusion of time.

Hemingway's first strategy in attempting to create an illusion of suspended time was to isolate the novel temporally and spatially. General Golz's orders for the blowing of the bridge are, to be sure, provisional, but in the dramatic development of the novel, the three-day action from Jordan's appearance with Anselmo to his final stand with the machine gun is as stylized and formally closed as the three act bull-fight. Using a seventy-hour time scheme for the novel's events and making that seventy-hour schedule apparent to the reader, Hemingway gives the appearance of employing horological time, but he does so only to transform it into his own time. There are several direct references to this transformation of time in the novel, the following fairly representative:

Maybe that is my life and instead of it being threescore years and ten it is forty-eight hours or just threescore hours and ten or twelve rather. Twenty-four hours in a day would be three-score and twelve for the three full days.

> I suppose it is possible to live as full a life in seventy hours as in seventy years; granted that your life has been full up to the time that the seventy hours start and that you have reached a certain age. (166)

Thus we are constantly reminded that this is not seventy clock hours of sequential time, but seventy hours scooped out of time with a quite arbitrary beginning and an end. Pilar's introduction of the omen she reads in Jordan's hand supports this time isolation; it is not minutes and hours that are passing in the novel, but Jordan's life. The seventy clock hours measure doom instead of time, and the movement of doom in fiction can only be presented as "suspended time."

We ought to note also Hemingway's pains to document the passing of the time in these seventy hours. The meal times are described in detail; the sleeping time during the two nights is so presented that the reader cannot possibly miss it; and the changes in weather and light during the three days and within each day are carefully delineated. The appearance of fighter and bomber planes in the sky, as well as the troop of Fascist cavalry on the ground, functions as much to punctuate the passing time as to develop the plot. And Jordan even gives his watch to Anselmo when he sends him to record the troop movements on the bridge. In short, if Hemingway wishes to suspend time in order to compress it in the novel, he cannot allow its passage within the scooped-out suspension to go unnoticed. The reader must be made aware of the swift and regular movement of time within the sequence of frozen time. Otherwise there will be no time for him to fuse.

But even as the novel is isolated temporally, it is also isolated spatially. The plot device of having the action take place behind the enemy lines makes a natural spatial demarcation. The action is placed, as it were, in another country—and one where the normal laws of human behavior do not apply. The guerrillas are by definition "irregulars," improvising their own expedients to structure a life lived outside of normal socially controlled habits and mores. The placing of sentries to guard this isolated space accentuates its fictional distance, as does the action of Andrés's difficulties in getting through the Loyalist lines to deliver his message to Golz. The placement of the bridge over a gorge between two mountains, the concealed remoteness of Pablo's cave, and the general impression that the reader receives of the entire locale of the action being cupped

in by a jagged mountain range effectively encloses the stage of the
novel in a manner parallel to the way the arbitrary segmenting of
time closes off the act played on that stage. Something of both
effects can perhaps be seen—as well as a sense of the circularity of
the enclosure—in a comparison of the opening lines of the novel
with those that end it:

> He lay flat on the brown, pine-needled floor of the forest, his chin on
> his folded arms, and high overhead the wind blew in the tops of the pine
> trees. The mountainside sloped gently where he lay; but below it was
> steep and he could see the dark of the oiled road winding through the
> pass. (1)

> Then he rested as easily as he could with his two elbows in the pine
> needles and the muzzle of the submachinegun resting against the trunk
> of the pine tree. . . . Robert Jordan lay behind the tree, holding onto
> himself very carefully and delicately to keep his hands steady. He was
> waiting until the officer reached the sunlit place where the first trees of
> the pine forest joined the green slope of the meadow. He could feel his
> heart beating against the pine needle floor of the forest. (471)

The two scenes are remarkably similar, both in Jordan's prone position of watching and in the general description of his surroundings.
But, in the seventy hours between the first and the last scene, the
pine needles have been covered with snow and also blood; and Jordan
has loved and killed and is now ready to be killed. He is, at the
end, where he was at the beginning; the arc of the circle is just at
the point of completion. And what the circle is meant to circum-
scribe is his whole life.

Because of the fictional requirement that a lifetime be compressed
into three days, Hemingway made a fuller dramatic use of the
memory flashback and of the interior monologue in this novel than
in any of his fictions. We know more about Robert Jordan's past
and about his thinking processes than about those of any other
Hemingway protagonist. This is still not very much, but the ex-
clusions in this case are justified on structural principles. Typically
the events that Jordan remembers or thinks about are directly or
indirectly related to the thematic necessities of the novel. Thus he
remembers saying good-bye to his father at a railway depot as a
prelude to his good-bye to Maria; his recollections of his grandfather's Civil War experience suggest a vertical identification in

time between his grandfather's war and the one he is in the midst of. The reflections on his father's suicide are dramatically motivated by his own awareness of the pressures that oppose him and the necessity that he places upon himself of performing well. Only in the reminiscences of Gaylord's and the somewhat over-protracted musings on democracy and communism does the tight structure tend to break. It seems that in this latter material Hemingway loses distance between himself and his protagonist (a flaw that becomes a catastrophe in *Across the River and into the Trees*); and the tenuous suspension of time and space is momentarily lost. The employment of the device, however, is almost mandatory; for if we are to believe that Jordan's life is squeezed into seventy hours, we must believe he had a life before the first of these hours began.

Hemingway broadens his use of this device to include memory recitals and straight third-person narratives, sometimes called the "set-pieces" in the novel. These include Pilar's description of the taking of the town from the Fascists, Maria's recollection of her parents' deaths and of her violation, and the description of El Sordo's stand on the hilltop. Each of these is unnecessary to the plot, and in the narration of each the actual dramatic momentum of the novel ceases. But the stoppage of linear time in these three cases is achieved without breaking distance and without losing the illusion of isolation. Each description, in a sense, broadens or elongates the time that has been caught and held in suspension; each constructs, as it were, a thicker density of time to be contracted and exploded at the bridge.

Simultaneously the suspension of space and time makes it possible for Hemingway to get the effect of always-time; the removal of the events and human actions makes a hiatus between the reader's normal sense of time and that of the novel, imparting to the latter a tinge of "mythic" or "make-believe" time. This tendency is strengthened by several devices. The recurrent references to gypsy and folk superstitions have an enduring quality quite harmonious to the long view of time. The stylized pidgin-Spanish dialogue with its "thee's" and "thou's" is purposely archaic in sound to reinforce the "long" time.[4] And the nature imagery that pervades the novel reflects ages of seasons in their relentless recurrence. In this passage, for example, Jordan is reacting to the snowstorm:

In the snowstorm you came close to wild animals and they were not afraid. They travelled across country not knowing where they were and the deer stood sometimes in the lee of the cabin. In a snowstorm you rode up to a moose and he mistook your horse for another moose and trotted forward to meet you. In a snowstorm it always seemed, for a time, as though there were no enemies. In a snowstorm the wind could blow a gale; but it blew a white cleanness and the air was full of a driving whiteness and all things were changed and when the wind stopped there would be the stillness. (182)

The style in this excerpt could easily be examined with results very similar to those in the opening paragraph of "In Another Country." There is a formal stylization, the same use of repetition and echoings from the King James Version, and the insistent coercion of the "always." Thus Hemingway has so patterned this novel to isolate it spatially and temporally, to cast vertical wells within the linear suspended time, and to arrange for a possibility of archaic or "eternal" identifications in his dialogue and in his nature descriptions.

Within this complex time frame the plot is stripped to simplicity. Jordan arrives with his orders at Pablo's cave, makes his arrangements, falls in love with Maria, has a slight obstructional deterrence from Pablo, explodes the bridge on schedule, and prepares to die when his broken leg makes it impossible for him to escape. The simplicity of the plot helps the process of time fusion, for the action starts slowly and accelerates increasingly to the final scene in the novel. It is pushed relentlessly by the ominous fatality of the palm reading and by the necessity to carry out the orders on schedule. The appearance of the cavalry troop and Pablo's treachery quicken the suspense, as does the knowledge that the Fascists are preparing to meet the attack. The switching of scenes toward the end of the novel between Andrés, who is trying to get his message through to Golz, and the scenes at the guerrilla camp are strongly reminiscent of D. W. Griffith's film splicing in *Intolerance,* and they serve the same function of heightening suspense and of speeding up the action by making every moment significant. The total effect of the plot acceleration crams the action intensively; it supersaturates the density of time within its enclosed and suspended space.

Finally, Hemingway explodes this charged pocket of time through a system of subtle identifications in which the character Maria becomes symbolic of Jordan's self-realization, of the universal rightness of the cause for which Jordan is offering his life, of Spain, and, ultimately, of ever-enduring Nature itself. An enormous load of meaning to place on one cropped head, it is not completely successful. But Jordan's experiences can be communicated only through his relationship to some one or thing apart from himself, and his transcendent sexual union with Maria is the most likely opportunity for becoming an objective correlative for the time fusion desired. We can point out the processes of these identifications analytically; the judgment of their success must be subjective.

The achievement of now-time that Jordan and Maria create in their lovemaking is suggested frequently in the novel, and perhaps nowhere more elaborately than in the following attempt to reproduce the sensations of a particularly fulfilling sexual union. Notice in this passage the purposeful discarding of horological time (the watch in the first sentence) and the suggestion of leitmotiv in Jordan's prone position in relation to the pine trees:

> Then they were together so that as the hand on the watch moved, unseen now, they knew that nothing could ever happen to the one that did not happen to the other, that no other thing could happen more than this; that this was all and always; this was what had been and now and whatever was to come. This, that they were not to have, they were having. They were having now and before and always and now and now and now. Oh, now, now, now, the only now, and above all now, and there is no other now but thou now and now is thy prophet. Now and forever now. Come now, now, for there is no now but now. Yes, now. Now, please now, only now, not anything else only this now, and where are you and where am I and where is the other one, and not why, not ever why, only this now; and on and always please then always now, always now, for now always one now; one only one, there is no other one but one now, one, going now, rising now, sailing now, leaving now, wheeling now, soaring now, away now, all the way now, all of all the way now; one and one is one, is one, is one, is one, is still one, is still one, is one descendingly, is one softly, is one lovingly, is one kindly, is one happily, is one in goodness, is one to cherish, is one now on earth with elbows against the cut and slept-on branches of the pine tree with the smell of the pine boughs and the night; to earth conclusively now, and with the morning of the day to come. (379)

With what seems an echoed influence from Joyce and Cummings, Hemingway attempts to do something in this passage similar to the older waiter's parody of the Lord's Prayer in "A Clean Well-

Lighted Place." As the effect of the short story gives tangibility or "somethingness" to the repeated "nothing" of the prayer, in the novel the words "now," "always," "one," and "is," should ideally merge into one composite symbol of mystical transport in which all is now one and always. Hemingway reinforces this purpose in Jordan's reflections immediately after this scene: "She said La Gloria. It has nothing to do with glory nor La Gloire that the French write and speak about. It is the thing that is in the Cante Hondo and in the Saetas. It is in Greco and in San Juan de la Cruz, of course, and in the others. I am no mystic, but to deny it is as ignorant as though you denied the telephone or that the earth revolves around the sun or that there are other planets than this" (380). This is a good example of the impossibility of rendering experience directly in language (especially sexual experience); but Hemingway's purpose and partial fulfillment can hardly be gainsaid.

Maria is thus the vessel of Jordan's complete self-realization; in his mergence with her he has achieved the immortality of becoming "other," of losing himself into something not himself. As he tells her in his final goodbye, "Thou art me now too. Thou art all there will be of me" (464). But we must investigate more closely what Maria is; for if she is only a mortal Spanish girl who is almost nineteen, Jordan's "immortality" is still susceptible to the destruction of time. First, her past experience as an innocent victim of brutal oppression identifies her strongly with the cause to which Jordan has committed himself; and this identification is strengthened by the "healing" virtues of Jordan's love for her. She has been inhumanly broken by her experience; her past mitigates against any chance of new life; but the cause promises to wipe out century-old oppression so that man may be given a new beginning. This theme of the new beginning is evident in Maria's acceptance of Pilar's folk wisdom: "Nothing is done to oneself that one does not accept and that if I loved some one it would take it away" (73). Hence Jordan's death leaves the vitality of the cause for which he dies untouched and even more resolute after his death.

Second, the symbolic connotations of Maria's name are obvious enough identifications with both Spain and the Virgin to need no further explication. Third, and more interesting, she is consistently identified with images of regenerative nature and of life. She is called "rabbit," Jordan's pet name for her; her cropped hair is imaged as a field of growing wheat; and, as Jordan holds her in his arms, she becomes purely and simply "life" to him: "But in the night he woke and held her tight as though she were all of life and it was being taken from him. He held her feeling she was all of life there was and it was true" (264).

But we must not overlook the fact that in losing his isolate self in Maria, Jordan gains eternal life beyond his insignificant mortality. He becomes the earth that abides forever, sinking his spirit in its impassive contempt for human time:

> Robert Jordan lay behind the trunk of a pine tree on the slope of the hill above the road and the bridge and watched it become daylight. He loved this hour of the day always and now he watched it; feeling it gray within him, as though he were a part of the slow lightening that comes before the rising of the sun; when solid things darken and the lights that have shone in the night go yellow and then fade as the day comes. The pine trees below him were hard and clear now, their trunks solid and brown and the road was shiny with a wisp of mist over it. The dew had wet him and the forest floor was soft and he felt the give of the brown, dropped pine needles under his elbows. (431)

This mergence is given final authority in the experience of "the earth moving" and in Hemingway's explicit statement of the theme several paragraphs before the novel ends: "Robert Jordan saw them there on the slope, close to him now, and below he saw the road and the bridge and the long lines of vehicles below it. He was completely integrated now and he took a good long look at everything. Then he looked up at the sky. There were big white clouds in it. He touched the palm of his hand against the pine needles where he lay and he touched the bark of the pine trunk that he lay behind" (471).

We suggested earlier that *For Whom The Bell Tolls* could almost be considered a pastoral idyll; it would be more accurate in the context of this discussion of time to call it a pastoral elegy—one strangely similar to Whitman's "When Lilacs Last in the Dooryard Bloom'd." Like that great poem, it envelops death and temporal violence in a transcendent serenity and harmony. And, like the poem also, eternal time and the seized moment of realization are merged and made one in the design of a poetic metaphor—profoundly evocative and cleanly humanistic.

It remains only to suggest how the time fusion becomes identical with the operation of the code. We mentioned earlier that just as the explosion of horological time must radiate from the focal center of the novel, the bridge, so the moment of confrontation must likewise integrally connect with it. But just as Maria is too slight to hold the burden of symbolic meaning placed on her, the bridge is not solidly enough fixed as the center of the novel to become a fully convincing "clean well-lighted place" in terms of the code. Within its limitations, however, it works extraordinarily well and the identifications almost occur. The major technique that Hemingway employs to this end is the futility of the attack and the abortive failure of the entire bridge-blowing operation: ". . . that bridge can be the point on which the future of the human race can turn." The Fascists have already moved their reinforcements up the road to counter the foreknown attack, however, and it matters little whether the bridge is blown up or not. In concrete military terms, the bridge is no longer the point on which the future of the war, or the human race, can turn. The explosion of the bridge, with all the human waste that accompanies it, is an absurdly meaningless event within the desperate flow of a losing war. It represents, in a grim and even sardonic way, the intrusion of *nada* into the illusions and courage of a group that banded together into a cohesive unit to destroy the bridge and create meaning.

But in nonmilitary terms, that is, in poetic terms, the *nada* is heroically bridged; the confrontation does become a point on which the future of the human race can turn; for mankind does conquer the futility of nonmeaning in its resolute bravery and achieved oneness. The individuals within the group have been forged into a whole; even Pablo realized in his temporary treachery that in "having done such a thing there is a loneliness that can not be borne." None of them achieves Jordan's mystical integration nor his imposition of meaning on the shadow; but General Golz's words into the telephone can stand as an emblem for the way the composite guerrilla group, representing the ideals of the Cause, and beyond that the determination of humanity to live lives of courage and dignity, have fronted the encroachments of "nothingness": "No. *Rien à faire. Rien. Faut pas penser. Faut accepter. . . . Bon. Nous ferons notre petit possible"* (429).

Chapter Seven

The Sun Also Rises: An Essay in Applied Principles

During the course of this book, we have purposely avoided discussing *The Sun Also Rises* (1926), Hemingway's first, and perhaps most completely successful novel, preferring to discuss it in isolation from any thematic or technical concerns. It is, in many ways, an anomalous work in Hemingway's lifetime of publication: characteristic Hemingway, it is an uncharacteristic Hemingway fiction. Written partly out of disgust with the empty Bohemianism of "The Lost Generation," it has made that Bohemianism eminently attractive to succeeding generations of readers. It was read originally as a roman à clef in which the major (and some of the minor) characters could be identified by those with the inside knowledge; time has made some of these very characters secure, living fictional beings.

Hemingway has insisted that *The Sun Also Rises* is a tragedy and not a "hollow or bitter satire,"[1] but criticism has been slow to accept either of his definitions. In fact, although some of the best Hemingway criticism has concerned itself with this novel,[2] there is a surprising lack of unanimity among critics on basic noncontroversial issues. Critics divide handsomely on determining the moral center of the book; some have found it in Pedro Romero, some in Jake Barnes, and there have even been spirited defenses of Robert Cohn. There have been attempts to read the book as an elegy on the death of love, and others to show that the sun does rise out of the wasteland.

When good critics disagree so violently, there must be much smoke and much fire, and the novel must rest on a special base of ambiguity. Our reading of *The Sun Also Rises* is no act of settlement or final explanation; however, our almost exclusive concern with the way Hemingway's art was formed and how it seems to work in special contexts brings general principles to what is unanimously agreed to be one of his superior artistic productions.

The difficulties of interpreting *The Sun Also Rises* stem in the main from two factors: the use of a particularly opaque first-person narrator; and the fact of Jake's wound, which has rendered him impotent but left him normally responsive to sexual desire. The first factor results in bewildering a reader trying to locate the norms of "truth" in the novel; that is, since the entire novel is related directly by Jake Barnes, the reader can never be sure how reliable Jake's observations and judgments are. He does not know whether to look at Jake ironically or sympathetically. And Hemingway has artfully (or accidentally) failed to provide the reader with hints or standards of measurement within the novel that direct the reader's point of view. Thus, if the reader accepts Jake's story as completely authoritative, he must accept as well Jake's friends and their empty reboundings from one Parisian cabaret to another, from France to Spain and back to France again. If he decides, on top of that, that Jake is Hemingway's sympathetic spokesman, he can only conclude that the "tragedy" of the novel is inherent in Jake's inability to join in the fun. Decisions that Jake is an unreliable narrator, or that he is meant to be unsympathetic, will lead to equally absurd readings in an opposite direction. He must be mostly reliable and mostly sympathetic. We will try to thread the precarious line of his maneuverings.

His wound separates Jake from the action in a way that makes this novel different from all Hemingway's longer fiction. Jake's impotency deprives him of a typical Hemingway love relationship and, because of the novel's milieu, forces him to be a spectator rather than a participator in the events of the novel. He can react intensely, but his actions will necessarily be passive; they will be struggles to "hold on" and to accept rather than to shape circumstances by the force of his direct will. Thus the novel is composed largely of "what happens" to Jake and how he copes with these happenings over which he is denied any control. In a sense this places him in a constant psychological situation of having to accept the absurd meaninglessness of his fate and somehow wrest some meaning from it. Hemingway makes special reference to his "biblical name," Jacob. This may suggest that like his namesake, Jake must wrestle until daybreak with an angel that is a demon; but, unlike his namesake, the "blessing" that will reward his powers to endure will merely ensure the prolongation of the struggle.

Jake's most elaborate statement of his code occurs during the fiesta at Pamplona. It is also close enough to the Hemingway code we have examined to stand as the value center of the novel:

I thought I had paid for everything. Not like the woman pays and pays and pays. No idea of retribution or punishment. Just exchange of values. You gave up something and got something else. Or you worked for something. You paid some way for everything that was any good. I paid my way into enough things that I liked, so that I had a good time. Either you paid by learning about them, or by experience, or by taking chances, or by money. Enjoying living was learning to get your money's worth and knowing when you had it. You could get your money's worth. The world was a good place to buy in. It seemed like a fine philosophy. In five years, I thought, it will seem just as silly as all the other fine philosophies I've had.

Perhaps that wasn't true though. Perhaps as you went along you did learn something. I did not care what it was all about. All I wanted to know was how to live in it. Maybe if you found out how to live in it you learned from that what it was all about. (148)

If we can accept this statement as being true for Jake, it should follow that the novel will be a recording of Jake's painful lessons in learning how to live in the world while getting his money's worth of enjoyment for the price exacted from him. We can then, at least as a point of departure, examine the story as an "epistemological" novel.

From this standpoint the novel contains one tutor, Count Mippipopolous, and one antitutor, Robert Cohn. The Count has presumably paid in full for his ability to enjoy his champagne, his chauffeur, and his expensive tastes in women (he offers Brett $10,000 to go to Biarritz with him). His somewhat incongruous arrow wounds testify that "he has been there" and has learned how to extract values from his experience. His role as model is pointed to in an early three-way conversation with Brett and Jake:

"I told you he was one of us. Didn't I?" Brett turned to me. "I love you, count. You're a darling."

"You make me very happy, my dear. But it isn't true."

"Don't be an ass."

"You see, Mr. Barnes, it is because I have lived very much that now I can enjoy everything so well. Don't you find it like that?"

"Yes. Absolutely."

"I know," said the count. "That is the secret. You must get to know the values."

"Doesn't anything ever happen to your values?" Brett asked.

"No. Not any more."

"Never fall in love?"

"Always," said the count. "I am always in love."

"What does that do to your values?"

"That, too, has got a place in my values."

"You haven't any values. You're dead, that's all."

"No, my dear. You're not right. I'm not dead at all." (60–61)

The Count is in the position of the Major's ideal man ("In Another Country") who has found things he cannot lose. He has stripped his stockpile of illusions to the barest minimum, transferring the capitalistic ethic of exchange values to the sphere of the emotions. But, as he corrects Brett, he is not "dead," nor are his emotional transactions mutely mechanical or sterile. His moral position can be compared to the gambler who bets beyond the law of percentage, who extends and backs his play with a calculated risk of losing because part of the gusto of living (to "enjoy everything so well") depends on the exhilaration of exposure. The "stuffed-animal" conversation between Bill Gorton and Jake, which occurs shortly after the above scene, reinforces this distinction. Bill drunkenly tries to persuade Jake to buy a stuffed dog:

"Mean everything in the world to you after you bought it. Simple exchange of values. You give them money. They give you a stuffed dog."

"We'll get one on the way back."

"All right. Have it your own way. Road to hell paved with unbought stuffed dogs. Not my fault." (72–73)

And several pages later Jake introduces Bill as a "taxidermist." " 'That was in another country,' Bill said. 'And besides all the animals were dead' " (75).

Beneath the current of wisecracking (and the dialogue here, as well as in the Burguete scenes, shows Hemingway's superb mastery of sophisticated stage talk), the Count's philosophy is contrasted and given higher valuation. A graded hierarchy of exchange value is implicitly established; the Count insists on a fair exchange; he will pay, but he wants his animals to be "live" and not stuffed. And he has trained himself to be an unillusioned connoisseur in distinguishing between life and its varied imitations. Bill's adaptation of the code is on a lower level of enjoyment. The "road to hell is paved with unbought stuffed dogs." He has no illusions about what he is paying for; he knows that all the animals are dead, but he is willing to forgo the supreme risk of paying for "life," by pursuing pleasures he can momentarily extract in the meaningless excitement of his "stuffed animals." His drunken trip to Vienna and his general behavior in Paris are a prelude to Frederic Henry's furlough in *A Farewell to Arms,* because Bill's commitment to enjoyment includes no real risk of himself. And his position is representative of most of the sophisticated carousers who find an adequate symbol for their desires in the San Fermin fiesta in Pamplona.

But there is also a lower level of gradation in the "exchange-value" metaphor. The road to hell can be traveled swiftly by those who buy stuffed animals, since this is a considered purchase of ultimate emptiness and non-meaning. But that same road, as Hemingway makes clear in his insertion of the scenes with Woolsey and Krum—or with the Dayton, Ohio, pilgrims—is also paved with unbought stuffed animals. To deny oneself the ephemeral pleasures, even though they are without meaning, without having a more substantial value to embrace is an even emptier behavior. There are degrees of rigor mortis in the death-in-life as we see in the following expertly understated conversation:

"Playing any tennis?" Woolsey asked.
"Well, no," said Krum. "I can't say I've played any this year. I've tried to get away, but Sundays it's always rained, and the courts are so damned crowded."
"The Englishmen all have Saturday off," Woolsey said.
"Lucky beggars," said Krum. "Well, I'll tell you. Some day I'm not going to be working for an agency. Then I'll have plenty of time to get out in the country."
"That's the thing to do. Live out in the country and have a little car." (36)

To use terminology hitherto employed, the Woolseys and the Krums are unknowing tourists in life, paying exorbitant prices for nothing; the Bill Gortons are professional tourists who pay without illusions for the nothingness that they are willing to settle for; and the Count is the non-tourist professional, determined to get his money's worth at the expense of exposing himself in the imposition of meaning on his emotional purchases.

This hierarchy of values is highlighted by the anti-tutor, Robert Cohn, who has the unfortunate burden of being "the horrible example" of the novel. He is Jake Barnes's double, the secret sharer who suffers cruel and comical ignominy to demonstrate to Jake the dangers inherent in "letting go" and falling into the pit of self-deception. First we should note the similarities between Jake and "his tennis friend." They are both writers, they both fall in love with Brett Ashley, they are both superior to the meaningless swirl of drinking, promiscuity, and aimless pleasure seeking that surrounds them. Unlike the others they realize there are stakes in the game that life has forced them to play; they are, in different ways, equally concerned to impose meanings on their purchases and receive their money's worth. But Cohn, unlike the Count, has never "been there"; and because of the faults of his temperament, Cohn never will be there. His arrow wounds are both superficial and self-inflicted; he refuses to pay the price of self-knowledge because he has become an expert in the illusion-creating art of self-deception.

Cohn's role of double is cast early in the novel when he tells Jake he can't stand to think that his life is ebbing away and he is "not really living it."

> "Listen, Jake," he leaned forward on the bar. "Don't you ever get the feeling that all your life is going by and you're not taking advantage of it? Do you realize you've lived nearly half the time you have to live already?"
> "Yes, every once in a while."
> "Do you know that in about thirty-five years more we'll be dead?"
> "What the hell, Robert," I said. "What the hell."
> "I'm serious."
> "It's one thing I don't worry about," I said.
> "You ought to." (11)

When Cohn proposes a trip to South America, Jake tells him that "going to another country doesn't make any difference. . . . You can't get away from yourself by moving from one place to another. There's nothing to that" (11). Cohn's adamant refusal to look nakedly at himself leaves him incapable of seeing anything external to himself with clarity. He demands that his experiences be measurable in terms of absolutes—his affair with Frances, his writing, his love for Brett; and when his fortunes become compounded in misery, he demands absolution for his sins of misjudgment. In a remarkable scene of reverse tutorial confrontation, he begs Jake to forgive his actions at Pamplona. The previously quoted conversation between Robert Jordan and Anselmo on forgiveness shows us how far outside the code Cohn stands:

He was crying without any noise.

"I just couldn't stand it about Brett. I've been through hell, Jake. It's been simply hell. When I met her down here Brett treated me as though I were a perfect stranger. I just couldn't stand it. We lived together at San Sebastian. I suppose you know it. I can't stand it any more."

. . .

"I guess it isn't any use," he said. "I guess it isn't any damn use."

"What?"

"Everything. Please say you forgive me Jake."

"Sure," I said. "It's all right."

"I felt so terribly. I've been through such hell, Jake. Now everything's gone. Everything." (194)

Robert Cohn capitulates unconditionally to the rule of *nada* through his refusal to give up his illusions; and although his intentions are far more admirable than those of the others who give in to the empty enjoyment of nothingness, his fate is to be the most despicable character Hemingway ever created; he is similar to but worse than Richard Gordon in *To Have and Have Not*.

The delicate web of differing values is subtly suggested in the death of Vincente Girones, the twenty-eight-year-old farmer from Tafalla who has come every year to the fiesta at Pamplona to join in the *encierro*, the running of the bulls through the streets to the bullring. Jake sees him tossed and gored as the bulls and the crowd of merrymakers sweep over and past him to the ring. When Jake returns to the café, he reports the event to the waiter:

The waiter nodded his head and swept the crumbs from the table with his cloth.

"Badly cogida," he said. "All for sport. All for pleasure. . . . A big horn wound. All for fun. Just for fun. What do you think of that?"

"I don't know."

"That's it. All for fun. Fun, you understand."

"You're not an aficionado?"

"Me? What are bulls? Animals. Brute animals. . . . You hear? Muerto. Dead. He's dead. With a horn through him. All for morning fun. Es muy flamenco."

"It's bad."

"Not for me," the waiter said. "No fun in that for me." (197–98)

Later Jake reports that the bull that gored Girones was killed by Pedro Romero and its ear was given to Brett, who left it with her cigarette butts in the bedside table of her hotel room. And later, after Bill has reported to Jake a full account of Cohn's activities on the night before, Jake tells him that a man had been killed in the runway outside the ring. " 'Was there?' said Bill" (204).

This episode, deceptively trivial in its presentation, is a measure of Hemingway's control over the dramatic irony with which the novel is narrated. Girones's death is the single event of absolute human importance in the entire novel. All the infidelities, quarrels, and carousals of the principal characters fade into insubstantiality in comparison with the man who "lay face down in the trampled mud." Even the courage and dexterity with which Romero performs in the ring becomes a theatrical gesturing in contrast to the finality and absurdity of this immutable death. And Bill's incapacity to react humanly to that death is a telling indication of his (and the others') deficiencies in a full knowledge and understanding of the code.

Girones is a symbol of the fatal and unchangeable stakes involved in the game that all the characters are playing. He leaves his wife and two children to run with the bulls, but he must pay with his life for his "fun." Like Robert Cohn, Girones is tossed and gored; it is probable that he dies "full of illusions"; but in terms of the code, he fails to get his money's worth for his death. Bill and the others also have become practiced in ignoring the prices they pay for their "fun." The consequences of their variety of self-deceit is a constant death-in-life because they have chosen to accept the rule of "nothingness," becoming servitors to its reign in the frenzy of their acceptance. Girones's death is the physical fact of their living deaths, and their inability to respond to it establishes clearly to what extent they have died.

Here we should perhaps deal with Brett's famous act of self-abnegation, her decision to send Romero away because she will not be "one of these bitches that ruins children." In the dramatic context of the novel, her action is meant to be taken seriously; and it leads directly to the definition of morality that Hemingway later voiced in his own person in *Death in the Afternoon:*

"You know I feel rather damned good, Jake."
   "You should."
   "You know it makes one feel rather good deciding not to be a bitch."
   "Yes."

"It's sort of what we have instead of God."
"Some people have God," I said. "Quite a lot."
"He never worked very well with me." (245)

It is too easy to accept this scene at face value, forgetting that it is filtered through Jake's narration and that its fictional meaning depends on the values with which Jake colors it. In our earlier discussion of the code, we noticed that Hemingway demanded certain basic prerequisites from his characters before he would allow their emotional reactions to be considered worthy gauges of morality. They would have to have learned the hard way what the stakes in the game involved, and they would have to be willing to shed their illusions in their fight to force meaning out of life. It is difficult to feel that Brett meets these qualifications. She has had an unenviable time with her previous husband; she claims to be in love with Jake; she is a near-alcoholic and a near-nymphomaniac. At the end of the novel she casts her lot—whether permanent or temporary it is impossible to determine—with Mike, who has made a career out of irresponsibility. We know of Brett what Jake chooses to divulge, and his position makes him a considerably biased observer.

He tells himself at one point that she thinks she is in love with him because he is something she cannot have. It is certainly true that her love develops after Jake's incapacitating wound. She despises Robert Cohn because he could not believe that their stay in San Sebastian "didn't mean anything" and because he allows his "suffering" to show. Yet if we are to accept her sacrifice of Romero as an act of positive morality and in terms of her own stated code, we must judge her as severely as she judges Cohn. She cannot believe her affair with Romero "didn't mean anything," and she makes no attempt to conceal her suffering. Jake's response to her speech on morality ("Some people have God.") may indicate his detachment from her use of the "we" in the previous sentence ("It's sort of what we have instead of God."). And similarly, the marvellously ambiguous ending of the novel would indicate Jake's holding himself apart from the illusions that Brett has voiced:

"Oh, Jake," Brett said, "we could have had such a damned good time together."
Ahead was a mounted policeman in khaki directing traffic. He raised his baton. The car slowed suddenly pressing Brett against me.

"Yes," I said. "Isn't it pretty to think so?" (247)

But Jake has learned—in part from Count Mippipopolous—that illusions (sure beliefs projected into the future) are the first things to discard if one wants to learn how to live life. To see this ambiguity clearly, we must reinvestigate Jake's role as narrator.

When we meet Jake at the beginning of the novel he is in the process of recovering from his wound and of attempting to learn how to live with it. His days are easily occupied with the seemingly simple tasks of newspaper correspondent and café habitué; the nights are more difficult for him to stand, since his wound, unlike the Count's, still throbs and gives him pain. He has detached himself completely from his Kansas City background and is relatively uninvolved with any of the Parisian set, although all claim him as a friend. He has three passions only: fishing, bullfighting, and Brett. The first two he is able to indulge in with full enjoyment—getting his money's worth and knowing when he has had it. The third is an impossibility on which he expends an inordinate amount of psychic energy and pain. Brett is something that he can neither afford nor even gamble for. And his meager pleasures for the price he pays become less and less. In fact, his relationship to Brett is a pathetic parallel to Vincente Girones's with the San Fermin fiesta. Like Girones, Jake exposes himself to the dangers of being gored and of being trampled "all for fun," except that the "fun" is pain. Brett is his fiesta, as we see in the image of Brett with the white garlic wreath around her neck surrounded by the circle of *riau-riau* dancers. And the lesson he learns from the sharp juxtaposition of his idyllic pleasures at Burguete and the misery of Pamplona is that he "was through with fiestas for a while" (232). Just as Frederic Henry has to learn that a truly human life demands involvement or "caring-ness," so Jake Barnes must learn to become uninvolved from useless and impossible illusions if he is to remain sane.

This, it seems to us, is the point of his breaking the code of the true aficionado that loses him the respect of Montoya. Hemingway tells us that "Aficion means passion. An aficionado is one who is passionate about the bull-fights" (131). But, as we have seen, Hemingway extends the concept of *aficion* to include the "passion" that the code requires for an honest confrontation of *nada*. And thus Jake falls from the ethics of the code badly in arranging the liaison between Brett and Romero. Montoya, who could forgive anything

of one who had *aficion,* cannot forgive the aficionado who has degraded his passion. In pursuing the vain illusion of Brett, Jake too
succumbs to self-deception and self-treachery, since he throws away
a self-respect that he does not need to lose. His decision to remain
at San Sebastian and the descriptions of his restrained enjoyment in
swimming, walking, reading, and eating are reminiscent of his
controlled pleasures while fishing in Burguete. His comments on
himself, after sending an answer to Brett's telegram, are not just
ironic; they are revelatory of the lesson he is learning: "That was
it. Send a girl off with one man. Introduce her to another to go off
with him. Now go and bring her back. And sign the wire with
love. That was it all right" (239). Here, even under the disguise
of self-dramatization, he is facing the truth of his actions and preparing himself for renunciation of the impossible illusion that Brett
represents. In this context he describes his arrival in Madrid in terms
strongly symbolic of the decision he is on the verge of making: "The
Norte station in Madrid is the end of the line. All trains finish
there. They don't go on anywhere" (239–40). Jake too has reached
the end of the line with this "vanity" that has sapped his emotional
strength.

In the ensuing conversation with Brett, Jake's role is the coun-
terpuncher. His answers to her remarks are restrained and couched
in a defensive irony that protests his detachment without exposing
him to attack. His appetite at Botin's is keen; and although he feels
the need to brace himself with wine, this is more an act of propi-
tiation to the pain of shedding an old self than a capitulation to
despair. And in the final ambiguous lines quoted earlier, the detachment is complete. The policeman directing traffic raises his
baton in a wonderfully suggestive gesture, both phallic and symbolic
of the new command that Jake has issued to himself; and the car
in which he and Brett are riding slows suddenly. "Yes. Isn't it
pretty to think so?" commemorates Jake's separate peace with himself and his new determination to live life by those passions within
the scope of his powers and conducive to his self-realization in pursuit
of them.

The structure and the ironic narrative perspective of *The Sun Also
Rises* are the subtle explicator and shaper of its meanings. Remembering Hemingway's explanation of the three acts of the bullfight,
we can find the hint of a parallel in the three-book division of *The
Sun Also Rises.* Book 1 is "the trial of the lances," Jake painfully

"pic-ed" by the barbs of his unresignable desire for a free expression of his natural wants; Book 2, the act of the banderillas at Pamplona, goads him beyond endurance into jealousy and self-betrayal; and Book 3, the final division of death, is the brave administering of quietus to that part of his life desire that he must learn to live without if he is to live at all. The mode of narration, in which the "lesson" of self-growth is presented obliquely and almost beneath the conscious awareness of the narrator-protagonist, creates the problem of interpretation, but it also insures the vitality and ironic tensions within which the novel changes its shape and suggests multiple meanings. Jake is both sympathetic and reliable narrator ultimately, but his emergence as a full-fledged, graduating tyro hero is gained only after he has fallen several times, forced himself to admit his failures to himself, and secured his own forgiveness. As we have seen in our previous discussions of Hemingway's fiction, "the irony of the unsaid" says most clearly and resonantly what the stripped usable values are, and what one has to pay for them.

On this base of interpretation we must now look briefly at a wider range of meanings that may explain the power and popular success of this novel. Surely the "story" we have outlined above is too bleak and spare in itself to have generated the response and wide acclaim that *The Sun Also Rises* has received since its publication. For this novel, more than any other of Hemingway's, has been cherished as a cultural document—a work of art that so miraculously conjoins with the spirit of the times as to seem both distillation and artistic resolution of the prevailing temper of the age from which it rises. Oscar Cargill points to one source of its cultural appeal in his *Intellectual America:* "*The Sun Also Rises* has no peer among American books that have attempted to take account of the cost of the War upon the morals of the War generation and . . . [there are] no better polemics against war than this, which was meant for no polemic at all."[3]

Coming four years after Eliot's *The Waste Land* and three years before Faulkner's *The Sound and the Fury, The Sun Also Rises*—like its two peers in American writing of the 1920s—succeeds in merging the unique psychological crisis of its author with the cultural crisis of its time. "After such knowledge what forgiveness?" is perhaps the agonizing question that informs the best writings of the 1920s. World War I had been the catalyst in releasing the stark factors of nothingness and absurdity at the root of traditional values.

And the theme that powerfully insinuates itself into the best literary documents of the postwar period is the emotional paralysis that results from the realization that life makes no sense except in those tenuous designs that enervated man imposes upon it. Within the reverberations of this theme *The Sun Also Rises* transcends its idiosyncrasies of unrepresentative locale and its restricted range of action to become a compelling and universalized metaphor for its era as well as ours.

The cause and the nature of Jake Barnes's wound force his experiences into a level of symbolic relevance that makes his slow, uncertain struggle to regain a positive stance toward life as much a parable as an "epistemological" romance. It is "the dirty war" that has crippled him, just as it has indirectly crippled the others who fritter and burn in the hells of the *bal musette* and in the pandemonic stampede of the *encierro*. Without the war as a causative background these would be merely empty and sick people who drain their lives away into the receding blue notes of a jazz orchestra; but the war was a fact, and it was one that stripped the veil of pious sanctimony and patriotic veneer from the spurious moralities and ethics of traditional American "boosterism" in religion, philosophy, and politics. The expatriates of *The Sun Also Rises* are sensitive recorders of the shock they have suffered and of the distance between themselves and those back in America who "lived in it [*nada*] and never felt it."

As characters who are truly "ex-patriated," they live in another country where all the stuffed values of the past in which they were trained are dead: " 'You're an expatriate. You've lost touch with the soil. You get precious. Fake European standards have ruined you. You drink yourself to death. You become obsessed by sex. You spend all your time talking, not working. You are an expatriate, see? You hang around cafés' " (115).

Our analysis of the hierarchy of exchange value in *The Sun Also Rises* shows that for many expatriates the war and the consequent moral vacuum were mere excuses for a life of empty sensationalism with the flimsy justification of arrogance and revolt. Yet for others— and especially Jake—the stock market of morality crashed and the bottom fell out of an instinctive rationale for life.

The Sun Also Rises is more than a polemic against war. It does show the battle casualties, and it does demonstrate that others than those in the direct line of fire were grievously crippled by flying shell fragments. But beyond this, and more important, it reasserts the basic truth of American culture (integral to that culture, if too frequently buried under concealing platitudes) that individual man is the puny maker of his meanings in life. If he does not impose them out of an integrity to the unvarnished truths of his own experience, then they will not exist at all—and unmeaning will flood into the vacuum of his irresolution. The "wilderness" of eighteenth-century American literature and the unfathomable "frontier" of the nineteenth century fuse and echo hollowly in the *nada* of the twentieth century, but the challenge is the same and the possible creative responses to that challenge are just as limited in number. It was probably a fortuitous accident that Hemingway's personal wound and relationship of estrangement from the Booth Tarkington mores of Oak Park should result in the compelling symbolism of *The Sun Also Rises,* but such are the graces of literary history.

Jake Barnes's wound paralyzes him at the roots of his being. He has the desire to act, coupled with a hypersensitive capacity to react; but he cannot make appropriate responses because his powers of creativity—his powers of self-generation—have atrophied as the symbolic result of his wound. He is not unlike Eliot's Gerontion or his Fisher-King, who sit in despair, praying for the miracle of rain. Nor is he wholly unlike Faulkner's Quentin Compson, whose similar despair and similar incapacity result from his inability to rid himself of a burdensome, life-denying past. But on a symbolic level Jake's struggle is not ineffectual; and it is in profound harmony with earlier American literary struggles with despair before the confrontation of nothingness. He creates his own miracle of rain, irrigating his dead lands out of the fructifying love of life to which his passion for nature (Burguete) and his admiration for human heroism (the bullfights) testify. And he is able to force himself to a new beginning, eradicating the determinism of his past—his wound, his self-treachery and degeneration with Brett—through self-forgiveness and faith in his own human resources that, like the earth, "abideth forever" in the granite veins of humanity.

Thus, *The Sun Also Rises* combines in one radical metaphor the two antithetical halves of the broad humanistic tradition that goes back to Ecclesiastes. It documents in full, unsparing detail the meaningless ant lives of petty, ephemeral humanity making its small noise of pleasure and sacrifice in the boundless and unheeding auditorium of eternity: "Vanity of vanities, saith the Preacher, vanity of vanities; all is vanity. What profit hath a man of all his labour which he taketh under the sun? One generation passeth away, and another generation cometh; but the earth abideth forever. The sun also ariseth, and the sun goeth down, and hasteth to his place where he arose."

Yet without compromising this merciless vision of the compounded vanities by which even the best of the human race lives, Hemingway erects a tenuous but believable bridge across the shadow of nothingness in Jake Barnes's determined wrestle for meaning. The title of the novel pays just obeisance to the cynical wisdom of the ancient Hebraic Preacher of Ecclesiastes; but the novel's exhortatory and unillusioned chronicling of man's heroic powers to create values out of himself echoes Emerson's similar considered faith that "The sun shines to-day also."

Chapter Eight
Hemingway: Man, Artist, and Legend

This chapter, in summing up, must attempt to indicate the nature and the extent of Hemingway's achievements and significance. While his work resists being snugly categorized in literary history, it demonstrates a configuration of shapes and designs that Hemingway criticism extends, refurbishes, and corrects. Two items that have emerged from this study need reemphasis, however, because they are basic to an understanding and appreciation of Hemingway's peculiar merits; and, oddly enough, both items have frequently been neglected or distorted in the bulk of Hemingway criticism. These are the profound organicism of his total work and the integral relationship of his achievement to the "classic" American literary tradition. Although these positions are argued implicitly (and sometimes, surreptitiously) within the body of this book, it may help to restate them more formally.

In his "A Portrait of Mister Papa," Malcolm Cowley describes Hemingway's technique of writing:[1] ". . . he writes a book like an exploring expedition setting out into unknown territory. He knows his approximate goal, but the goal can change. He knows his direction, but he doesn't know how far he will travel or what he will find on a given day's journey." Cowley's metaphor is an interesting choice because it echoes the title, *The Undiscovered Country*, that Hemingway provisionally gave *For Whom the Bell Tolls*;[2] and it also echoes the image, "in another country," that we have seen to be rich in connotations and possibilities in Hemingway's work. And in our discussion of the "inner symbolic drama" of chapter 3, as well as in the explications of "Big Two-Hearted River" and of *The Old Man and the Sea*, we saw that, more often than not, Hemingway's fiction seems rooted in journeys into himself much more clearly and obsessively than is usually the case with major fictional writers. Indeed, the subject of his fiction is almost always an exposition of his dynamic relation to the world at the time he is writing. In Cowley's terms, Hemingway's writing is an exploring expedition into the unknown territory of those deeper layers of awareness and unconsciousness that the act of creativity may sometimes release. And if there is truth in these conjectures, they may illuminate the extraordinarily "round" shape of Hemingway's work.

In our successive analyses of style, structure, thematic interest, and treatment of time, we hope it became clear that each of these single prose techniques was subordinate and functional to an overriding purpose; that no single one of them developed its rhythms or designs out of the runaway braggadocio of a virtuoso performance. Hemingway's style has been frequently singled out for praise or derision; his metaphysic of time has been commented upon; his particular concern with violence and brutality has become identified in the popular mind with his work as a whole; and it has been imitated by literally legions of writers. The clipped, understated dialogue and the pervasive irony of perspective that he introduced in the 1920s effected a major shift in the direction prose fiction took after the 1920s.

But no criticism, hostile or favorable, of any isolated aspect of his work throws light on what those works ultimately are, because each aspect—when Hemingway is at his best—is a single functionary in the total aesthetic communication of his vision. The style is the man, but the style is also the structure and the metaphysic of time and the code and the thematic use of certain material. Perhaps half a dozen times in Hemingway's writing career, these individual elements fused into a magical symbolic construction where each is indistinguishable from the others. These are his great achievements, but their individual parts can no more be approached in isolation from the others than can a Shakespearean sonnet be judged on the basis of its diction or its imagery alone. And even in the bulk of Hemingway's work where the total fusion does not take place, these technical functionaries are still single instruments toward the effecting of his purpose.

The organic quality of Hemingway's fiction is an inevitable product of a writer who typically and intensively turned his view internally when he wrote. He did not write stories to promulgate a code of heroism or to exhibit an eccentrically manicured prose style or to provide sensationalistic images for the titillation of those in his audience who never left Oak Park. His writing was his way of approaching his identity—of discovering himself in the projected metaphors of his experience. He believed that if he could see himself clear and whole, his vision might be useful to others who also lived in his world. In order to project those metaphors cleanly ("without faking"), he had to subject the total techniques of his writing to the natural rhythms of his own personality.

On this level, all the devices of his fiction succumb to the tyrannous eye and control of "the meter-making argument"—the shaping spirit that creates form out of experience and ideally allows no intruding elements to falsify that form and betray that experience. In *Death in the Afternoon* Hemingway seems to be pointing to this ideal in his retort to Aldous Huxley:

> If a writer can make people live there may be no great characters in his book, but it is possible that his book will remain as a whole; as an entity; as a novel. . . . No matter how good a phrase or a simile he may have if he puts it in where it is not absolutely necessary and irreplaceable he is spoiling his work for egotism. Prose is architecture, not interior decoration, and the Baroque is over. . . . People in a novel . . . must be projected from the writer's assimilated experience, from his knowledge, from his head, from his heart and from all there is of him. If he ever has luck as well as seriousness and gets them out entire they will have more than one dimension and they will last a long time. (191)

Whatever else it means, the profound resultant organicism of his work indicates that Hemingway had the "seriousness" if not always the "luck."

From this viewpoint the oft-repeated criticism of individual components of his work—style, code, etc.—fail to deal with their stated targets in an essential way, for they fail to appreciate how each is conditioned and controlled by the other accompanying techniques. It is easy to parody Hemingway's prose style; it is difficult to parody Hemingway. It is similarly easy to extract a Hemingway "code" from his fiction to demonstrate its "primitivism," or "sadism," or "masochism," or sheer adolescence; chapters 5 and 6 defend the code from such attacks and demand, at least, that it be judged aesthetically in its total context. And it is the simplest of literary-critical standpoints to dismiss Hemingway as a writer who fails to demonstrate development in his work—although such criticism rarely makes it clear what development is and why it is a good thing.[3] We should suppose that development might mean that the idea-content of a writer's work exhibits a process of change over a period of years accompanied by an experimental variation in stylistic devices to record that change. If this is development, our examination of the changes and deepening of complexity that we noticed in the comparison of "The Undefeated" with *The Old Man and the Sea* would make it clear that Hemingway's work developed in clarity and complexity as his hoard of experience became richer.

But the critics of Hemingway's arrested development impose their own definitions of what idea-content in a work of art consists of; and, having fashioned an arbitrary inner sanctum of artistic excellence, they patronizingly or apologetically proclaim his failure to attain entrance to it. They usually make the false assumption that idea-content must mean an interest in and a capacity to dramatize conceptual ideas. In practice they demand that Hemingway's work demonstrate a linear development (a maturation) in the figuring forth of those philosophical or sociological concepts that the particular critic feels passionate about. But as we have seen, this demand requires of Hemingway's art a content it does not possess naturally and, further, requires of art in general a special talent that would almost automatically exclude from first-class achievement such writers as Emerson and Whitman, the Shakespeare of the sonnets, and most of the British Romantic poets. Like them, Hemingway wrote his fiction out of a research into himself, trusting the shock of emotional recognition to tell him when he had located that recondite self, and trusting further in the organic rhythms of his own nature to blend the techniques of his craft into a clean and "whole" artistic vehicle of communication. Hence the profound organicism of his total form and content—itself a product of the organic relation that his life imposed on his literary products—must be taken into account if his work is to be judged in terms of what it is, rather than what some special interest decides it should have been.

We have also stressed Hemingway's integral attachment to the basic American literary tradition as the place in which his achievements can most properly and fruitfully be appreciated. Hemingway characteristically confused this issue with his ex cathedra remarks on the "classic" American authors of the nineteenth century in *Green Hills of Africa;* in it he allowed status to Mark Twain, Henry James, and Stephen Crane but disposed of Emerson, Melville, Hawthorne, and their like. We may defend him partially by suggesting that his job was to be a writer rather than a literary historian or critic, but the whole sequence of literary evaluations is another indication of

Hemingway's incompetence in the handling of abstractions foreign to his immediate experience.

At any rate, as regards Hemingway's relation to the American tradition, there is no question of influence in any direct way. He was the type of writer who, like Emerson, had an enormous talent for picking up what he needed (largely as a substantiation of what he already knew intuitively); he read omnivorously, seeking a reflection of himself and his immediate needs; and he was as likely to find these reflections in one place as in another. Thus, when he responds to a question of influence with the following list of culture heroes drawn from the areas of literature, music, painting, and religious mysticism, he is being honest as well as puckishly playful: "Mark Twain, Flaubert, Stendhal, Bach, Turgenev, Tolstoi, Dostoevski, Chekhov, Andrew Marvell, John Donne, Maupassant, the good Kipling, Thoreau, Captain Marryat, Shakespeare, Mozart, Quevedo, Dante, Vergil, Tintoretto, Hieronymus Bosch, Breughel, Patinier, Goya, Giotto, Cezanne, Van Gogh, Gaugin, San Juan de la Cruz, Góngora—it would take a day to remember everyone."[4] And when a writer is as over-influenced as the above listing suggests, it is probably more fruitful to think of him as an "original," or as almost without meaningful influences.

Yet this has been the typical situation of the American writer. Concerned ultimately with the artistic process of a quest for identity, he has used anything he could get his hands on—from books on the history of whaling to treatises of phrenological research. With some few and obvious exceptions, the major American writers have responded to literary influence as a one-way transaction. They adapt their external materials to their own obsessive uses; they adamantly resist being formed or molded by those materials. And with a writer as organic in his development as Hemingway, this resistance to the formative impress of influences would be particularly strong and unyielding. But Hemingway's place in that chain of great American writers that stretches from Jonathan Edwards seems secure and beyond question. It is not a matter of influence so much as what we might almost think of as inalienable birthright. The *nada* that challenged and stimulated Hemingway's art was, as we saw in our discussion of *The Sun Also Rises,* just the new manifestation of the same *nada* that was wilderness for the Puritans and unknown frontier for the nineteenth century. The function of the American artist— we are tempted to say the "only" function of the American artist—

has been to create order out of the primordial chaos that wilderness, frontier, or *nada* represent. And he has had to do this out of an awesome loneliness, unsupported by the sustaining guides of religious, philosophical, or social traditions.

The chaos has been external and internal, and inexorable in its encroachments on those tenuous structures of order that individual men have erected out of their painful isolation. It has demanded an endless series of new beginnings—a constant series of creative acts that might bring being (identity, value) out of nothingness. The shape of the literature that has resulted from this overweening challenge has been inevitably eccentric. Its accent has been colloquial or folkloristic; its forms have tended strongly to the abstract, the symbolic, the mythic. Its social purposes have been unashamedly moralistic, aiming at a direct stimulation of the heroic image of man in the minds and hearts of its audience. To use a phrase of Emerson's that would be palatable to Puritans, Transcendentalists, and twentieth-century non-categorizables alike, it has sought to effect an "active soul" in its readers and it has used almost any means to gain this end. It has "hoaxed" and exhorted, chanted hypnotic incantations, and delivered allegorical moral sermons. It has been overtly purposive in its concern with bringing the new Adam to life; and it has also frequently disguised its concern in the form of stories of adventure, ghost tales, fables, and fantasies. And it has usually been characterized by a peculiar ironic humor—sometimes as blatant as Mark Twain's, sometimes as hidden as Whitman's. In the novel this tradition has created that most flexible of literary forms, the romance, the ideal fictional instrument for the projection of warring states of mind, for dramatizations of the desperate grapplings for identity.[5]

At its heart Hemingway's work can be best appreciated in terms of this tradition. His characteristic employment of fantasy projections, his faith in the validity of an inner rather than an outer reality, his attitudes towards organicism in form and content, and his employment of his writing as an instrument rather than an end would all seem to indicate that it is in this tradition of romance rather than in terms of European realism that his successes and failures be measured. And within this tradition the imperatives of his temperament led him toward the aesthetic resolutions of Emerson and Whitman rather than to those of Hawthorne and Melville. What we have called his "anti-intellectualistic" bias—the fact of his temperament that led him to place his reliance on the primacy of his emotions—necessarily gave him an unshakeable faith in himself, and in faith as well. And while he was keenly aware of the web of multiple ironies through which reality manifests itself, his primal faith required a positive confrontation of those ironies—an act of will—rather than an indirect confrontation—an act of intellect. Hence, although the question of influences is generally irrelevant, his work should be considered in the light of that American literary tradition of which he is an organic part as well as a brilliant continuation.

If one measure of an artist's success is the influence he exerts on his contemporaries and successors, then Hemingway is certainly the most important twentieth-century writer in this respect. Although we can do little more than indicate the fact here, it would not be much of an exaggeration to say that after 1930 no writer in any country of the world failed to feel Hemingway's influence.[6] His prose style lost little of its power when translated into the major western languages, and the sensuous appeal of his descriptions of action made his work as popular abroad as in America. As early as October, 1927, he was writing to his editor, Maxwell Perkins, that he then had "2 British, 1 Danish, 1 Swedish, 1 French, and 1 German publisher."[7] His international popularity increased rather than waned throughout his lifetime, embracing Asia and Africa as well as Europe. And his translated works were more than popular; the Nobel Prize Committee justly pointed to his powers of stylistic influence when they praised his "forceful and style-making mastery of the art of modern narration."

Even in translation the superficial characteristics of his style and flexible irony proved incredibly contagious on writers seeking a new mode of approach to literature as well as on writers seeking a more electric appeal to a mass audience. His influence has included such serious figures as Graham Greene, André Malraux, Albert Camus, Elio Vittorini, Giuseppe Berto, James T. Farrell, and John Steinbeck. On a more widespread level, it included beginning writers of the 1930s and 1940s to such an extent that creative writing workshops and classes were frequently exercises in Hemingway prose. And in the manufacture of action-stories for the mass media throughout the world, Hemingway's influence is and has been of enormous weight on popular journalism, pulp writing of all varieties, and scripts for motion pictures and television. In fact, the proliferating imitations of the superficial characteristics of his work by writers who copy him without capturing the forming spirit behind him have made it increasingly difficult for Hemingway's achievements in his own work to be judged without the dilution of this popular image. At least this explanation may account for some of the critical resistance to his art.

Hemingway's creative output over a lifetime of serious, steady writing is not very large. Some five dozen stories, five works of nonfiction, one *novella*, and seven novels make up the sum. Of these his reputation will probably rest ultimately on *The Sun Also Rises, A Farewell to Arms, For Whom the Bell Tolls, The Old Man and the Sea*, and some eight to ten short stories. But the volume of his work is somewhat larger than this list indicates because his individual efforts have a fragmentary quality, even when they are whole within themselves. The separate stories, like the separate aspects of his fictional techniques, are, in a sense, functionaries to the composite unity of his oeuvre. Even when the names of the characters change and their backgrounds slightly differ, there is still a sense in which each is a new unit in the fully constructed mosaic of Hemingway's life work. This is not to suggest that he created a Yoknapatawpha County in his fiction but that, as a deeply committed organic writer, he produced in the total of his efforts something like a fictional *Leaves of Grass*. And, as with Whitman, the impress of his individual works is cumulative in its strength and artistic subtlety.

In the attempt to assess Hemingway's ultimate significance as a major twentieth-century writer, another factor intrudes to make his work more important than the intrinsic value that his finely wrought short stories and novels possess. Hemingway's legendary personality, as he lived it in the newspapers and in the public eye, is inextricably intertwined with his fictional themes and images. His life is in his books, as with all serious artists; but his books inevitably reflect back to his life. Unlike the works of his two great American con-temporaries, Eliot and Faulkner, Hemingway's work does not stand by itself—complete, austere, impersonal, self-defined. We are not interested in a Faulknerian "hero" or an Eliotic "code"; but countless readers have accepted the Hemingway hero as a living reality, and they have subjected the Hemingway code to their own versions of employment. In Hemingway's case, his life and his literary efforts were so much of a single piece and his public life was so romantically

close to the heroic derring-do of his fictional heroes that this mergence of life and literature cannot be dismissed by literary criticism.
To do so would be to fail to appreciate the extraliterary dimension
that Hemingway's fiction contains for his audience. Paradoxically
it may even be an aesthetic deficiency for an artist not to submerge
himself completely in his work; but art is large as well as long, and
Hemingway's personality will doubtless continue to be a factor in
the appeal of his works, even as Mark Twain's personality persists
in his.

In summing up such a protean figure and such a paradoxical
accomplishment, it is difficult to strike the right-sounding chord
that will be just to his strengths without overrating them—and
honest to his weaknesses without making more of them than they
actually are. Almost all of Hemingway's significant contemporaries
possessed talents beyond his ability. Faulkner's fecundity of imagination and invention far surpassed his. He never learned how to
dramatize and give poetic life to the abstractions of ideas as Eliot
could so handsomely do. He lacked Thomas Wolfe's torrential self-
confidence. He was completely without the fine sense of scenario
and the light touch of wit that could bring straight exposition to
life, as in F. Scott Fitzgerald's work. He did not have the dogged
seriousness of vision and historical curiosity that his friend John Dos
Passos possessed. He could not tell a story with the effortless charm
that came to Steinbeck so naturally. And he never knew how to
create the kind of scene in which social normality parades in convincing figures—the kind of scene that Sinclair Lewis or John P.
Marquand could do with their left hands. In fact, he lacked almost
all the tools that fiction writers have traditionally employed as their
basic stock in trade. He had only what seems a tormented zeal to
find out who he was by writing it out of himself, a measurement
of personal integrity that rarely faltered, and a genius for adapting
the limited resources and materials that he did possess into a brilliantly harmonic fusion.

Gertrude Stein and William Faulkner have both implied in different ways that the great failure of Hemingway was his desire to
play it safe—to stay within the limits of what he could do rather
than to attempt something beyond his grasp. The perception is an
acute one, for it points to the admittedly narrow range of Hemingway's accomplishments. But the criticism in the perception misses
the real point entirely, and the miss must have given Hemingway

a good deal of pleasure. For although his range was limited, we doubt that he was playing it safe. Like Santiago, that other fisherman who knew many tricks, Hemingway went too far out in every one of his serious fictions; he extended himself beyond his resources and powers; and he fought his way home on sheer nerve and desperate faith. Part of his public role was to act as though he were a confident natural force with immeasurable reserves in store that he had not even inventoried.

The struggle of his last nine years, his suicide, the recurrent images in his fiction of the man who keeps the light burning at night in a vain attempt to ward off the horrors of "nothing"—these strongly suggest that Hemingway's natural talents were "zero at the bone," and that he created himself out of that "nothing" under immense pressure in the writing of his prose. Indeed, his writing career argues cogently that whatever philosophical validity the Hemingway code may have possessed, its pragmatic functioning for him was cardinal and irrefutable. It enabled him to adopt the role of what we might call *"jongleur* of pain," a role that he imagined so poignantly in describing Belmonte in the Pamplona bullring. He exhausted himself beyond his natural means, but he maintained that "grace under pressure," which, for him, was one of the conditions from which immortality might come.

But rather than end on such a subdued note, let us remember that if his range was narrow, it was not shallow. Art is long and it is large and it can also be deep; and if the sum of Hemingway's achievement was to project in compelling symbols his own human situation, his popularity attests to the fact that his was not a unique human condition. Too fragmented to make a rebellious vain rush against life and too proud to accept the inevitability of defeat and resignation, Hemingway found in himself and communicated to countless readers a stance of heroism—positive, unillusioned, and defiantly humanistic.

Chapter Nine
Of Memory and Melancholy: The Posthumous Works

Posthumous publications create difficult editorial problems. And for the work of a writer like Hemingway, so zealous to protect the integrity of his literary terrain, the problems expand exponentially. The titles under consideration in this chapter—*A Moveable Feast, The Dangerous Summer, African Journal,* and *Islands in the Stream*— are a mixed legacy of blessing and curse.[1] On the one hand we can be grateful for the generous addition of materials, some of it surely equal in quality to his best efforts and much of it useful in illuminating the complexities of his personality, his life, and the deeper mechanisms from which his work was crafted. There are, however, severe textual questions that can never be satisfactorily resolved.[2] Other hands have intervened between his pen and publication. Other authorities have chosen to cull, blend, shape, recombine, add, and subtract material that, at his death, was unfinished, inchoate, unapproved by his editorial intelligence. The topography of Hemingway's posthumous work is rife with intrusions on the signal privacy of his creative processes. Obviously we welcome the publication of these materials, but not without notice of the patchwork nature of their assemblage. An appreciation of Hemingway's posthumous work must first acknowledge the situation surrounding its initial creation—what seems to have been the author's deteriorating psychophysical condition—and, second, the economic pressures on his estate to publish the manuscripts he left behind. Those pressures, coupled with a genuine public demand, have resulted in a substantial body of posthumous work that richly supplements—albeit problematically—the Hemingway canon.

The appearance of *Ernest Hemingway: Selected Letters* provided an eminently moveable feast for a public hungry for more and more tidbits of information and insight about Hemingway's contradictory, but always charismatic, personality. There are letters for readers who glory in Hemingway's hostility toward such people as Gertrude

Stein, Sherwood Anderson, older sister Marcelline, critic-biographer Charles Fenton, and third wife Martha Gellhorn. Similarly, readers interested in the depths of his friendships can find letters aplenty to Maxwell Perkins, Bernard Berenson, Charles Scribner, Sr., and Charles T. "Buck" Lanham. Hemingway petulant, indignant, cocky, obscene, affectionate, arrogant, rowdy, sincere, comic, and more: he dons and doffs all the masks of his personality. But when this voluminous collection of his letters is added to the posthumous works, we may begin to feel overwhelmed by the details of the Hemingway life. Must we learn in *African Journal* that Hemingway had replaced his old hip-hugging Jinny flask with a new square one? Must we learn in *A Moveable Feast* that it was Hemingway who rose early and sterilized the bottles and nipples and milk for son Bumby? Must we learn from *Islands in the Stream* the names of the cats at the Finca Vigía or how to make a daiquiri? Is it necessary for Hemingway to tell us in *The Dangerous Summer* that Marceliano's was his favorite "secret place" in Pamplona to "eat and drink and sing after the encierro" (*DS,* 139)?

Such a glut of biographical information may prompt clamorous wishes for a stringent editor, for someone to intervene on our behalf between the trunks of documents Hemingway obsessively saved and our need or capacity to read and absorb them. It is only fair to acknowledge the various known editors who anticipated and answered that wish: Aaron E. Hotchner for editing *The Dangerous Summer;* Ray Cave for *African Journal;* and Mary Hemingway for her collaborative efforts with L. H. Brague, Jr., on *A Moveable Feast,* and with Charles Scribner, Jr., on *Islands in the Stream.*[3] But sated though we as readers may be, we have also been screened from certain information. Baker's three-pound-five-ounce book of selected letters puts the matter plainly: presumably for literary, legal, or ethical reasons, Baker has decided what we will and will not read. But what may constitute a representative sample of letters to Professor Baker, a scholar to whom all Hemingway students are deeply indebted, may not be a representative sample to another reader of the correspondence. If, for instance, his seemingly comprehensive biography disappoints an expectation that he will comment upon Hemingway's relationships with each of his sons during the 1950s, then it may be equally disappointing that *Selected Letters* includes only one of the threescore letters Hemingway wrote Adriana Ivancich, the Italian countess who inspired the character of Renata in

Across the River and into the Trees.[4] It may even seem an odd omission for there to be no indication that *Selected Letters* contains only one-sixth of Hemingway's available letters. If the "strength" of an iceberg lies in the seven-eighths beneath an ocean's surface, it is likely that the other five-sixths of Hemingway's letters contain some strong matters.

Of the posthumous work, only *African Journal* is prefaced and footnoted with comments that describe the state of the manuscript, indicate where and how it was altered, and identify Hemingway's marginal instructions to himself. For a "popular" magazine, the text in *Sports Illustrated* is surprisingly scholarly. Ray Cave states not only that its three installments comprise only one-fourth of an 850-page, 200,000-word manuscript, but he also signals with asterisks, ellipses, spacing, dashes, and oversized capitals those places where the manuscript has been cut or rearranged. His meticulousness constantly reminds us that the text has been "stringently" edited. Although we may wonder what the missing three-fourths contains, we at least know it exists.[5]

Such editorial scrupulousness is absent in the other three posthumous works. It was six years after publication of *The Dangerous Summer* before Aaron Hotchner's role as editor was commonly known. And even though we learned that he cut some 55,000 words from the roughly 120,000-word manuscript, it has only been with the publication of Scribner's hardbound version that we have also learned that for the 30,000-word version published in *Life,* unidentified magazine editors excerpted their three installments from the "polished manuscript" of "about 70,000" words which Hotchner had prepared.[6] For the 45,000-word version published by Scribner's, neither James A. Michener's "Introduction" nor any front matter identifies the editors at Scribners responsible for the cuts in or changes and additions to the *Life* version.[7] Not until scholars analyze the manuscript materials now available in the Hemingway Collection at the John F. Kennedy Library in Boston will we know what Hotchner cut, whether he rearranged segments, and whether, say, the inclusion of the episode in which he poses as Antonio Ordóñez's *sobresaliente* or substitute matador was at the cost of more valuable episodes.

Even thornier problems exist in the other edited books published by Charles Scribner's Sons, books whose skimpy prefatory notes some scholars and critics find scandalously misleading. Mary Hemingway's "Note" in the front matter of *A Moveable Feast*, for example, declares that Hemingway "finished the book in the spring of 1960," implying that the published book reproduces that "finished" text. We now know better.[8] We know, for example, that she made significant cuts and alterations, that to Hemingway's "finished" typescript she added material he had not written or had chosen to leave out, that the ending was one she doctored from his rejected drafts. Her "Note" in the front matter of *Islands in the Stream* admits that she and Charles Scribner, Jr., "made some cuts in the manuscript." But she chooses to ignore other alterations, especially the decision to assign the narrative to Thomas Hudson. That is, when Hemingway stopped working on the drafts of the sections that became *Islands*, he was undecided whether to leave "Bimini" a first-person narrative, as told by George Thomas, a painter living on Bimini and visited by Roger Hancock and Roger's three sons, or to convert the narrative to a limited third-person, telling it through the painter's perspective but not his voice. Nor had Hemingway decided whether to change George's or Roger's name to Thomas Hudson.[9] One can legitimately question Mrs. Hemingway's decisions and argue, for example, that the discontinuity in the character of Thomas Hudson the painter and Thomas Hudson the Q-boat commander in the second and third sections would have been less perplexing had she chosen to keep Roger Davis as the father of the three sons and to have had the second and third section be about him. Clearly she took the responsibility to resolve the problems that needed resolving. But perhaps the better course may have been not to make the disingenuous claim, "The book is all Ernest's."

Commercial interests may have prompted the publication by Scribner's of both *Feast* and *Islands*. And we are happy to have them as additions to the shelf of Hemingway's works; however, to discuss them as works bearing upon any overview of his canon must be done only in the context of knowing that they have been edited in ways that Maxwell Perkins never dreamt of. And even if the editors were motivated by the best of intentions, we can no more allow ourselves the illusion that we are reading pure Hemingway than we can suppose that his early journalism for the *Kansas City Star* or the *Toronto Star* was untouched by city-desk editors.

The final installment of *African Journal*, Hemingway's account of his 1953–54 safari, concludes with a curious anecdote. Hemingway recalls a brief conversation with his paternal grandmother:

> I had a truly lovely grandmother with a face like an angel if angels were eagles and she had told me, after writing an excuse for my absence from high school and caring for me for six days when I had picked up a concussion acquired when boxing under another name than my own since nobody, then, would pay to see a boy named Hemingway fight, "Ern, promise me to do what you truly want to do. Do it always. I am an old woman now and I have always tried to be a good wife to your grandfather and as you know he can be a difficult man. But I want you to remember, Ern. Can you remember now, Ern?"
> "Yes, Grandmother. I can remember everything except six rounds."
> "They don't matter," she said. "Remember this now. The only things in life that I regret are the things that I did not do."
> "Thank you very much, Grandmother. I'll try to remember."[10]

This passage strongly implies that Hemingway followed his grand-mother's not-very-original advice. Surely the biographies and mem-oirs that now proliferate on library shelves portray a man who—adventurously or self-indulgently as the case may be—rarely curbed a desire. Hemingway's four marriages, continental migrations, and seemingly insatiable appetite for vigorous activity—to observe it keenly or to plunge into it himself—repeatedly show him doing the things he truly wanted to do, lest he regret not having done them. But grandmother Hemingway's admonition is secondary to another urging in Hemingway's recollection. As the curiously long parenthetical interruption in the quotation above suggests, he is compelled to record precisely when his grandmother admonished him ("after writing an excuse for my absence from high school"), why she wrote the excuse (because she had cared "for me for six days"), why he needed care (because he "had picked up a concussion acquired when boxing"), how he had been boxing (under an assumed name), and even why he did so (because his own name on a boxing card would not have brought paying customers to the ring). To ask whether the details in the parenthetical interruption are either nec-essary or true—and they probably are not—is to miss the point. The point is that they underscore an urgency underlying both the recalled conversation and Hemingway's posthumous work: his need to honor the reiterated word: "remember."

Hemingway was proud of his capacity to remember accurately, boasting often about his "rat-trap" memory. His boast may have been well founded, for Mary Hemingway testifies, remarking on *African Journal*—with some astonishment—"I had a record of the whole safari in my diary, but Ernest just carried it back to Cuba in his head. I have checked my diary to verify things, and he was consistently correct."[11] But among the interesting features of *African Journal* is the interweaving of recent and old remembrances. Into its fabric of Mary Hemingway's difficulties in killing a condemned lion Hemingway intersperses reminiscences: of a cider mill in the Michigan of his boyhood, of "secret" restaurants he patronized in Paris during the 1920s, of his 1930s African safari, and of such people as Ezra Pound, Ford Madox Ford, Marlene Dietrich, George Orwell, and Jane Mason Gingrich.[12] In a like manner, *The Dangerous Summer* finds Hemingway at the *barrera* throughout the summer of 1959, chronicling the competition between Spain's leading matadors, Antonio Ordóñez and Luis Miguel Dominguín. But in the background to this rivalry are comparisons of matadors past and present, of bullfighting classic and modern, of Ordóñez father and son, of Pamplona in the 1920s and the 1950s. Across the scenes that Hemingway's eyes witness flit shadows of earlier scenes and ghosts of other matadors, memory adding a dimension to what otherwise might pass as mere reportage: "No one in our time cites twice recibiendo. That belongs to the times of Pedro Romero, that other great torero of Rondo who lived two hundred years ago. But Antonio had to kill [the bull] in this way as long as he would charge" (203). Of the posthumous works only *Islands in the Stream* is classified as fiction. But in it, too, are broad ribbons of remembrance. The first section, "Bimini," finds Hemingway journeying back to his early Paris years and to experiences with John Dos Passos and his own sons in the mid-1930s. The second section, "Cuba," returns to events and acquaintances from his life as a "Cuban" and frequenter of Havana's establishments. The third section, "At Sea," recalls his experiences as a Q-boat commander during the early years of World War II.[13] Of the posthumous publications *A Moveable Feast,* Hemingway's memoir of his apprentice years in Paris from 1921 to 1925, relies strongest upon memory and shows most openly that deeply rooted obsession we have remarked upon earlier, his compulsive journeying into himself. By tracing that journey in these works, we can follow the patterns that diminish their artistic effects and perhaps expose their pervasive melancholy.

> It is only when you can no longer believe in
> your own exploits that you write your memoirs.
>
> —"Pamplona Letter," *transatlantic review*, October 1924

Some of the appeal of *A Moveable Feast* is due to the almost universal interest in portraits of established artists as young apprentices. A novice bent on learning his craft, Hemingway and his recent bride resolutely struggle against hunger and poverty as he confronts a gallery of complex (and famous) people and temptations, both of which seem determined to perplex or thwart his artistic hopes.[14] His account of voyaging forth in Paris reminds us of the autobiography of another young American, runaway Ben Franklin, making his way up Market Street with loaves of bread in his arms, drawing derisive laughter from onlookers—among them his future wife. Hemingway's memoir also calls to mind other mainstream American autobiographies, part of whose intent is to record the helps and hindrances that eased and impeded a writer's development: *The Education of Henry Adams* and *Narrative of the Life of Frederick Douglass*, Richard Wright's *Black Boy* and Henry James's three volumes, *A Small Boy and Others*, *Notes of a Son and Brother*, and *The Middle Years*. Unlike another writer, one of whose motives for writing his autobiography was "to make acknowledgement of the debts which my intellectual and moral development owes to other persons,"[15] Hemingway seems motivated by the obligation to record the advanced schooling he received from a host of flawed tutors: instruction on taboo topics from an opinionated lesbian (Gertrude Stein), warnings and advice from an influential poet who seriously misjudges others' characters and who admits to having "never read the Rooshians" (Ezra Pound), exploitation and egotism from a respected author and editor (Ford Madox Ford), false promises from a literary entrepreneur (Ernest Walsh), poor role-modeling from artists with Bohemian affectations or supportive coteries (Wyndham Lewis and T. S. Eliot), seductive treachery from the wealthy and their hangers-on (Pauline Pfeiffer, John Dos Passos, and Gerald and Sara Murphy), and most shocking of all, wholesale irresponsibilities from a phenomenally talented contemporary (F. Scott Fitzgerald).

Opposite these tutors are a few devoted supporters: a library-book-store owner who believes in Hemingway as a mother might her son (Sylvia Beach), a fond wife (Hadley Richardson), and a gentle, shy editor who not only broke his own rules by including in his annual collection of previously published *Best American Short Stories* Hemingway's unpublished "My Old Man," but even dedicated to Hemingway the 1923 volume in which it appeared (Edward O'Brien). Then, too, there are a few good friends, like Evan Shipman the poet, fellow horserace enthusiast Mike Ward, and professional soldier "Chink" Dorman-Smith.

Projecting himself as tyro, Hemingway capitalizes upon the sympathy that customarily attaches to such a figure, typecasting in domestic terms those people surrounding himself. Labels readily identify nurturing and negative mother figures (Beach and Stein), good and bad father figures (Pound and Ford), sibling rooters and rivals (Shipman and Fitzgerald). Even if readers know few or none of these literary personages, the labels of domestic conflict will influence their emotional alliances. That we sympathize with the tyro is not surprising, especially when we find him so strongly characterized as the most—if not the only—responsible individual in the entire cast.[16] Indeed, by the end of *A Moveable Feast,* our sympathy for tyro-Hemingway has been so aroused that he evokes some of the same emotional pathos that Nick Adams draws from us in such stories as "Indian Camp," "Ten Indians," "The Battler," "A Way You'll Never Be," and "Now I Lay Me." Over a four-page recollection of events, people and scenes from the winter of 1924–25 in Schruns, Hemingway's last chapter incantatorily repeats the phrase "I remember . . . I remember . . . I remember." This nostalgic tremolo draws a full measure of pathos for a worthy, sensitive young man whose first, idyllic marriage is about to crumble:

I remember the smell of the pines and of the sleeping on the mattresses of beech leaves in the woodcutters' huts and the skiing through the forest following the tracks of hares and of foxes. In the high mountains above the tree line I remember following the track of a fox until I came in sight of him and watching him stand with his right forefoot raised and then go carefully to stop and then pounce, and the whiteness and the clutter of a ptarmigan bursting out of the snow and flying away and over the ridge.

I remember all the kinds of snow that the wind could make and their different treacheries when you were on skis. Then there were the blizzards when. . . .

[That] winter of the avalanches was like a happy and innocent winter in childhood compared to the next winter, a nightmare winter disguised as the greatest fun of all, and the murderous summer that was to follow. (206–7)

Not to respond sympathetically to Hemingway's vivid, lyrically edged, and nostalgically sweet evocation of a mythified interval in his life is to be deaf to the magic of Hemingway's prose at its best. But to respond too sympathetically to tyro-Hemingway is, of course, to be blindsided by his creator, to ignore a sizable fact: all memoir writers sort out and select the events they choose to write about, magnify and filter and distort with varying lenses the defects and felicities of those people they deem worthy of their pens' potentially immortalizing power. We might justifiably extend Emerson's "There is properly no history, only biography," by adding a corollary: "There is properly no autobiography, only fiction." Whether Franklin, Adams, Douglass, Wright, James, or Thoreau (exaggerating his "solitude" at Walden Pond,[17]) the autobiographer fictionally reconstructs not only events and other people, but himself as well, creating a self-portrait in harmony with his deeper wishes and anxieties. As Alfred Kazin remarks, "a basic function of such writing is to cure oneself of guilt and self-division[,] . . . to find salvation, to make one's own experience come out right."[18] So intent is Hemingway upon making his "own experience come out right" that he supervises—literally oversees—our emotions, thereby diminishing the aesthetic pleasures *Feast* could have given. As we might expect from a personality attracted to domestic melodrama, Hemingway invokes our anger toward Stein and Ford and Dunning, our disappointment in Pound and Fitzgerald, our gratitude for Beach and Hadley and Shipman, our indignation at pilot-fish Dos Passos and the rich. Such emotional pointing is absent in the Nick Adams stories. In "Indian Camp," for example, we may well feel pathos for a young boy possibly traumatized by witnessing the gore of a caesarian delivery and a suicide. But Hemingway also lets us smile bemusedly at Nick's naive confidence that he'll never die, just as he allows our smile at Nick's belated realization in "Ten Indians" that his heart was broken by Trudy's alleged infidelity. Likewise, we sympathize with Nick's insomnia in "Now I Lay Me," for we cannot be sure that he has fully recovered from his war trauma. But the story also invites a measure of annoyance toward him because of his refusal to marry, his misogyny apparently linking marriage and trauma. In the Nick Adams stories, *A Farewell to Arms,* and *The Sun Also Rises,* Hemingway creates tyros whose conduct allows us to question and to respond to it in alternative ways. In contrast, *Feast* asks us to find fault only in others' behavior. Tyro-Hemingway seems to do nothing to justify others' ill treatment of him or to warrant alternative responses from us. Nothing he does deserves Dunning's chasing and hurling milk bottles after him or Ernest Walsh's reneging on the pledge to award Hemingway *This Quarter's* first prize, "a very substantial sum." His trusting naivete should not permit the rich to infiltrate and befoul his happy domestic nest, victimizing him and Hadley.

That Hemingway "supervises" his memoirs is also evidenced in the narrative voice that tells us about tyro-Hemingway: that is, tutor-Hemingway's. The overlay to Hemingway's projection of himself as tyro is his self-appointment as tutor to evaluate and reveal the shortcomings of the tyro's acquaintances. The presence of tutor-Hemingway makes one wonder whether tyro-Hemingway was as naive and unsuspecting as he is presented to be. Was he disingenuous, a sham tyro? Consider the episode of Wyndham Lewis. After Hemingway and Pound finish a boxing session at which Lewis has been present and which Lewis has insisted they not halt because of him, Hemingway records, "We had a drink of something and I listened while Ezra and Lewis talked about people in London and Paris. I watched Lewis carefully without seeming to look at him, as you do when you are boxing . . ." (109). It may be that Hemingway intends to suggest only that he does what all fiction writers do: he observes people and events carefully so as to add them to the retentive pool from which his imagination draws. But Hemingway also reveals some conspiratorial habit, some eavesdropping penchant, one at odds with his self-portrait as merely a responsible, hardworking apprentice writer. Even more, Hemingway, having stepped out of the sparring ring, still has his guard up. And if Lewis, unknown to Hemingway, knows that Hemingway is carefully watching him, then it is unlikely Lewis would warm to the person behind the inquisitorial gaze, a man who later describes him as having the eyes of an "unsuccessful rapist." Such intentness upon observing someone else reveals Hemingway's indifference to, if not antipathy for, a genuine relationship with a stranger. It also reveals a preference for forming some conclusion about another person, rather than engaging with him in an experience before assessing him. In an earlier chapter Hemingway was seen as a lyric writer whose exceptional forte was not to describe what he saw, but to describe himself seeing and to convey, thereby, the complex of feeling that was invoked in him. It would appear that our lyric writer has yielded in part to a didactic writer, whose stock in trade is to convey the single feeling invoked in him, to administer instruction worth learning, to issue verdicts and judgments, to esteem his own character and codes, to express self-righteous intolerance of others and their values. For all of its genuine felicities in recapturing the sensuousness of a lost time, *Feast* is marred by such defensive self-consciousness. Tutor-Hemingway's rancid pride in observing others while being unobserved seems blind to tyro-Hemingway's disingenuousness. Observe tutor-Hemingway observing tyro-Hemingway as he, in turn, observes Scott Fitzgerald upon their first meeting in the Dingo Bar: "Scott did not stop talking and since I was embarrassed by what he said—it was all about my writing and how great it was—I kept on looking at him closely and noticed instead of listening. . . . I do not think that Dunc [Chaplin] or I followed the speech very closely, for it was a speech and I kept on observing Scott. . . . I looked at him some more. . . . I wasn't learning very much from looking at him now . . ." (149–50). De Tocqueville's remark seems apposite: "those who have written their memoirs have only shown us their bad actions or weaknesses when they happen to have mistaken them for deeds of prowess and fine instincts."

A reading of *Feast* might see its doubling-up of tyro and tutor as proof that it resembles the other tyro-tutor structures we examined in an earlier chapter. To do so might equate tutor- and tyro-Hemingway in *Feast* with narrator- and actor-protagonist Frederic Henry in *Farewell*. The equation might also clarify tyro-Hemingway's epistemological progress, for we might measure his movements along a continuum of such tutors as Henry's Rinaldi, the Priest, Count Greffi, and Catherine. But tutor-Hemingway, leaving little doubt about what his epistemological expedition enables him to learn, violates the tactic of Hemingway's accomplished tutor-tyro fictions: to keep from making explicit the knowledge that the tutor acquires. It may be that Frederic Henry learns to care, learns what caringness is about, learns to say farewell to "not-caringness." But we have no surety that he learns such lessons. For we do not know what he does after Catherine dies, after he walks back in the rain to the hotel, after he tells or writes his story. Similarly, Jake Barnes may achieve a separate peace with himself and find a new determination to live his life in the pursuit of passions both within the scope of his powers and conducive to his self-realization. But again we are uncertain: we are at a loss to know what Jake does after he "rescues" Brett in Madrid, knowledge vital to proving his separate peace and new determination. In contrast to these novels' uncertain epistemological messages, the lesson of the young artist, like that of the old fisherman Santiago, boldly insists that we register its didactic messages: beware false tutors; allow but little self-indulgence; observe new experiences carefully so as to be able to evaluate them; never overpraise your peers; and with everything you do—be it writing, skiing, watching people or the horse and bike races—work ever so diligently at it so as to derive the pleasures of intense work. Such didacticism veers sharply away from the ironies we have found so characteristic of Hemingway's best work.

Tutors oversee tyros in all four of the posthumous works. But the other three tutors are anxious. Identifying the causes of their anxiety may account for each work's diminished emotional resonance. In *African Journal* tutor-Hemingway accepts the two needs of his tyro-wife, "Miss Mary": her unexplainable need to kill a gerenuk and her well-understood (but unexplained) need to kill the condemned, marauding lion: "Everyone understood why Mary must kill her lion. But it was hard for some of the elders who had been on many hundreds of safaris to understand why she must kill it in the old straight way. All of the bad elements were sure it had something to do with her religion, like the necessity to kill the gerenuk at approximately high noon. It evidently meant nothing to Miss Mary to kill the gerenuk in an ordinary and simple way" (1:4–5). Tutor-Hemingway also accepts the responsibility of assisting her, even though he knows that she will have to overcome the handicaps of her disabling dysentery, her lack of height to see over the tall grass into which a wounded lion may seek cover, the huge black-maned lion's intelligence and experience, and her own unpredictable aim: ". . . at point-blank range she had shot fourteen inches higher than she had aimed, downing the [wildebeest] with a perfect high spinal shot" (1:9). Her handicaps, of course, jeopardize the welfare of those who might have to risk going in after a wounded lion.

The contrived mystery of why Mary must kill the lion partly explains the failure of *African Journal* to engage us deeply. Perhaps we might simply agree that her motive lies in some compulsive need for self-validation, frequent among hunters, athletes, and outdoorsmen. But for Hemingway to permit such a motive strips her of mystery, assigns her some common compulsion and ordinary obsession. That is, Mary's compulsion to kill a gerenuk and the lion seems intended as an easy psychological symptom. It signals that in her psyche lies some significant neurotic tendency that she has fought against but must now come to terms with. Yet Hemingway asks us to guess this or to assign it to her gratuitously. He does not develop her character sufficiently to warrant his request and our compliance. Nor does he structure his materials in such a way as to surround her symptoms with clues that will point regressively to the recent or long-ago event that she can no longer dodge but must now confront through the acts of a hunter.

The contrived burden of responsibility that the anxious tutor assigns himself also explains *African Journal's* failure. Rather than focus on objective correlatives that might disclose the tyro's complexity, Hemingway focuses on himself focusing on her. He writes minutely of precautions he must take to safeguard her, of solicitousness he must proffer her to keep peace in camp, of duplicity he must engage in to assure her that it was she who killed the lion, that the shots fired by him and Game Ranger Denis Zaphiro (nicknamed G. C. for Gin Crazed), were only finishing shots: "I drank [from the flask] and then lay down by the lion and talked to him very softly in Spanish and begged his pardon for having killed him and while I lay beside him I felt for the wounds. There were four. Mary had hit him in the foot and in one haunch. While I stroked his back I found where I had hit him in the spine and the larger hole G. C.'s bullet had made well forward in his flank behind the shoulder. . . . I drew a fish in front of him with my forefinger in the dirt and then rubbed it out with the palm of my hand" (2:35).[19] In all of this the anxious tutor implies that his scrupulous behavior is clue to Mary's psychological fragility. Should he suspend even momentarily the delicacy with which he must conduct himself, she may crumble, her hunting—like Nick's fishing in the swamp— suddenly become "tragic." But to give such implications credibility and probability requires fuller characterization of Miss Mary than Hemingway provides and a good deal less triviality of subject matter. Indeed, *African Journal* is far removed in time and place from *in our time*'s "miniature" about the execution of the six cabinet ministers, which we examined in detail much earlier. Still, our observation that the only character of real interest is the narrating voice holds true. Mary's compulsive need to satisfy some lethal but ethically controlled obsession ("she must kill it in the old straight way") may have prompted Hemingway to write *African Journal*. But beneath that stimulus seems to lie his need to portray—if not aggrandize— himself as a man whose revelation of deep anxieties gives the lie to the public portraits of himself—the cool, controlled, inviolable man—that he helped popularize.

The anxious tutor also hovers over *The Dangerous Summer*, bringing Hemingway's well-schooled *afición* to the chronicle of lethal competition between two brothers-in-law. Appealing to our interest in professional athletes and performers at work, he caters to our overt wish to appreciate and observe their tricks, skill, or artistry. He also caters to our covert wish to witness the injury or mishap to which all performers are susceptible. Skillful though Hemingway is at describing the drama of a summer's various bullfights, he tries too hard to have us share his dread that some goring will destroy Spain's reigning matador, Luis Miguel Dominguín, or, worse, the challenger, Antonio Ordóñez. Repeatedly he wraps events in the tissue of his anxiety. Accompanying his continual worrying about the safety of the men are "presentiments or forebodings" (85). Over the outcome of the summer's bullfighting rivalry he shares "apprehensions" with Juanito Quintano (the fictionalized Montoya of *The Sun Also Rises*). A driver whose driving "chilled me and spooked me hollow" (66) especially rattles Hemingway when he catches him crossing himself "fervently" before beginning a drive to Madrid. And on the way to the bullring at Aranjuez to watch Ordóñez, Hemingway dashes into the road to pluck up a girl who had slid from a crashing cycle into two-way traffic. Fearful that she had fractured her skull, "I was very careful to carry her gently and carefully and at the same time not to get blood on my suit. I did not care about the suit but what had happened to the girl was a bad enough omen without taking evidence of it into the first row of seats at the bullring."[20]

In Hemingway's eyes Antonio represents the classic matador, exemplifies the valor artist par excellence. And so he counts heavily upon our emotional identification with Antonio and tries to prevent us from feeling indifference toward someone so significant to him. Yet unless we have followed the career of a celebrated athlete for some time, the threat or reality of an injury to him or her—bullfighter, baseball player, or long-distance runner—moves us little. The hazards of performing, after all, are usually rewarded with enormous salaries or glamorous publicity. So the problem *Dangerous Summer* presents is to explain Hemingway's excessive concern for Antonio. Referring to his custom of visiting Antonio briefly in his dressing room before a bullfight, Hemingway acknowledges the futility of his visits: "But nobody can help a bullfighter immediately before the fight; so we tried to cut the time of acute anxiety down. I prefer the term anguish, controlled anguish, to anxiety" (142). Understandably Hemingway identifies with Antonio, who embodies Hemingway's long-standing ideals, a matador whose artistry in the bullring is similar to writers whose artistry, in turn, compels them to take risks that jeopardize their reputations: Antonio "was very pleased, always, to call the faena writing" (103). But a simpler explanation of Hemingway's role as anxious tutor is that he represents a brooding parent, worried lest some accident deprive him of an exemplary "son." While Hemingway's anxiety over Mary in *African Journal* expresses the worry of both a devoted husband and a fond big brother taking care of a favored little sister, his worry here expresses a father's guilt-tinged fears for a risk-taking son.[21] Indeed, sounding like a parent who has sworn off getting involved with a son's or daughter's personal life, Hemingway admits, "I had lost much of my old feeling for the bullfight. But a new generation of fighters had grown up and I was anxious to see them. I had known their fathers, some of them very well, but after some of them died and others lost out to fear or other causes I had resolved never to have a bullfighter for a friend again because I suffered too much for them and with them when they could not cope with the bull from fear or the incapacity that fear brings" (48–49).

Comparing Hemingway's anxious tutor with a brooding parent would be farfetched were it not the explicit subject matter of *Islands in the Stream,* the last novel on which Hemingway worked. For now, however, we might suggest that the potentially interesting emotional tensions of *African Journal* and *Dangerous Summer* fall far short of engaging the reader's concerns. Unable to share in, or even sympathize with, Hemingway's excessive anxieties, and unpersuaded that his African and Spanish storms are much more than tempests in a tea-pot-boiler, the reader is likely to become bored by the travelogue and irritated by a fuss so grossly disproportionate to its causes.

"After thirty a man wakes up sad every morning . . . until the day of his death." Yes, Emerson again. *African Journal* begins with just such a morning, the departure from the safari of Philip Percival, better known as the white hunter Pop of *Green Hills of Africa*. His departure leaves to Hemingway the responsibility of seeing that Miss Mary kill the marauding lion: "It was all mine on a windless morning of the last day of the month of the next to the last month of the year" (1:45). An odd way to say November 30. But in the oddity must lurk Hemingway's concern with his own "last days" and "last months." How does a writer of international acclaim deal with the awareness that his own last days, months, or years may be upon him, that his last writings may not meet his own standards for publication, that his creativity may have ebbed beyond return?[22] No Henry James, Hemingway does not seek to relive his creative years by turning back to revise his work for some New York edition. But he does seek them by turning back to settings and activities whose intensely felt experience and varied subjects had once fueled his creative energies and tested his developing aesthetic. To consider the posthumous works in the sequence of their interrupted composition—*Islands in the Stream, African Journal, A Moveable Feast,* and *The Dangerous Summer*—is to see Hemingway regressing to the 1930s and 1920s: fishing again the Gulf Stream, hunting again the plains beneath Kilimanjaro, walking again the streets of Paris, and sitting again at *barreras* in Spain to absorb the unfolding drama in the *plaza de toros*. The return to those activities and settings, actually or in memory, seems prompted by a wish to reload the imagery and emotions of recollected events and so to trigger fresh creation. By displaying the capacity and retentiveness of his memory in *African Journal* and *A Moveable Feast,* Hemingway implies the strength of another faculty, namely creative invention.

But the emotional and aesthetic shortcomings of the posthumous work are strong evidence that Hemingway's use of art was failing him. His heavy reliance upon remembering suggests that his choice or need to write about memories of past events finds less value in the products of memory (what he remembers) or their reliability (the truth of what he remembers) than in the activity of remembering (how he remembers) and the ability of remembering (that he remembers). It is this last pair of memory functions that is so crucial to the composing process in Hemingway's creativity.[23] And inasmuch as remembering is a way of knowing things—and letting others know that we know things—Hemingway's use of tutors suggests a greater confidence in telling what he has learned than in revealing experiences whose epistemological or existential problems await readers' solutions. This is, of course, a significant shift away from the successful techniques of his best work. Together, the compulsive remembering and the anxious tutors are sufficient symptoms of some deeply imbedded sorrow or guilt—or both—that disclose in these works a sizeable component of melancholy. Not a new component in his repertory, any retrospective of his canon should spotlight its melancholy, if only by looking upon his writings as a literature of loss. There are such literal losses as Jake Barnes's sexual capacity, Harry Morgan's arm, Robert Jordan's leg, Santiago's marlin, Frederic Henry's lover, and the major's young wife in "In Another Country." Coupled to this pulse of explicit mourning over separation are Jake's fiesta-ending depression, Frederic's dejection over life's irrational inequities, the older waiter's litany response to the Lord's Prayer, Harry Morgan's embitterment at a politically malignant world, Manolin's despondency that his absence from Santiago's skiff during the ordeal with the marlin and sharks may result in Santiago's death, and Robert Jordan's deep shame at his father's suicide, which stain only his compensatory deeds can bleach out.

To find melancholy a major component of Hemingway's art should not surprise us. After all, the melancholy beneath an "imagination of disaster" bulks large in the tradition of American literature, as nearly any list of classic texts would suggest: Hawthorne's *Scarlet Letter*, Melville's *Moby-Dick*, Twain's *Mysterious Stranger*, Cather's *The Professor's House*, Faulkner's *Absalom! Absalom!*, James's *Portrait of a Lady*, Steinbeck's *Grapes of Wrath*, Wright's *Native Son*, the dramas of Eugene O'Neill and Tennessee Williams, and most of the poetry of T. S. Eliot, Theodore Roethke, and Robert Lowell.

Melancholy commands our attention in *Islands in the Stream*. Here the anxious tutor is literally a brooding parent, and his preoccupation, whether adequately accounted for or not, helps us see that such a countenance has hovered over much of what Hemingway has written. Tempting though it is to speculate on the origin of that countenance, we leave that challenge to biographers and biographical critics. Our task is to attend to the melancholy that unifies the novel and to suggest why such a flawed novel warrants genuine regard.

Setting aside the excellent Conradian pursuit of a "secret sharer" in the "At Sea" section,[24] the novel as a whole suffers from insisting that we pity Thomas Hudson, a sometime artist whose loss of all three sons informs the novel. The anxious tutor-father who broods over his tyro-sons figures in all of the major episodes during the sons' five-week visit in "Bimini": the conversations on raising oldest son Tom in Paris among renowned artists, the pretense of letting youngest son Andrew get drunk in a public bar so as to shock and dismay tourists, the hammerhead shark's nearly fatal attack on spear-fishing middle son David, and the three sons' attendance upon a young woman with whom Hudson's visitor and former companion, Roger Davis, falls in love. But son David's six-hour ordeal, fighting but losing at boat-side a huge marlin (a replay of Santiago's ordeal), best displays the problem of Hemingway's anxious tutor. Hemingway superbly renders the psychological drama of the adult men and two siblings who surround David's initiatory experience. The men coach and help him, their display of parental concern complemented by the fraternal anxiety of his brothers. Both groups realize the danger to which David is exposed and agonize over his painful ordeal. The oddity in the episode is the role of Thomas Hudson, David's father. He leaves to Roger Davis and to Eddy, the boat's cook and a known rummy, the actual coaching of David. Admirably unpossessive in his trust of Roger and Eddy's coaching skills, Hudson is also strangely derelict in his duties as the boy's father. His hands-off role here does not match with his professed love of and anxiety over the boys. Indeed, the editorial decision to make Hudson the boys' father—rather than to leave them Roger's sons, as the manuscripts first established—invites puzzlement over Hudson's role, puzzlement that would not occur were we to regard him as merely Roger's friend.

When compared with Hudson's attempts to suppress his sorrow in the novel's second section, "Cuba," the puzzlement we feel for Hudson's curiously unfatherly conduct during David's ordeal seems negligible. Whether attending his lonesome cats, reflecting upon sad memories ignited by landmarks during his car ride into Havana, or conversing with the gallery of sorrow-filled characters he meets, Hudson's behavior shows him to be deeply depressed. The cause for such depression, news that his third son Tom has been killed in the war, is certainly grounds for depression. But this section of the novel occurs three weeks after that news, and clearly he has not disclosed it to any of his crew during the outing from which they have just returned on the previous day. Willie, the closest of his Q-boat crew members, scolds him at the Floridita Bar for having been a "grief-hoarder," for not having divulged the news during the two weeks of their most recent submarine-hunting cruise. Even during Hudson's day-ending chance reunion with his famous actress ex-wife, to whom he finally reveals the news of their Tommy's death, Hudson's protectiveness of her shows that he arrogates to himself the role of chief mourner. Although his behavior seems understandable enough, it borders on neurosis. Publicly parading himself before others as a man who can absorb the loss of his last son, he invites regard for his stoicism. But it is not stoicism. Rather, he deliberately puts himself into situations that force friends and acquaintances to probe the cause of his unusual behavior, as when Honest Lil pleads, "You can tell me, you know. Henry tells me about his sorrows and cries in the night. Willie tells me dreadful things. They are not sorrows, so much as terrible things. You can tell me. Everyone tells me. Only you don't tell me" (274). And once they learn the cause of his grief they express what he most wants—if only to reject it: pity.

Hudson's behavior seems aimed at demonstrating how to cope with deep personal loss. But his lesson is warped by self-pity, and his inability to reconcile himself to his last son's death and his determination to suppress his grief suggest some underlying guilt. That guilt is manifest in his conduct while chasing the fleeing German submarine crew in the last section. Concerned though he seems, both for the welfare of his crew and for the slain or injured crewmen left behind by the fleeing German submarine captain, Hudson's sleep-denying, duty-ridden ways worry his crew, Ara exhorting him, "Now that you have ceased to be careful of yourself I must ask you to be, please. For us and for the ship" (358). Careless of his own safety, he justifies his actions in the name of duty. Taking an unnecessary risk, he sails the disguised craft down a narrow channel rather than anchor it at the head of the channel and send out a reconnaisance party. That risk exposes him and his crew to the Germans' ambush. Not surprisingly, he alone is wounded by the gunfire and he guarantees that his wounds will be lethal by stipulating that his crew return to defuse a boobytrapped turtleboat before they take him to an island hospital. The result of his suicidal behavior certainly releases him from grieving further and from facing whatever guilt lies beneath his melancholy.

T. S. Eliot's claim, "The more perfect the artist, the more completely separated in him will be the man who suffers and the mind which creates," may indicate the artistic flaw that spoils *Islands*. Hemingway's lack of separation from Thomas Hudson, "the man who suffers," is evident in the absence of the controlling forms of irony that recur in Hemingway's successful fiction. Thomas Hudson is not a created character whom we may scorn or towards whom Hemingway invites alternative responses. He is no Nick Adams, or Frederic Henry, or Jake Barnes, or even Harry Morgan. Rather, Hemingway's narrator expects us to appreciate Hudson's melancholy and to revere him as someone who—stripped of his parental duties because of the early and untimely deaths of his three sons—turns to patriotic duties and dies carrying them out. His presumably noble conduct, aligning him with Robert Jordan and Santiago, asks only for a sentimental response.

Nevertheless, the genuineness of *Island*'s melancholy may guarantee the novel's value as a major work in Hemingway's career. Less an accomplished work of art that draws upon the skills of dialogue and varied techniques of irony than a memory-driven, thinly disguised autobiographical confession, the book reveals some deep anguish seeking outlet. Thomas Hudson's sufferings show Hemingway trying to get outside himself, trying to disguise and metamorphose some personal anxieties by assigning them to Hudson—as none of the other posthumous and more expressly autobiographical documents do. And inasmuch as Hemingway began the novel as early as 1946,[25] we can assume that his melancholy was not just a phenomenon of his last few years. He was unable, however, to gain from the writing process the cathartic effect of projecting personal emotions onto an invented character. At least this seems a reasonable conclusion, given the depression of his final years and his inability to complete the novel before the other projects and works of his last decade sidetracked him. What remains for us, then, from this novel and from the overlay of memory and melancholy in the other posthumous works, is a somberly different profile of Ernest Hemingway than we are accustomed to—one that highlights lines of anguish in his brow, shows darker rings beneath his eyes, and reveals troubled memory-images flitting like vexatious shadows across the sidewise search of his vision.

Notes and References

Chapter One

1. Johnson J. Hooper, *Simon Suggs Adventures* (1845; rpt., Philadelphia, 1881), 26. Quoted in Pascal Covici, Jr., *Mark Twain's Humor* (Dallas: Southern Methodist University Press, 1962), 7; Covici's analyses have indirectly stimulated the following discussion.

2. *The Short Stories of Ernest Hemingway* (New York, 1954), 148; hereafter cited in the text as *SS*.

3. See Carlos Baker, *Ernest Hemingway: A Life Story* (New York, 1969). For other other biographies and reminiscences, see the bibliography.

4. See Philip Young, *Ernest Hemingway* (New York, 1952) or his revised and expanded *Ernest Hemingway: A Reconsideration* (University Park, 1966) for the most thorough and persuasive examination of this aspect of his work.

5. John Peale Bishop, "Homage to Hemingway," *New Republic*, 11 November 1936, 40; rpt. in his *Collected Essays* (New York: Scribner's, 1948), 38.

6. Edmund Wilson, "Ernest Hemingway: Gauge of Morale," *Atlantic*, July 1939, 42; rpt. in his *The Wound and the Bow* (Boston: Houghton Mifflin, 1941), 226, in *Ernest Hemingway: The Man and His Work*, ed. John K. M. McCaffery (Cleveland, 1950; New York, 1969), 220–21, and in *Hemingway: The Critical Heritage*, ed. Jeffrey Meyers (Boston, 1982), 305.

7. Lillian Ross, *New Yorker*, 13 May 1950. Republished as *Portrait of Hemingway* (New York, 1961) with the note that the author had no intention of presenting a derogatory portrait and that she and Hemingway were perfectly satisfied with the one presented; rpt. in *Hemingway: A Collection of Critical Essays*, ed. Robert P. Weeks (Englewood Cliffs, N.J., 1962), 17–39.

8. Arturo Barea, "Not Spain But Hemingway," *Horizon* 3 (1941): 360; rpt. in *Hemingway and His Critics*, ed. Carlos Baker (New York, 1961), 211, in *The Literary Reputation of Hemingway in Europe*, ed. Roger Asselineau (New York, 1965), 209, in *The Merrill Studies in "For Whom the Bell Tolls*," comp. Sheldon Norman Grebstein (Columbus, Ohio, 1971), 89, and in Meyers, *Heritage*, 359.

9. See "American Bohemians in Paris a Weird Lot," *Toronto Star Weekly*, 25 March 1922; quoted in Charles A. Fenton, *The Apprenticeship*

of Ernest Hemingway (New York, 1954), 124–25; rpt. in *By-Line: Ernest Hemingway,* ed. William White (New York, 1967), 23–25. See also *Green Hills of Africa* (New York, 1935), 19–27—hereafter cited in the text as *GH*—for a good specimen of a Hemingway pronouncement.

10. His most notorious main event was with Max Eastman (11 August 1937); see Carlos Baker, *Hemingway: The Writer as Artist,* 4th ed. (Princeton, 1972), 233. For literary purposes, a more significant preliminary event may have taken place at Pamplona, July 1925; see Harold Loeb, *The Way It Was* (New York, 1959), 294–97; rpt. in Bertram D. Sarason, *Hemingway and THE SUN Set,* (Washington, D.C., 1972), 136–44. For rounds with publisher Joseph Knapp and poet Wallace Stevens see Baker, *Life Story,* 273 and 285, respectively; a fuller account on the round with the publisher is in Leicester Hemingway, *My Brother, Ernest Hemingway* (Cleveland, 1961), 165–67; for Hemingway's version of the fight with Stevens, see his letter to Sara Murphy in *Ernest Hemingway: Selected Letters 1917–1961,* ed. Carlos Baker (New York, 1981), 438–40.

11. Alfred G. Aronowitz and Peter Hamill, *Ernest Hemingway: The Life and Death of a Man* (New York, 1961), 216–18; for Betsky's account, see "A Last Visit," *Saturday Review,* 29 July 1961, 22.

12. See Fenton's *Apprenticeship,* chapter 1, for the best picture of Oak Park; but see also Marcelline Hemingway Sanford, *At the Hemingways: A Family Portrait* (Boston, 1962); and Baker, *Life Story,* 1–29.

13. Malcolm Cowley, "A Portrait of Mister Papa," *Life,* 10 January 1949, 86–101; rpt. in McCaffery, *The Man and His Work,* 26–48.

14. Hemingway married Hadley Richardson in 1921, divorced her in 1927 to marry Pauline Pfeiffer, was divorced by her in 1940 when he married Martha Gellhorn, divorced her in 1945 and married Mary Welsh in 1946. For a sympathetic account of Hadley's life, see Alice Hunt Sokoloff, *Hadley: The First Mrs. Hemingway* (New York, 1973); for a superior study of the various wives and women in Hemingway's life see Bernice Kert, *The Hemingway Women* (New York, 1983).

15. *A Farewell to Arms* (New York, 1929), 185; hereafter cited in the text as *F.*

16. An important distinction between *anti-intellectual* and *anti-intellectualist* is made by Morton White in "Reflections on Anti-Intellectualism," *Daedalus* (Summer 1962): 457–68. The best articulated dismissals of Hemingway as thinker are Robert Evans, "Hemingway and the Pale Cast of Thought," *American Literature* 38 (1966): 161–76; rpt. in *Ernest Hemingway: A Collection of Criticism,* ed. Arthur Waldhorn (New York, 1973), 112–26; and Otto Friedrich, "Ernest Hemingway: Joy Through Strength," *American Scholar* 26 (1957): 470, 518–30; rpt. in *The Merrill Studies in "A Farewell to Arms,"* comp. John Graham (Columbus, Ohio, 1971), 46–54.

17. See especially Wyndham Lewis, "The Dumb Ox: A Study of Ernest Hemingway," *American Review* 3 (1934): 289–312 and *Life and Letters* 10 (1934): 33–45; rpt. as "The Dumb Ox in Love and War," in his *Men Without Art* (1934; New York: Russell & Russell, 1964), 17–41, in *Twentieth Century Interpretations of "A Farewell to Arms": A Collection of Critical Essays,* ed. Jay Gellens (Englewood Cliffs, N.J., 1970), 72–90, and in Meyers, *Heritage,* 186–209. All subsequent specimens of this viewpoint are merely footnotes to this classical essay in expert vituperation.

18. Hemingway's courage has never seriously been impugned, at least not since the Max Eastman episode. His generosity with younger writers up until World War II is generally acknowledged; for an instance of which, see Arnold Samuelson, *With Hemingway: A Year in Key West & Cuba* (New York, 1984).

19. Baker, *Life Story,* 44–45.

20. See "The Adventures of Nick Adams," 29–54, in Young's *Reconsideration* for the most cogent exposition of the "trauma" theory.

21. W. M. Frohock, *The Novel of Violence in America* (Dallas: Southern Methodist University Press, 1957, rev. ed.), 194.

22. So Hemingway admitted in a letter to Baker, *Hemingway,* 142n.

23. *Death in the Afternoon* (New York, 1932), 147; hereafter cited in the text as *D.*

24. Colonel Cantwell's demand for a corner table in restaurants and his consciousness of protecting his flanks in bars is an absurd extension of this. If Hemingway means this to be comical, he fails; if he means it to be serious, it cannot but be taken comically.

25. For the relationship between Hemingway and Anderson see John T. Flanagan, "Hemingway's Debt to Sherwood Anderson," *Journal of English and Germanic Philology* 54 (1955): 507–20; James Schevill, *Sherwood Anderson: His Life and Work* (Denver: University of Denver Press, 1951), 226–28; Scott Donaldson, *By Force of Will: The Life and Art of Ernest Hemingway* (New York, 1977), 194–97; Anthony F. R. Palmieri, "A Note on the Hemingway-Anderson Rupture," *Fitzgerald/Hemingway Annual 1978,* 349; his "The Hemingway-Anderson Feud: A Letter from Boni," *Hemingway Review* 1 (1981): 56–58; and Ray Lewis White, "Anderson's Private Reaction to *The Torrents of Spring,*" *Modern Fiction Studies* 26 (1980–1981): 635–37. Gertrude Stein articulately argues the feud with Hemingway in her *The Autobiography of Alice B. Toklas* (New York, 1933), to which Hemingway responds in *Green Hills,* 65–66; in *A Moveable Feast* (New York, 1964), 11–21, 25–30, and 119; and in *Selected Letters,* 736, 781, and 794–95. The Stein rift seems to have received at least a token reconciliation during the liberation of Paris in 1944, according to Hemingway, *Selected Letters,* 650.

26. The list could be considerably longer. As representatives let these suffice: Harold Loeb, Max Eastman, Sinclair Lewis. To these could be added literary critics and biographers as well as the generals and statesmen who receive Hemingway's disapproval in *Across the River Into the Trees* (New York, 1950); hereafter cited in the text as *A*.

27. This may help explain the inclusion of such figures as counts Mippipopoulos and Greffi in *The Sun Also Rises* and *A Farewell to Arms*, since their age makes equality of relationship out of the question for either character.

28. Jake Barnes's relationship to Lady Brett is a possible exception, but biologically he is not a lover. See Baker, *Hemingway*, 109–16, for a spirited but unconvincing defense of Hemingway's female characterizations, and, for an equally spirited and unconvincing attack of them, Judith Fetterley, "*A Farewell to Arms*: Ernest Hemingway's Resentful Cryptogram," in her *The Resisting Reader: A Feminist Approach to American Fiction* (Bloomington: Indiana University Press, 1978), 46–71. The statement concerning Frederic Henry is qualified in chapter 4, but not changed significantly.

29. The full impact of World War I on the American literary scene can hardly be indicated here. Good introductions to the period are Frederick J. Hoffman, *The Twenties: American Writing in the Postwar Decade* (New York: Viking Press, 1955) and Paul Fussell, *The Great War and Modern Memory* (New York: Oxford University Press, 1975).

30. Concerning Hemingway's running away from home, see Madelaine Hemingway Miller, *Ernie: Hemingway's Sister "Sunny" Remembers* (New York, 1975): "I have read that Ernie ran away from home. Our parents always knew where he was and helped him plan and pack for his trips. And he always sent back the self-addressed postcards Dad gave him on departure . . . (95)."

31. Quoted in Baker, *Hemingway*, 71.

32. *A Farewell to Arms* averaged close to twenty thousand sold copies per month in the first four months of its appearance (Baker, *Hemingway*, 411).

33. By Edmund Wilson, who reprints it and three letters from Hemingway in his *The Shores of Light: A Literary Chronicle of the Twenties and Thirties* (New York: Farrar, Straus and Young, 1952), 115–25; rpt. in *Ernest Hemingway: Five Decades of Criticism*, ed. Linda Welshimer Wagner (East Lansing, 1974), 222–23, in *Ernest Hemingway: The Critical Reception*, ed. Robert O. Stephens (New York, 1977), 1–3, and in Meyers, *Heritage*, 63–65.

34. *Life*, 5, 12, and 19 September 1961, 77–109, 60–82, and 74–90.

35. The drawing power of Hemingway's name may be indicated by a partial listing of the magazines in which he published: *Atlantic Monthly, Collier's, Cosmopolitan, Esquire, Fortune, Holiday, Ken, Life, Scribner's,* and *Vogue.* And this was before it became fashionable for national magazines to peddle culture. The influence of the movie version of Hemingway's fictions should also be taken into account, for which see Gene D. Phillips, *Hemingway and Film* (New York, 1980) and Frank M. Laurence, *Hemingway and the Movies* (Jackson, 1981).

36. Sean O'Faolain, *The Vanishing Hero: Studies of the Hero in the Modern Novel* (London: Little Brown, 1956), 164.

37. This is an enormously large and complicated subject. See Herbert Marcuse's arguments in *Eros and Civilization* (Boston: Beacon Press, 1955).

38. For a tour de force exposition on the sense of smell, see Pilar's explanation of the smell of death-to-come in *For Whom the Bell Tolls* (New York, 1940), 254–57; hereafter cited in the text as *FW*. Hemingway can be profitably compared to Whitman ("Song of Myself") in their respective concerns with an imaginative re-creation of the five senses.

39. Benjamin Franklin, Ezra Pound, and Norman Mailer are probably also exceptions: the first can be ignored here since he was not a "creative" writer in the usual sense; the second is a special case, and, at any rate, he never enjoyed wide popularity; the third, who allows few readers to ignore him, may deserve inclusion along with Twain and Whitman.

40. As mentioned above, Wyndham Lewis, "The Dumb Ox," best articulates the negative view; for a positive view see Elliot Paul, "Hemingway and the Critics," *Saturday Review,* 6 November 1937, 3–4; rpt. in McCaffery, *The Man and His Work,* 94-98. For another pairing, see the short exchange in *Folio* 20 (1955): 18–20 and 20–22 between Leon Edel, "The Art of Evasion" and Philip Young, "Hemingway: A Defense"; rpt. in Weeks, *Collection,* 169–74.

41. A good comprehensive view of the American literary scene in the 1930s with a special focus on Leftist movements is Daniel Aaron, *Writers on the Left: Episodes in American Literary Communism* (New York: Harcourt Brace & World, 1961).

42. *The Old Man and the Sea* (New York, 1952), 66.

43. Lillian Ross, *Portrait,* 37; rpt. in Weeks, *Collection,* 24.

44. Quoted in Baker, *Hemingway,* 339.

45. See "A Man of the World" and "Get a Seeing-Eye Dog," Hemingway's contributions to the *Atlantic Monthly* Jubilee edition (November 1957): 64–68; for two articles that value the stories as "the true capstone to his career," see Julian Smith, "Eyeless in Wyoming, Blind in Venice: Hemingway's Last Stories," *Connecticut Review* 4 (1971): 9–15; and Delbert E. Wylder, "Internal Treachery in the Last Published Short Stories of

Ernest Hemingway," in *Hemingway In Our Time*, eds. Richard Astro and Jackson J. Benson (Corvallis, 1974), 53–65.

46. According to Reverend D. Richard Wolfe (Columbia City, Ind.), who spent four days in close contact with Hemingway in the psychiatric ward of the Mayo Clinic (Spring, 1961), Hemingway appeared to be a man "in despair." He seemed thoroughly disoriented and spiritually listless; nor did he appear to be searching for away out of his despair (telephone conversation, DRW and ER, 28 August 1962). That this situation was not a temporary result of his treatment has been well documented in Baker, *Life Story*, 553–64; A. E. Hotchner, *Papa Hemingway: A Personal Memoir* (New York; 1966), 276–335; and Mary Welsh Hemingway, *How It Was* (New York, 1976), 482–503.

47. Ross, *Portrait*, 48; rpt. in Weeks, *Collection*, 30.

Chapter Two

1. Compare with Whitman: "For well dear brother I know / If thou wast not granted to sing thou would'st surely die." Whitman, of course, had never heard of the "trauma theory" of literary creativity.

2. Two early articles on Hemingway's aesthetic are still valuable: Robert C. Hart, "Hemingway on Writing," *College English* 18 (1957): 314–20; and C. Hugh Holman, "Hemingway and Emerson: Notes on the Continuity of an Aesthetic Tradition," *Modern Fiction Studies* 1 (1955): 12–16. For subsquent explorations of Hemingway's aesthetic see Emily Stipes Watt, *Ernest Hemingway and the Arts* (Urbana, 1971); Gerry Brenner, *Concealments in Hemingway's Works* (Columbus, 1983), 8–16, 65–106; and Brian Way, "Hemingway the Intellectual: A Version of Modernism," in *Ernest Hemingway: New Critical Essays,* ed. A. Robert Lee (Totowa, N.J., 1983), 151–71.

3. Compare with Emily Dickinson's famous kinetic test for authentic poetic experience.

4. It might be argued that Hemingway uses the Roman soldier's speech in this story as a technique of characterization; but as his impersonal narrators and public statements show, Hemingway's sports usage is obsessively marked. See Ross, *Portrait;* Jackson J. Benson, *Hemingway . . . The Writer's Art of Self-Defense* (Minneapolis, 1969), 73–88; John Reardon, "Hemingway's Esthetic and Ethical Sportsmen," *University Review* 34 (1967): 13–23; rpt. in Wagner, *Five Decades*, 131–44; and Robert W. Lewis, Jr., "Hemingway's Concept of Sport and 'Soldier's Home,' " *Rendezvous* 5 (1970): 19–27; rpt. in *The Short Stories of Ernest Hemingway: Critical Essays,* ed. Jackson J. Benson (Durham, N.C., 1975), 170–80.

5. *The Sun Also Rises* (New York, 1926), 214–15; hereafter cited in the text as *TS*.

6. Pilar's recollection of Finito in *For Whom the Bell Tolls*, 182–90, is similar in feeling and in its dramatically intrusive character.

7. Hemingway's poem "Mitrailliatrice," *Poetry* (January 1923): 193; rpt. in *88 Poems*, ed. Nicholas Gerogiannis (New York, 1979), comes very close to suggesting that death is in the typewriter.

8. Three studies of "Snows" warrant consideration: Oliver Evans, " 'The Snows of Kilimanjaro': A Revaluation," *PMLA* 76 (1961): 601–7; rpt. in *Hemingway's African Stories: The Stories, Their Sources, Their Critics*, ed. John M. Howell (New York, 1969), 150–57; Marion Montgomery, "The Leopard and the Hyena: Symbol and Meaning in 'The Snows of Kilimanjaro,'" *University of Kansas City Review* 27 (1961): 277–82; rpt. in Howell, *African Stories*, 145–49; and Gennaro Santangelo, "The Dark Snows of Kilimanjaro," in Benson, *Short Stories*, 251–61.

9. Hemingway adapted the epigraph from Hans Meyer, *Across East African Glaciers*, changing the antelope in the original to a leopard, according to Robert O. Stephens, "Hemingway's Riddle of Kilimanjaro: Idea and Image," *American Literature* 32 (1961): 84–87; rpt. in Howell, *African Stories*, 93–94. But also see Alice Hall Petry, "Voice Out of Africa: A Possible Oral Source for Hemingway's 'The Snows of Kilimanjaro,'" *Hemingway Review* 4 (1985): 7–11.

10. Hemingway takes special care to emphasize that Harry is not just thinking of writing, but actually is writing: " 'I've been writing,' he said. 'But I got tired' " (*SS*, 74). Immediately after that the death-hyena climbs on his chest.

11. Hemingway made a practice of referring to the lucrative movie version as "The Snows of Zanuck." See his African articles, "The Christmas Gift," *Look*, 20 April and 4 May 1954; rpt. in White, *By-Line*, 425–69. See also Phillips, *Hemingway and Film*, 6–16, 106–19.

12. Ross, *Portrait*, 56; rpt. in Weeks, *Collection*, 24.

13. *The Old Man and the Sea* (New York, 1952), hereafter cited in the text as *OM*.

14. The inventories of Hemingway's libraries have considerably broadened the base for influence and source studies; see "Hemingway's Bones," the introductory chapter of Michael S. Reynolds, *Hemingway's Reading: 1910–1940, An Inventory* (Princeton: Princeton University Press, 1981), 3–36; and James D. Brasch and Joseph Sigman, *Hemingway's Library: A Composite Record* (New York, 1981).

15. Fenton's *Apprenticeship* has been the most valuable source for any work on Hemingway's formative years; for the Lardner relationship, see 22–26. But for significant new materials see Peter Griffin, *Along with Youth: Hemingway, The Early Years* (New York, 1985).

16. Quoted in Fenton, *Apprenticeship*, 56.

17. For discussions of Hemingway's satiric and comic abilities, see Benson, *Self-Defense*, 28–42, and Sheldon Norman Grebstein, *Hemingway's Craft* (Carbondale, 1973), 171–201.

18. Fenton, chapters 2, 4, and following; see also Scott Donaldson, "Hemingway of *The Star*," *College Literature* 7 (1980): 263–81; rpt. in *Ernest Hemingway: The Papers of a Writer*, ed. Bernard Oldsey (New York, 1981), 89–107.

19. Quoted in Baker, *Hemingway*, 31.

20. Wilson, *The Shores of Light*, 117.

21. "An Interview with Ernest Hemingway," *Paris Review* 18 (1958): 85; rpt. in *Writers at Work: The "Paris Review" Interviews*, 2nd series, ed. George Plimpton (New York: Viking, 1963), 236–37, in Baker, *Critics*, 35, and in Wagner, *Five Decades*, 36.

22. A fine discussion of the Stein relationship is in Fenton, *Apprenticeship*, 150–58. For an interesting parallel between Stein and Pilar, see Raymond S. Nelson, *Hemingway: Expressionist Artist* (Ames, Iowa, 1979), 38–40.

23. Several illuminating studies of Hemingway's style warrant recognition: John Graham, "Ernest Hemingway: The Meaning of a Style," *Modern Fiction Studies* 6 (1960–61): 298–313; rpt. in *Ernest Hemingway: Critiques of Four Major Novels*, ed. Carlos Baker (New York, 1962), 183–92, in Graham, *Studies*, 88–105, and in Waldhorn, *Criticism*, 18–34; Harry Levin, "Observations on the Style of Ernest Hemingway," *Kenyon Review* 13 (1951): 581–609; rpt. in his *Contexts of Criticism* (Cambridge: Harvard University Press, 1957), 140–67, in Weeks, *Collection*, 72–85, and in Baker, *Critics*, 93–115; Richard Bridgman, "Ernest Hemingway," in his *The Colloquial Style in America* (New York: Oxford University Press, 1966), 195–230; rpt. in Wagner, *Five Decades*, 160–88; Grebstein, *Hemingway's Craft*, 141–70; and James Rother, "Modernism and the Nonsense Style," *Contemporary Literature* 15 (1974): 187–202. For the most comprehensive study of Hemingway's style, see Richard K. Peterson, *Hemingway: Direct and Oblique* (The Hague and Paris, 1969).

24. Robert Penn Warren, "Ernest Hemingway," *Kenyon Review* 9 (1947): 28; rpt. in his *Selected Essays* (New York: Random House, 1951), 93, and in Wagner, *Five Decades*, 118.

25. Baker, *Hemingway*, 155.

26. The distinction can be suggested by a comparison between the African landscapes of *Green Hills of Africa* and the same landscapes in "The Snows of Kilimanjaro" and in "The Short Happy Life of Francis Macomber." In spite of Hemingway's most strenuous efforts, the background in the first book is unconvincing and unalive, but it becomes almost an active character in the short stories. The difficulty with *Green Hills* is the absence of any significant tension, or forcefield, to bring places into a

focus. It is very hard for a reader to become terribly concerned about whether Hemingway's friend Karl does or does not shoot a bigger kudu than Hemingway. For positive readings of *Green Hills* see Robert W. Lewis, Jr., *Hemingway on Love* (Austin, 1965), 57–75; and Brenner, *Concealments*, 81–97, 103–6.

27. Saul Bellow, "Hemingway and the Image of Man," *Partisan Review* 20 (1953): 342. Bellow's comment accurately prophesies and interprets Hemingway's suicide.

28. D. H. Lawrence, *Studies in Classic American Literature* (1923; New York: Viking, 1964), 62–63.

Chapter Three

1. Hemingway's poetry is collected in Gerogiannis, *88 Poems.*

2. For a more thorough explication of this subject see Earl Rovit, "The Shape of American Poetry," *Jahrbuch für Amerikastudien* 6 (1961): 122–33.

3. Philip Young's chapter "The Hero and the Code," in his *Reconsideration*, 55–78, is an excellent introduction. For other studies of the code, see Delmore Schwartz, "Ernest Hemingway's Literary Situation," *Southern Review* 3 (1938): 769–82; rpt. in McCaffery, *The Man and His Work*, 99–113, and in Meyers, *Heritage*, 243–56; Warren, "Ernest Hemingway," 1–28; rpt. in Wagner, *Five Decades*, 80–118; and James B. Colvert, "Ernest Hemingway's Morality in Action," *American Literature* 27 (1955): 372–85.

4. Ernest Hemingway, "The Denunciation," *Esquire*, November 1938, 112; rpt. in *The Fifth Column and Four Stories of the Spanish Civil War* (New York, 1969), 97.

5. Baker, *Hemingway*, 131. For additional commentary on Nick Adams, see Philip Young, " 'Big World Out There': The Nick Adams Stories," *Novel: A Forum on Fiction* 6 (1972): 5–19; rpt. in Benson, *Short Stories*, 29–45, and Joseph M. Flora, *Hemingway's Nick Adams* (Baton Rouge, 1982).

6. One could argue that the bull in "The Undefeated" and the lion in "The Short Happy Life of Francis Macomber" are perfectly representative "tutors" in action. In Hemingway's renditions, their thoughts are as intelligent as those of Manuel.

7. Young, *Reconsideration*, 64. See also Robert P. Weeks, "Wise-Guy Narrator and Trickster Out-Tricked in Hemingway's 'Fifty Grand,' " *Studies in American Fiction* 10 (1982): 83–91.

8. Two excellent discussions of this phase of modern fiction are Ihab Hassan, *Radical Innocence* (Princeton: Princeton University Press, 1961) and R. W. B. Lewis, *The Picaresque Saint* (Philadelphia: Lippincott, 1959).

9. A possible exception to the rule is Schatz in "A Day's Wait."

10. Baker's discussion in *Hemingway*, 283–87, is especially valuable on this subject.

11. A survey of such studies includes Isaac Rosenfeld, "A Farewell to Hemingway," *Kenyon Review* 13 (1951): 147–55; rpt. in Meyers, *Heritage*, 385–93; Richard Drinnon, "In the American Heartland: Hemingway and Death," *Psychoanalytic Review* 52 (1965): 5–31; David Gordon, "The Son and the Father: Patterns of Response to Conflict in Hemingway's Fiction," *Literature and Psychology* 16 (1966): 122–38; rpt. in his *Literary Art and the Unconscious* (Baton Rouge: Louisiana State University Press, 1976), 171–94; Richard B. Hovey, *Hemingway: The Inward Terrain* (Seattle, 1968); Irvin D. and Marilyn Yalom, "Ernest Hemingway—A Psychiatric View," *Archives of General Psychiatry* 24 (1971): 485–94; Richard E. Hardy and John G. Cull, *Hemingway: A Psychological Portrait* (Sherman Oaks, Ca.: Banner Books, 1977), especially 47–56 and 81–92; Brenner, *Concealments;* and Jeffrey Meyers, "Lawrence Kubie's Suppressed Essay on Hemingway," *American Imago* 41 (1984): 1–18.

12. *To Have and Have Not* (New York, 1937), 221; hereafter cited in the text as *TH*.

13. There is actually a further confusion in the end of the novel in which Henry identifies with his stillborn son: "Poor little kid. I wished the hell I'd been choked like that" (*F*, 327); he also rejects himself as father, claiming that he has no feeling of fatherhood. The most interesting detail is his looking into a mirror with his white gown and beard: "I looked in the glass and saw myself looking like a fake doctor with a beard" (*F*, 319). Dr. Clarence Hemingway and, presumably, Dr. Adams as well wore beards.

14. Baker, *Life Story*, 198–99.

15. The dates of the publication of *To Have and Have Not* are a little confusing because the first two sections of the novel had been previously published as stories, "Part One: Harry Morgan (*Spring*)" as "One Trip Across" in *Cosmopolitan*, April 1934, 20–23, 108–22; "Part Two: Harry Morgan (*Fall*)" as "The Tradesman's Return" in *Esquire*, February 1936, 27, 193–96. Although he published these as stories, as early as 1933, Hemingway had conceived of them as part of a novel, as a letter to Archibald MacLeish, 27 February 1933, indicates (*Selected Letters*, 381). The novel was published in October, 1937, the third part apparently drafted as early as the summer of 1936, for Hemingway showed some 30,000 words of it to Arnold Gingrich in early July, 1936 (*Selected Letters*, 447–49). For Hemingway's own estimate of the novel and of his having cut some 100,000 words from it, see his letter to Lillian Ross, 28 July 1948, in *Selected Letters*, 648–49.

16. Critical studies of this story continue to pile up; see " 'Macomber' Bibliography," comp. William White in *Hemingway notes* 5 (1980): 35–38, for a list of 101 items and articles. More recently see Bert Bender, "Margot Macomber's Gimlet," *College Literature* 8 (1981): 12–20; Geoffrey Meyers, "A Queer, Ugly Business: The Origins of 'The Short Happy Life of Francis Macomber,' " *London,* November 1983, 26–37; Mark Spilka, "A Source for the Macomber 'Accident': Marryat's *Percival Keene,*" *Hemingway Review* 3 (1984): 29–37; and Roger Whitlow, *Cassandra's Daughters: The Women in Hemingway* (Westport, Conn.: Greenwood Press, 1984), 59–68.

17. Baker, *Hemingway,* 238–39n.

18. The value of psychoanalytic criticism to the study of literature is well argued by Frederick Crews, "Anaesthetic Criticism," in *Psychoanalysis and Literary Process,* ed. Frederick Crews (Cambridge, Mass.: Winthrop Publishers, 1970), 1–24; David J. Gordon, "Introduction" and "The Unconscious in Literary Art," in his *Literary Art and the Unconscious,* xiii–xxx, 3–51; C. Barry Chabot, "Psychoanalysis as Literary Criticism / Literary Criticism as Psychoanalysis" and "Groundings in Theory: The Cohesive Life, the Whole Story," in his *Freud on Schreber: Psychoanalytic Theory and the Critical Act* (Amherst: University of Massachusetts Press, 1982), 49–107; and Meredith Anne Skura, *The Literary Use of the Psychoanalytic Process* (New Haven: Yale University Press, 1981).

Chapter Four

1. Some of Hemingway's fiction—generally his lesser achievements—falls into none of these forms: *The Torrents of Spring,* "Mr. and Mrs. Elliot," "A Canary for One," and "Homage to Switzerland." In these exceptions Hemingway seems to be playing with a satirical approach to fiction. But see Julian Smith, "'A Canary for One': Hemingway in the Wasteland," *Studies in Short Fiction* 5 (1968): 355–61 and Delbert E. Wylder's excellent study of *The Torrents of Spring* in his *Hemingway's Heroes* (Albuquerque, 1969), 11–30.

2. For readings by critics who find this story valuable, see Richard B. Hovey, " 'Now I Lay Me': A Psychological Interpretation," *Literature and Psychology* 15 (1965): 70–78; rpt. in Benson, *Short Stories,* 180–87; Julian Smith, "Hemingway and the Thing Left Out," *Journal of Modern Literature* 1 (1970–1971): 169–72; rpt. in Wagner, *Five Decades,* 188–200, and in Benson, *Short Stories,* 135–47; and Flora, *Nick Adams,* 114–24.

3. Although indebted to Malcolm Cowley ("Nightmare and Ritual in Hemingway," the introduction to *The Portable Hemingway* [New York, 1945]; rpt. in Weeks, *Collection,* 41–42), Philip Young's illuminating and provocative reading of this story (*Reconsideration,* 43–48) set the stan-

dard to which subsequent studies are footnotes. To see the lengths to which the story can be exhausted, see Flora, *Nick Adams*, 145–75.

4. The Harry Morgan sections of *To Have and Have Not* are also variants of the tutor story.

5. Broch's discussion of this point, as well as his description of the "style of old age," are extraordinarily relevant to *The Old Man and the Sea*. See his introduction to Mary McCarthy's translation of Rachel Bespaloff's *On the Iliad* (New York: Pantheon Books, 1947).

6. For a fine collection of essays on *The Old Man and the Sea* see *Twentieth Century Interpretations of "The Old Man and the Sea": A Collection of Critical Essays*, ed. Katharine T. Jobes (Englewood Cliffs, N.J., 1968). At opposite ends of the spectrum on the novel's worth, see Robert P. Weeks, "Fakery in *The Old Man and the Sea*," *College English* 24 (1962): 188–92; rpt. in Jobes, *Collection*, 34–40; and Bickford Sylvester, "Hemingway's Extended Vision: *The Old Man and the Sea*," *PMLA* 81 (1966): 130–38; rpt. in Jobes, *Collection*, 81–96.

7. "Interview," *Writers at Work*, 229; rpt. in Baker, *Critics*, 29, and in Wagner, *Five Decades*, 30–31. Still the best discussion of Hemingway's "symbolism" is E. M. Halliday, "Hemingway's Ambiguity: Symbolism and Irony," *American Literature* 28 (1956): 1–22; rpt. in Baker, *Critiques*, 61–74, Waldhorn, *Criticism*, 35–55, and Weeks, *Collection*, 52–71. Notwithstanding Halliday's essay, symbolic critics will pluck ripe Christian symbols from *The Old Man and the Sea*: John Bowen Hamilton, "Hemingway and the Christian Paradox," *Renascence* 24 (1972): 141–54, and Sam S. Baskett, "Toward a 'Fifth Dimension' in *The Old Man and the Sea*," *Centennial Review* 19 (1975): 269–86.

8. The remark is quoted in Baker, *Hemingway*, 323n.

9. See Chapter 2, note 2. See also Linda W. Wagner, "The Poem of Santiago and Manolin," *Modern Fiction Studies* 19 (1973–1974): 517–29; rpt. in her *Hemingway and Faulkner: Inventors/Masters* (Metuchen, N.J.: Scarecrow Press, 1975), 111–24.

10. It is an interesting commentary on Transcendentalism that Hawthorne, in so many ways hostile to its precepts, should give the most lucid fictional expositions of its principles. See also "The Great Stone Face."

11. For a more comprehensive explanation of "the epistemological story," see Earl Rovit, "American Literature and 'The American Experience,' " *American Quarterly* 13 (1961): 115–25.

12. Valuable commentary on *A Farewell to Arms* is abundant. Among earlier discussions see Baker, *Hemingway*, 94–116; Norman Friedman, "Criticism and the Novel: Hardy, Hemingway, Crane, Woolf, Conrad," *Antioch Review* 17 (1958): 352–55; rpt. in Gellens, *Interpretations*, 105–107; James F. Light, "The Religion of Death in *A Farewell to Arms*," *Modern Fiction Studies* 7 (1961): 169–73; rpt. in Graham, *Studies*, 39–45;

and Charles Vandersee, "The Stopped Worlds of Frederic Henry," in Graham, *Studies*, 55–65. For recent discussions that draw upon manuscript studies, see Michael S. Reynolds, *Hemingway's First War: The Making of "A Farewell to Arms"* (Princeton, 1976); Bernard Oldsey, *Hemingway's Hidden Craft: The Writing of "A Farewell to Arms"* (University Park, 1979); and Millicent Bell, "*A Farewell to Arms*: Pseudoautobiography and Personal Metaphor," in *Ernest Hemingway: The Writer in Context*, ed. James Nagel (Madison, 1984), 107–28.

13. Ferguson occupies an almost Jamesian role in this novel, serving as norm of commonsense or as guide to the obvious. Mark Twain's abuse of the guide Ferguson in *Innocents Abroad* makes it possible that Hemingway is having a private joke in his naming and employment of this character.

14. The remark is quoted in Baker, *Hemingway*, 98n.

Chapter Five

1. The following discussion is indebted to the thinking of Hannah Arendt, particularly to her book *The Human Condition* (Chicago: University of Chicago Press, 1958); peripheral to it, but not without influence, is Hazel E. Barnes, *The Literature of Possibility* (Lincoln, Neb.: University of Nebraska Press, 1959).

2. Sean O'Faolain, *Short Stories: A Study in Pleasure* (Boston: Little, Brown and Co., 1961), 77; rpt. in Weeks, *Collection*, 113.

3. The story's confusing dialogue begat a minor industry of scholarship, no fewer than 20 articles having danced attention on the problem. For a quick tour of the industry, start with William E. Colburn, "Confusion in 'A Clean, Well-Lighted Place,' " and F. P. Kroeger, "The Dialogue in 'A Clean, Well-Lighted Place,' " *College English* 20 (1959): 241–42 and 240–41, respectively; then see David Lodge, "Hemingway's Clean, Well-Lighted Puzzling Place," *Essays in Criticism* 21 (1971): 33–56; and Charles E. May, "Is Hemingway's 'Well-Lighted Place' Really Clean Now?" *Studies in Short Fiction* 8 (1971): 326–30; end with Warren Bennett, "The Manuscript and the Dialogue of 'A Clean, Well-Lighted Place,' " *American Literature* 50 (1979): 613–24; David Kerner, "The Foundation of the True Text of 'A Clean, Well-Lighted Place,' " *Fitzgerald/Hemingway Annual 1979*, 279–300; and C. Harold Hurley, "The Manuscript and the Dialogue of 'A Clean, Well-Lighted Place': A Response to Warren Bennett," *Hemingway Review* 2 (1982): 17–20.

4. Baker, *Hemingway*, 124.

5. Excellent discussions on this point are Joseph Beaver, " 'Technique' in Hemingway," *College English* 14 (1953): 325–28; and Reardon, "Hemingway's Esthetic Sportsmen."

6. D. S. Savage, *The Withered Branch: Six Studies in the Modern Novel* (London: Eyre & Spottiswoode, 1950), 24, 27, and 31, respectively; rpt. in Gellens, *Interpretations*, 92, 95, and 98.

7. Jean Paul Sartre, "American Novelists in French Eyes," *Atlantic Monthly* (August 1946): 118. Relevant discussion of Hemingway's influence on Camus and his relationship to existentialism include Richard Lehan, "Camus and Hemingway," *Wisconsin Studies in Contemporary Literature* 1 (1960): 37–48; his *A Dangerous Crossing: French Literary Existentialism in the Modern American Novel* (Carbondale, 1973), 46–68; Philip Thody, "A Note on Camus and the American Novel," *Comparative Literature* 9 (1957): 243–49; and John Killinger, *Hemingway and the Dead Gods: A Study in Existentialism* (Lexington, 1960).

Chapter Six

1. Among the studies on Hemingway's handling of time, the following are valuable: Frederick I. Carpenter, "Hemingway Achieves the Fifth Dimension," *PMLA* 69 (1954): 711–18; rpt. in Baker, *Critics,* 192–201, in Waldhorn, *Criticism,* 83-91, and in Wagner, *Five Decades,* 279–87; Graham, "The Meaning of a Style"; and O'Faolain, "A Clean, Well-Lighted Place." Attempts to relate Hemingway's metaphysic of time to that of Henri Bergson have been ignored, not because the affinities in the two schemes are disputable, but because equal affinities exist between Hemingway's use of time and Emerson's.

2. Levin, "Observations on the Style," 601; rpt. in Baker, *Critics,* 109, and in Weeks, *Collection,* 80.

3. Among many interesting readings of *For Whom the Bell Tolls,* several warrant being singled out: Baker, *Hemingway,* 223–63; William T. Moynihan, "The Martyrdom of Robert Jordan," *College English* 21 (1959): 127–32; rpt. in Grebstein, *Studies,* 94–101; Linda W. Wagner, "The Marinating of *For Whom the Bell Tolls,*" *Journal of Modern Literature* 2 (1972): 533–46; rpt. in her *Five Decades,* 200–12; rev. and expanded in her *Inventors/Masters,* 86–106; Robert E. Fleming, "Hemingway's Treatment of Suicide: 'Fathers and Sons' and *For Whom the Bell Tolls,*" *Arizona Quarterly* 33 (1977): 121–32; A. Robert Lee, " 'Everything Completely Knit Up': Seeing *For Whom the Bell Tolls* Whole," in his *New Critical Essays,* 79–102; and Patrick Cheney, "Hemingway and Christian Epic: The Bible in *For Whom the Bell Tolls,*" *Papers on Language & Literature* 21 (1985): 170–91.

4. For discussions of Hemingway's use of Spanish in this novel, see Edward Fenimore, "English and Spanish in *For Whom the Bell Tolls,*" *ELH* 10 (1943): 73–86; rpt. in McCaffrey, *The Man and His Work,* 184–99; Barea, "Not Spain But Hemingway"; Robert O. Stephens, "Language Magic and Reality in *For Whom the Bell Tolls,*" *Criticism* 14 (1972): 151–

64; rpt. in Wagner, *Five Decades*, 266–79; and F. Allen Josephs, "Hemingway's Poor Spanish: Chauvinism and Loss of Credibility in *For Whom the Bell Tolls*," in *Hemingway: A Revaluation*, ed. Donald R. Noble (Troy, N.Y., 1983), 205–23.

Chapter Seven

1. Baker, *Hemingway*, 81.
2. The number of penetrating readings of *The Sun Also Rises* quickly climbs into double digits. Acknowledging in advance the inadequacy of doing justice to them, we list here only a handful: Earl H. Rovit, "Ernest Hemingway: *The Sun Also Rises*," in *Landmarks of American Writing*, ed. Hennig Cohen (Washington, D.C.: U.S. Information Agency, Voice of America Forum Series, 1969), 341–52; Mark Spilka, "The Death of Love in *The Sun Also Rises*," on *Twelve Original Essays on Great American Novels*, ed. Charles Shapiro (Detroit: Wayne State University Press, 1958), 238–56; rpt. in Weeks, *Collection*, 127–38, in Baker, *Critics*, 80–92, in Baker, *Critiques*, 18–25, and in *The Merrill Studies in "The Sun Also Rises*," comp. William White (Columbus, Ohio, 1969), 73–85; Baker, *Hemingway*, 75–93; Arthur L. Scott, "In Defense of Robert Cohn," *College English* 18 (1957): 309–14; Benson, *Self-Defense*, 30–43; Dewey Ganzel, "*Cabestro* and *Vaquilla*: The Symbolic Structure of *The Sun Also Rises*," *Sewanee Review* 76 (1968): 26–48; Claire Sprague, "*The Sun Also Rises*: Its 'Clear Financial Basis,' " *American Quarterly* 21 (1969): 259–66; Wirt Williams, "*The Sun Also Rises*: Passivity as a Tragic Response," in his *The Tragic Art of Ernest Hemingway* (Baton Rouge, 1981), 40–64; and R. W. Stallman, "*The Sun Also Rises*—But No Bells Ring," in his *The Houses That James Built and Other Literary Studies* (East Lansing: Michigan State University Press, 1961), 173–93. Two books are vital tools to a full understanding of the novel. for a historical account of, reminiscences by, and interviews with, people who knew or were characters in the novel, see Sarason, *The SUN Set*; for a careful analysis of the compositional stages the novel went through—including reproductions from Hemingway's notebooks and quotations from subsequent drafts—see Frederic Joseph Svoboda, *Hemingway & "The Sun Also Rises": The Crafting of a Style* (Lawrence, 1983).
3. Oscar Cargill, *Intellectual America* (New York: Macmillan, 1948), 357–58.

Chapter Eight

1. Malcolm Cowley, "A Portrait of Mister Papa," *Life*, 10 January 1949, 94; rpt. in McCaffery, *The Man and His Work*, 45.
2. Baker, *Hemingway*, 239n.
3. There are many specimens of this overall attack on Hemingway. A particularly good example—because it contains almost all of the anti-

Hemingway shibboleths in a wonderfully patronizing dress—is Dwight Macdonald's "Ernest Hemingway," *Encounter* 18 (1962): 115–21. This article is also of interest because it shows how easy it is to parody Hemingway's style while capturing none of his seriousness or his concern with truth. For sustained arguments of the development of Hemingway's work, see Lewis, *Hemingway on Love*, and Brenner, *Concealments*.

4. Plimpton, "An Interview," 27; rpt. in *Writers at Work*, 227, in Baker, *Critics*, 27, and in Wagner, *Five Decades*, 29. The influences on Hemingway's writing have received more serious attention within the last decade; see Reynolds, *Hemingway's First War*; Robert W. Lewis, "Hemingway in Italy: Making It Up," *Journal of Modern Literature* 9 (1982): 209–36; and Mark Spilka, "Victorian Keys to the Early Hemingway, Part I—*John Halifax, Gentleman*; Part II—*Fauntleroy and Finn*," *Journal of Modern Literature* 10 (1983): 125–50, 289–310, respectively; and his "Victorian Keys to the Early Hemingway: *Captain Marryat*," *Novel: A Forum on Fiction* 17 (1984): 116–40.

5. For a fuller exposition of this American literary tradition, see Earl Rovit, "American Literature and 'The American Experience.' " See also Richard Chase, *The American Novel and Its Tradition* (Garden City, N.Y.: Doubleday, 1957); Daniel G. Hoffman, *Form and Fable in American Fiction* (New York: Oxford University Press, 1961); Charles Feidelson, Jr., *Symbolism and American Literature* (Chicago: University of Chicago Press, 1953); and R. W. B. Lewis, *The American Adam* (Chicago: University of Chicago Press, 1955).

6. For an indication of Hemingway's influence on an international level see Baker, *Critics*, 1–18; Deming Brown, "Hemingway in Russia," *American Quarterly* 5 (1953): 143–56; rpt. in Baker, *Critics*, 145–61; Mario Praz, "Hemingway in Italy," *Partisan Review* 15 (1948): 1086–1100; rpt. in Baker, *Critics*, 116–30; the *In Memoriam* tribute in *Saturday Review*, 29 July 1961, which contains remarks by Salvador de Madariaga, Frank Moraes, Carlos Levi, Ilya Ehrenburg, and Alan Pryce-Jones, 18–21; the tribute in *Der Spiegel*, 12 July 1961, 45–52; Asselineau, *Literary Reputation*; Wayne E. Kvam, *Hemingway in Germany: The Fiction, The Legend, and The Critics* (Athens, 1973); Moira Monteith, "A Change in Emphasis: Hemingway Criticism in Britain Over the Last Twenty-Five Years," *Hemingway Review* 1 (1982): 2–19; and John Raeburn, *Fame Became of Him: Hemingway as Public Writer* (Bloomington, 1984).

7. Baker, *Critics*, 1.

Chapter Nine

1. Admittedly *The Dangerous Summer* is not posthumous. Its three installments, "The Dangerous Summer," "The Pride of the Devil," and "An Appointment with Disaster," appeared in 1960 in successive issues

of *Life* magazine on 5, 12, and 19 September, pages 77–109, 60–82, and 74–90, respectively. But it deserves discussion, not only because of Scribner's recent publication of an expanded and somewhat laundered version of it, but because it relates to—if, in fact, it does not complete—the posthumous writing on which Hemingway worked during his last decade. This may be the appropriate place to remark that in this chapter we might be expected to discuss *The Nick Adams Stories* (New York, 1972). But the new material in this collection, too scant to warrant much consideration, sheds little perspective on the already well-established features of Nick's character and Hemingway's art. The accessibility of the Hemingway papers in Boston's Kennedy Library and elsewhere will tease publishers and Hemingway's sons with the prospect of profiting from publication of other posthumous works. But of those known, it is doubtful that *Garden of Eden* can be sufficiently reconstructed to make anything but a fragmentary novel of it. [For a description and excerpts, see Aaron Latham, "A Farewell to Machismo," *New York Times Magazine* 16 October 1977: 52, 55, 80, 82, 90.] Although the "complete" versions of both *African Journal* and *The Dangerous Summer* would be valuable to students and scholars, it seems doubtful that either work will be published in its entirety. Scribner's publication of a 45,000-word version of *The Dangerous Summer*, however, virtually guarantees that we can expect to see published—at a commercially advantageous interval—a hardbound edition of *African Journal*. *A Moveable Feast* (New York, 1964); hereafter cited in the text as *MF*; *The Dangerous Summer* (New York, 1985); hereafter cited in the text as *DS*; *African Journal*, *Sports Illustrated*, parts 1-3, 1971-72; hereafter cited in the text as *AJ*; *Islands in the Stream* (New York, 1970); hereafter cited in the text as *IS*.

2. See Hershel Parker, *Flawed Texts and Verbal Icons: Literary Authority and American Fiction* (Evanston, Ill.: Northwestern University Press, 1984), whose trenchant arguments about authorial intentionality are as relevant to the posthumous Hemingwayana as to *The Sun Also Rises, A Farewell to Arms,* and *To Have and Have Not.*

3. See, respectively, A. E. Hotchner, *Papa Hemingway*, 261–76; Ray Cave, "Introduction to An *African Journal*," *Sports Illustrated* 20 December 1971, 40–41; and Baker, *Hemingway*, 358, 383–84.

4. For reproduced pages from auction sale and dealers' catalogs that reveal the existence of such letters, see Matthew J. Bruccoli and C. E. Frazer Clark, Jr., comps., *Hemingway at Auction, 1930–1973* (Detroit, 1973), 133–35, 208. Although the existence of these letters may not be common knowledge, it seems scholarly neglect that in his "Notes and Acknowledgements" to *Selected Letters* Professor Baker omits mention of letters and sets of letters which he has chosen to refrain from including. For instance, why include only two letters from the exchange of some 70 between Hemingway and Malcolm Cowley? For a corrective to this latter

omission, see James D. Brasch, "Invention from Knowledge: The Hemingway-Cowley Correspondence," in Nagel, *The Writer in Context,* 201–36.

5. In a telephone conversation Ray Cave confirmed that he was solely responsible for the *Sports Illustrated* installments, products of two weeks of work in Key West on the original manuscript (RC to GB, 8 April 1985).

6. James A. Michener, "Introduction," *The Dangerous Summer* (New York, 1985), 13–14.

7. A note in the *Hemingway Review* 4 (1985): 57, identifies Charles Scribner, Jr. and Michael Pietsch as the editors of this version.

8. Gerry Brenner, "Are We Going to Hemingway's *Feast?*" *American Literature* 54 (1982): 528–44.

9. See item 103 in the Hemingway Collection, John F. Kennedy Library, Boston, Mass.

10. "Part 3: Imperiled Flanks," *Sports Illustrated,* 10 January 1972, 50. Parts 1 and 2, "Miss Mary's Lion," appeared in the issues for 20 December 1971, 41–70 and 3 January 1972, 26–46. Part 2 has since appeared in *The Enduring Hemingway,* ed. Charles Scribner, Jr. (New York, 1974), 571–613.

11. Ray Cave, "Introduction to An *African Journal,*" 40.

12. For Jane Mason Gingrich's role in Hemingway's life, see Baker, *Life Story,* 222, 228, 244, 285–86; Kert, *The Hemingway Women,* 235–36, 240–44, 247–50, 269–71; and Jeffrey Meyers, *Hemingway: A Biography* (New York, 1985), 242–56.

13. For a brief discussion of some of the discrepancies between the facts and fictions of "Bimini," see Patrick Hemingway, "*Islands in the Stream*: A Son Remembers," in Nagel, *The Writer in Context,* 13–18. See Norberto Fuentes, *Hemingway in Cuba,* trans. Consuelo E. Corwin (Secaucus, N.J., 1984) for commentary both on the Havana places and people who figure in "Cuba," 221–37, and on the background, people, and itinerary of "At Sea," 190–217.

14. The poverty is rejected by Matthew J. Bruccoli, *Scott and Ernest: The Authority of Failure and the Authority of Success* (New York, 1978): "The hunger was authentic, but the poverty was largely illusory. Hadley was a small heiress. At the time of their marriage she had an income of $3000 a year from a trust fund. . . . [T]he Hemingways were not paupers and did not have to rely on his earnings for eating money," 12.

15. John Stuart Mill, *Autobiography,* ed. Currin V. Shields (New York: Bobbs-Merrill, 1957), 3.

16. Brenner, *Concealments,* 220–23.

17. Leon Edel, "The Mystery of Walden Pond," in his *Stuff of Sleep and Dreams: Experiments in Literary Psychology* (New York: Harper & Row, 1982), 47–65.

18. "The Self as History: Reflections on Autobiography," in *Telling Lives: The Biographer's Art,* ed. Marc Pachter (1979; Philadelphia: University of Pennsylvania Press, 1981), 79.

19. For Mary's version of the killing see *How It Was,* 363–64.

20. *Life,* 5 September 1960, 102; this episode, had it not been deleted from the hardbound edition, would have appeared on page 88, just before the paragraph on the drying mud around the old bullring at Aranjuez.

21. For discussion of this equation see José Luis Castillo-Puche, *Hemingway in Spain: A Personal Reminiscence,* trans. Helen R. Lane (Garden City, N.Y., 1974), 154, 165, et passim; and Brenner, *Concealments,* 208–17.

22. Hemingway's back-to-back brushes with death while trying to fly out of Africa after the 1953–54 safari would certainly have been regarded by him as presentiments of his own end. For an account of those crashes, see Mary Hemingway, *How It Was,* 376–83.

23. For differentiations among—and philosophical arguments about—the many functions of memory, see Brian Smith, *Memory* (New York: Humanities Press, 1966).

24. Brenner, *Concealments,* 197–99.

25. Baker, *Hemingway* 379–84, 389, 397.

Selected Bibliography

PRIMARY SOURCES

1. Novels

The Torrents of Spring. New York: Charles Scribner's Sons, 1926. Paperback. Scribner, 1972.

The Sun Also Rises. New York: Charles Scribner's Sons, 1926. Paperback. Scribner, 1960.

A Farewell to Arms. New York: Charles Scribner's Sons, 1929. Paperback. Scribner, 1962.

To Have and Have Not. New York: Charles Scribner's Sons, 1937. Paperback. Scribner, 1966.

For Whom the Bell Tolls. New York: Charles Scribner's Sons, 1940. Paperback. Scribner, 1960.

Across the River and into the Trees. New York: Charles Scribner's Sons, 1950. Paperback. Scribner, 1970.

The Old Man and the Sea. New York: Charles Scribner's Sons, 1952. Paperback. Scribner, 1965; Bantam, 1965.

Islands in the Stream. New York: Charles Scribner's Sons, 1970. Paperback. Bantam, 1972; Scribner, n.d.

2. Short Stories

Three Stories and Ten Poems. Paris and Dijon: Contact Publishing Co., 1923. Reprint. Bloomfield Hills, Mich.: Bruccoli Clark Books, 1977.

in our time. Paris: Three Mountains Press, 1924.

In Our Time. New York: Boni & Liveright, 1925. Revised edition. New York: Charles Scribner's Sons, 1930. Paperback. Scribner, 1962.

Men Without Women. New York: Charles Scribner's Sons, 1927. Reprint. World Publishing Co., 1946. Paperback. Scribner, 1970.

Winner Take Nothing. New York: Charles Scribner's Sons, 1933. Paperback. Scribner, 1968.

The Fifth Column and the First Forty-Nine Stories. New York: Charles Scribner's Sons, 1938. Reprint. *The Short Stories of Ernest Hemingway*. Scribner, 1954. Paperback. 1964.

The Fifth Column and Four Stories of the Spanish Civil War. New York: Charles Scribner's Sons, 1969. Paperback. Bantam, 1970; Scribner, 1972.

The Nick Adams Stories. Preface by Philip Young. New York: Charles Scribner's Sons, 1972. Paperback. Bantam, 1973; Scribner, 1973.

A Divine Gesture. New York: Aloe Editions, 1974. Paperback reprint of the prose fable "A Divine Gesture." *The Double Dealer* 3 (1922): 267–68.

The Faithful Bull. Pictures by Michael Foreman. London: Hamish Hamilton Childrens Books, 1980. Reprint of the prose fable "The Faithful Bull." *Holiday,* March 1951, 51.

3. Nonfiction

Death in the Afternoon. New York: Charles Scribner's Sons, 1932. Paperback. Scribner, 1969.

Green Hills of Africa. New York: Charles Scribner's Sons, 1935. Paperback. Scribner, 1962.

The Spanish Earth. Cleveland: J. B. Savage Co., 1938.

Men at War. Edited with an introduction by Ernest Hemingway. New York: Crown Publishers, 1942. Paperback. Avon, 1952; Berkeley, 1958 abridged.

The Wild Years. Edited by Gene Z. Hanrahan. New York: Dell, 1962. Paperback. Seventy-three articles from the *Toronto Star Weekly* and the *Toronto Daily Star.*

A Moveable Feast. New York: Charles Scribner's Sons, 1964. Paperback. Bantam, 1965; Scribner, 1971.

By-Line: Ernest Hemingway, Selected Articles and Dispatches of Four Decades. Edited by William White. New York: Charles Scribner's Sons, 1967. Paperback. Bantam, 1968; Scribner, n.d. Gathers nine North American Newspaper Alliance (NANA) dispatches from the Spanish Civil War and sixty-eight articles from *Toronto Star Weekly* and *Toronto Daily Star, Transatlantic Review, Esquire, PM, Colliers, Holiday, True,* and *Look.*

Ernest Hemingway, Cub Reporter: Kansas City Star Stories. Edited by Matthew J. Bruccoli. Pittsburgh: University of Pittsburgh Press, 1970. Twelve articles from December 1917 through April 1918.

Ernest Hemingway's Apprenticeship: Oak Park, 1916–1917. Edited by Matthew J. Bruccoli. Washington, D.C.: NCR Microcard Editions, 1971. High school writings: thirty-nine articles, three stories, five poems, and class prophecy.

The Dangerous Summer. Introduction by James A. Michener. New York: Charles Scribner's Sons, 1985. Expanded and altered version of the edited manuscript from which *Life* magazine published its three installments in 1960, cited below.

4. Poetry

88 Poems. Edited by Nicholas Gerogiannis. New York: Harcourt Brace Jovanovich/Bruccoli Clark, 1979. Paperback reprint. *Complete Poems.* University of Nebraska Press, 1983. First authorized edition of Hemingway's collected poetry; supersedes *The Collected Poems of Ernest Hem-*

ingway. San Francisco: Haskell House, 1970. (First hardcover edition of pirated editions.) Paperback. Gordon Press, 1972.

5. Letters

Hemingway at Auction, 1930–1973. Compiled by Matthew J. Bruccoli and
C. E. Frazer Clark, Jr. Detroit: Gale Research Co., 1973. Reproduces
pages from (and prices brought by items in) 115 auction-sale and
dealers' catalogs of Hemingway's books, manuscripts, and letters
between 1930 and 1973. More than 150 letters, inscriptions, and
manuscript and typescript pages are described, summarized, excerpted, reproduced, and indexed.
Ernest Hemingway: Selected Letters, 1917–1961. Edited by Carlos Baker.
New York: Charles Scribner's Sons, 1981. Paperback. Scribner, 1982.
Judiciously samples nearly 600 of Hemingway's 3500 available letters.
"The Finca Vigía Papers." Compiled by Norberto Fuentes. In his *Hemingway in Cuba*. Secaucus, N.J.: Lyle Stuart 1984. Prints "Hemingway's Lost Love Letters to Mary" (November through December 1944)
and forty-five other letters to and from Hemingway, 1924–57.

6. Selected Writings

The Viking Portable Hemingway. Edited by Malcolm Cowley. New York:
Viking Press, 1944.
The Hemingway Reader. Selected by Charles Poore. New York: Charles
Scribner's Sons, 1953. Paperback. Scribner, 1965.
The Snows of Kilimanjaro and Other Stories. New York: Charles Scribner's
Sons, 1962. Paperback. Scribner, 1962.
The Enduring Hemingway: An Anthology of a Lifetime in Literature. Edited
by Charles Scribner, Jr. New York: Charles Scribner's Sons, 1974.
Includes, among much else, the second part of the posthumous *African
Journal*.
Ernest Hemingway on Writing. Edited by Larry W. Phillips. New York:
Charles Scribner's Sons, 1984. Paperback. Quality Paperback Books,
1984. Compiles over 200 excerpts from Hemingway on writing.
Along with Youth: Hemingway, The Early Years. Peter Griffin. New York:
Oxford University Press, 1985. Includes five previously unpublished
stories, several poems, summaries of and excerpts from early writings,
and generous servings of correspondence from and to Hemingway.

7. Uncollected Stories

"Nobody Ever Dies!" *Cosmopolitan*, March 1938, 28–31, 74–76. Re-
printed in *Cosmopolitan*, April 1959, 78–83.
"A Man of the World." *Atlantic Monthly*, November 1957, 64–66.
"Get a Seeing-Eyed Dog." *Atlantic Monthly*, November 1957, 66–68.

"The Mercenaries." *New York Times Magazine,* 18 August, 1985, 17–18. Included in Peter Griffin, *Along with Youth,* 104–12.

"Crossroads: An Anthology." *New York Times Magazine,* 18 August 1985, 19–20. Included in Peter Griffin, *Along with Youth,* 124–27.

"The Ash Heel's Tendon." *New York Times Magazine,* 18 August 1985, 21, 23, 59, 61. Included in Peter Griffin, *Along with Youth,* 174–80.

8. Uncollected Nonfiction

The Dangerous Summer. Edited by Aaron E. Hotchner et al. Part 1, "The Dangerous Summer," *Life,* 5 September 1960, 77–109; Part 2, "The Pride of the Devil," *Life,* 12 September 1960, 60–82; Part 3, "An Appointment with Disaster," *Life,* 19 September 1960, 74–96.

African Journal. Edited by Ray Cave. Part 1, "Miss Mary's Lion," *Sports Illustrated,* 20 December 1971, 41–70; Part 2, "Miss Mary's Lion," *Sports Illustrated,* 3 January 1972, 26–46; Part 3, " Imperiled Flanks," *Sports Illustrated,* 10 January 1972, 22–50. Part 2 is included in *The Enduring Hemingway.*

"The Art of the Short Story." *Paris Review* 23 (Spring 1981): 85–102.

9. Miscellaneous Materials: Audiotape Cassette (AC), Film (F), Filmstrip (FS), Record (R), Videotape Cassette (VC).

The rapid distribution of films on videocassettes should make most of Hollywood's versions of Hemingway's fictions—some listed here—inexpensive and available by decade's end.

A Farewell to Arms. Directed by Henry King. Hollywood: Paramount, 1932. F, VC: B&W, 78 min. Stars Gary Cooper and Helen Hayes.

————. Directed by Charles Vidor. Hollywood: Twentieth Century–Fox, 1957. F: color, 151 min. Stars Rock Hudson and Jennifer Jones.

————. Adapted by Ernest Canoy. New York: NBC Star Playhouse (Radio Broadcast), n.d. Distributed: Anaheim, Calif.: Mark 56 Records, 1976. R: 50 min. Stars Fredric March and Florence Eldridge.

Ernest Hemingway Cassette Library. Narrated by Alexander Scourby. Old Greenwich, Conn.: Listening Library, n.d. AC: 6 cassettes include "The Killers," "Fifty Grand," "A Clean Well-Lighted Place," "The Gambler, the Nun, and the Radio," "The Snows of Kilimanjaro," "The Short Happy Life of Francis Macomber," "Capitol of the World," and "The Undefeated."

Ernest Hemingway Reading. New York: Caedmon Records, 1965. AC, R: 45 min. Includes "Nobel Prize Acceptance Speech," "Second Poem to Mary," "In Harry's Bar in Venice," "The Fifth Column: Introduction," "Work in Progress," and "Saturday Night in the Whorehouse in Billings, Montana."

The Killers. Directed by Robert Siedmak. Hollywood: Universal, 1946.
F: B&W, 102 min. Stars Burt Lancaster.

————. Directed by Don Siegel. Hollywood: Universal, 1964. F: color,
95 min. Stars Lee Marvin, Angie Dickinson, and Ronald Reagan.

My Old Man. London: Encyclopedia Brittanica Educational Corp., 1976.
F: color, 27 min.

Soldier's Home. The American Short Story Series. Learning in Focus—Coronet Instructional Films, 1977. F: color, 39 min.

The Old Man and the Sea. Read by Charlton Heston. New York: Caedmon
Records, 1976. AC, R: 143 min.

The Short Happy Life of Francis Macomber. Adapted by Ernest Canoy. NBC
University Theatre Series, 21 November 1948; rebroadcast 5 June
1949. Distributed: Logan, Iowa: Nostalgia Broadcasting Co., n.d.
AC: 60 min.

The Sun Also Rises. Directed by Henry King. Twentieth Century—Fox,
1957. F: color, 129 min. Stars Tyrone Power and Ava Gardner.

————. Directed by James Goldstone. Twentieth Century—Fox Television, 1984. F: color, 4-hour miniseries. Stars Hart Bochner and
Jane Seymour.

Under My Skin. Hollywood: Twentieth Century—Fox, 1950. F: B&W, 68
min. Stars John Garfield and Luther Adler. Based on short story "My
Old Man."

SECONDARY SOURCES

1. Bibliographies

Benson, Jackson J., comp. "A Comprehensive Checklist of Hemingway
Short Fiction Criticism, Explication and Commentary." In his *The
Short Stories of Ernest Hemingway: Critical Essays.* Durham, N.C.: Duke
University Press, 1975. Comprehensively lists entries through 1974.

Clarke, Graham, comp. "Hemingway in England: Bibliography." *Hemingway Review* 1 (Spring 1982): 76–84. Chronologically lists all English editions of Hemingway's works as well as selected reviews,
essays, articles, and books published in England on Hemingway.

Hanneman, Audre, comp. *Ernest Hemingway: A Comprehensive Bibliography.*
Princton: Princeton University Press, 1967. Indispensable; meticulously describes and scrupulously cross-references entries through 1965;
hard-to-use index and excessive excerpts of book reviews are minor
defects.

————. *Supplement to Ernest Hemingway: A Comprehensive Bibliography.*
Princeton: Princton University Press, 1975. Adds overlooked entries
and those from 1966 through 1973.

Wagner, Linda Welshimer, comp. *Ernest Hemingway: A Reference Guide.* Boston: G. K. Hall, 1977. Easy-to-use, indexed, and annotated, chronologically lists books and articles on Hemingway through 1975.

White, William, comp. "Hemingway Checklist." In *Fitzgerald/Hemingway Annual,* 1975: 351–68; 1976: 260–72; 1977: 255–66; 1978: 449–63; 1979: 463–83. For complete entry of *Fitzgerald/Hemingway Annual,* see section 5, Collections.

――――――. "Hemingway: A Current Bibliography." In *Hemingway notes* 5 (Fall 1979): 34–35; 5 (Spring 1980): 38–40; 6 (Fall 1980): 39–40; 6 (Spring 1981): 39–40.

――――――. " 'Macomber' Bibliography." In *Hemingway notes* 5 (Spring 1980): 35–38. Lists 101 items on "The Short Happy Life of Francis Macomber."

――――――. "Current Bibliography." In *Hemingway Review* 1 (Fall 1981): 64–68; 2 (Fall 1982): 90–94; 2 (Spring 1983): 63–65; 3 (Fall 1983): 73–76; 3 (Spring 1984): 57–60; 4 (Fall 1984): 61–64; 4 (Spring 1985): 61 –63; 5 (Fall 1985): 60–64.

2. Other Reference Works

August, Jo, comp. *Catalog of the Ernest Hemingway Collection at the John F. Kennedy Library.* 2 vols. Boston: G. K. Hall, 1982. Vol. 1: Manuscripts, Outgoing Correspondence, Incoming Correspondence A-L; Vol. 2: Incoming Correspondence M-Z, Photographs, Newspaper Clippings, Other Material. Unindexed, descriptive listing of documents accessible to researchers as of January 1982.

Brasch, James D., and Joseph Sigman, comps. *Hemingway's Library: A Composite Record.* New York: Garland Publishing, 1981. Well indexed and comprehensive, scrupulously lists some 7700 books in Hemingway's various libraries; *the* book for source and influence studies, with an excellent sixty-page introduction.

3. Memoirs, Biographies, and Reminiscences

Arnold, Lloyd R. *Hemingway: High on the Wild.* Caldwell, Id.: The Caxton Printers, 1968. Paperback. Grosset & Dunlap, 1977. Photographer-friend reminisces on Hemingway's fall recreational visits to Sun Valley, Idaho, 1939–41, 1946–48, and 1958–61; excellent photographs.

Baker, Carlos. *Ernest Hemingway: A Life Story.* New York: Charles Scribner's Sons, 1969. Paperback. Bantam, 1970; Avon, 1980. Detailed and well-documented, the authorized, discreet, all-but-definitive biography.

Berg, A. Scott. *Max Perkins: Editor of Genius.* New York: E. P. Dutton, 1978. Paperback. Pocket Books, 1979. Includes Hemingway's relationship with his editor at Scribner's.

Bruccoli, Matthew J. *Scott and Ernest: The Authority of Failure and the Authority of Success.* New York: Random House, 1978. Paperback. Southern Illinois University Press, 1978. Traces the Fitzgerald-Hemingway relationship, replete with quoted correspondence on and between the two, but unindexed.

Burgess, Anthony. *Ernest Hemingway and His World.* New York: Charles Scribner's Sons, 1978. British novelist's picture-filled short biography.

Callaghan, Morley. *That Summer in Paris: Memories of Tangled Friendships with Hemingway, Fitzgerald, and Some Others.* New York: Coward-McCann, 1963. Paperback. Dell, 1964; Penguin, 1979. Includes reminiscences on Hemingway in Toronto, 1923, and in Paris, 1929.

Castillo-Puche, José Luis. *Hemingway entre la vida y la muerte.* Barcelona: Ediciones Destino, 1968. Translated as *Hemingway in Spain: A Personal Reminiscence of Hemingway's Years in Spain by His Friend.* Translated by Helen R. Lane. Garden City, N.Y.: Doubleday & Co., 1974. Insightful and impressionistic reminiscences of a psychologically troubled Hemingway in Spain between 1954 and 1960.

Ferrell, Keith. *Ernest Hemingway: The Search for Courage.* New York: M. Evans & Co., 1984. Excellent biography for young adults.

Fuentes, Norberto. *Hemingway in Cuba.* Translated by Consuelo E. Corwin. Edited by Larry Alson. Introduction by Gabriel García Márquez. Secaucus, N.J.: Lyle Stuart, 1984. Baggy but fascinating account of Hemingway's twenty-two years in Cuba; identifies Cuban sources for Hemingway's fictions, inventories the contents of Finca Vigía, and prints "The Finca Vigía Papers": sixty documents that include Hemingway letters to Gregory Hemingway and Adriana Ivancich as well as his early "love letters" to Mary Hemingway.

Griffin, Peter. *Along with Youth: Hemingway, The Early Years.* Foreword by Jack Hemingway. New York: Oxford University Press, 1985. Uses previously withheld materials—including letters and five stories printed herein—to give the fullest picture yet of Hemingway's development into the 1920s.

Hemingway, Grace Hall. *Heritage: For My Children.* N.p.: Autolycus Press, 1974. Mother's 1940 brief "chronicle" traces her side of the family back two hundred years and five generations.

Hemingway, Gregory H., M.D. *Papa: A Personal Memoir.* Preface by Norman Mailer. Boston: Houghton Mifflin Co., 1976. Paperback. Pocket Books, 1977. Youngest son's memoir of times with "Papa."

Hemingway, Leicester. *My Brother, Ernest Hemingway.* Cleveland : World Publishing Co., 1961. Paperback. Crest, 1963. Fifteen-year younger brother's recounting of many hand-me-down tales of Ernest at home, of "me and Ernie" at Key West, and of later years.

Hemingway, Mary Welsh. *How It Was.* New York: Knopf, 1976. Paperback. Ballantine, 1977. Fourth wife's diary-driven account of life with Hemingway, 1944–61.

Hotchner, A. E. *Papa Hemingway: A Personal Memoir.* New York: Random House, 1966. Paperback. Bantam, 1967. Reprinted with postscript and new subtitle, *The Ecstasy and Sorrow.* New York: William Morrow & Co., 1983. Paperback. Quill, 1983. Memoir of Hemingway's last fourteen years, with provocative postscript.

Ivancich von Rex, Adriana. *La torre bianca* (The white tower). Milan: Arnaldo Mondadori Editore, 1980. Italian noblewoman recollects her ambivalent relationship with Hemingway, 1949–60.

Kert, Bernice. *The Hemingway Women.* New York: Norton & Co., 1983. Perceptive and sympathetic, looks closely at Hemingway's mother, his first three wives, and other women important in his life and work; exceptionally good on Martha Gellhorn.

Klimo, Vernon (Jake), and Will Oursler. *Hemingway and Jake: An Extraordinary Friendship.* Garden City, N.Y.: Doubleday & Co., 1972. Paperback. Popular Library, 1973. A Key West fishing chum's sensationalized reminscences.

Mc Lendon, James. *Papa: Hemingway in Key West.* Miami, Fla.: E. A. Seeman Publishers, 1972. The best of the remembrances by a friend during the Key West Years, 1928–40; indexed.

Meyers, Jeffrey. *Hemingway: A Biography.* New York: Harper & Row, 1985. A trenchant, irreverent, and illuminating critical biography that draws heavily upon archival materials, candid interviews, FBI files, and extensive research.

Miller, Madelaine Hemingway. *Ernie: Hemingway's Sister "Sunny" Remembers.* New York: Crown Publishers, 1975. Favorite "kid" sister's photograph-filled, fond memoir.

Montgomery, Constance Cappel. *Hemingway in Michigan.* New York: Fleet, 1966. Focuses on Hemingway summers in northern Michigan, 1900–21.

O'Connor, Richard. *Ernest Hemingway.* New York: McGraw-Hill Co., 1971. American Writers Series biography for young readers.

Ross, Lillian. *Portrait of Hemingway.* New York: Simon & Schuster, 1961. The brief, controversial, and ambiguous *New Yorker* "Profile" of 13 May 1950.

Samuelson, Arnold. *With Hemingway: A Year in Key West & Cuba.* New York: Random House, 1984. Memoir, April through October, 1934, of life at the Hemingway's in Key West and aboard the *Pilar.*

Sanford, Marcelline Hemingway. *At the Hemingways: A Family Portrait.* Boston: Atlantic-Little, Brown, 1962. Older sister's lively, anecdote-filled version of growing up in the Hemingway households.

Sarason, Bertram D. *Hemingway and the SUN Set*. Washington, D.C.: Microcard Editions, 1972. Interviews with and accounts by various people who became characters in *The Sun Also Rises*.

Sokoloff, Alice Hunt. *Hadley: The First Mrs. Hemingway*. New York: Dodd, Mead & Co., 1973. Sympathetic account of Elizabeth Hadley Richardson's life.

4. Critical Studies

Baker, Carlos. *Hemingway: The Writer as Artist*. 4th ed. Princeton: Princeton University Press, 1972. Paperback. Princeton, 1972. Marred by bardolatry and symbol hunting, but the wealth of biographical facts and details on the composition history of Hemingway's works make this the first book for every serious student.

Baker, Sheridan. *Ernest Hemingway: An Introduction and Interpretation*. New York: Holt, Rinehart & Winston, 1967. Paperback. Brief, balanced, and well-written, analyzes Hemingway's works through *Old Man and the Sea*.

Benson, Jackson J. *Hemingway . . . The Writer's Art of Self-Defense*. Minneapolis: University of Minnesota Press, 1969. Extends the idea that Hemingway exorcises through art his personal emotional problems.

Brenner, Gerry. *Concealments in Hemingway's Works*. Columbus: Ohio State University Press, 1983. Psychoanalytic afterwords, chronological groupings, and revisionist readings buttress three theses: Hemingway's sustained experimentation, esthetic of concealed art, and father-fixation.

Broer, Lawrence R. *Hemingway's Spanish Tragedy*. Tuscaloosa: University of Alabama Press, 1973. Argues Hemingway's conversion to Hispanic values, especially "particularismo" (extreme anarchistic individualism) and "pundonor" (primitive aggressiveness).

De Falco, Joseph. *The Hero in Hemingway's Short Stories*. Pittsburgh: University of Pittsburgh Press, 1963. Emphasizes the psychological dynamics of the short fiction.

Donaldson, Scott. *By Force of Will: The Life and Art of Ernest Hemingway*. New York: Viking, 1977. Paperback. Penguin, 1978. Topically organized and well researched, weaves biographical details and literary issues into easy-to-use but critically conventional reference text.

Fenton, Charles A. *The Apprenticeship of Ernest Hemingway: The Early Years*. New York: Farrar, Straus & Cudahy, 1954. Paperback. New American Library, 1961. Invaluable scholarship: meticulously traces Hemingway's development from journalist to artist between 1916 and 1923.

Flora, Joseph M. *Hemingway's Nick Adams*. Baton Rouge: Louisiana State University Press, 1982. Reconstructs the Nick Adams "chronicle," arguing that the Nick of the twenty-six "stories" is a recovering, not a wounded, hero.

Grebstein, Sheldon Norman. *Hemingway's Craft.* Carbondale: Southern Illinois University Press, 1973. Attends exclusively to Hemingway's craftsmanship: his fictional structures and sophisticated use of narrators, dialogue, and style.

Gurko, Leo. *Ernest Hemingway and the Pursuit of Heroism.* New York: Thomas Y. Crowell Co., 1968. Paperback. Apollo, 1969. Somewhat simplistic judgments and moral certainty about the anguished searching of Hemingway's heroes.

Hovey, Richard B. *Hemingway: The Inward Terrain.* Seattle: University of Washington Press, 1968. A mildly Freudian approach to the works through *Feast*.

Joost, Nicholas. *Ernest Hemingway and the Little Magazines: The Paris Years.* Barre, Mass.: Barre Publishers, 1968. Companion work to Fenton, traces Hemingway's successes and rebuffs, 1922–26, as a budding poet and fiction writer.

Killinger, John. *Hemingway and the Dead Gods: A Study in Existentialism.* Lexington: University of Kentucky Press, 1960. Paperback. Citadel, 1965. A provocative discussion of the links between existentialists and Hemingway's concerns with individualism and crisis situations.

Kvam, Wayne E. *Hemingway in Germany: The Fiction, The Legend, and The Critics.* Athens: Ohio University Press, 1973. The German critical response to Hemingway from the 1920s through the 1960s.

Laurence, Frank M. *Hemingway and the Movies.* Jackson: University Press of Mississippi, 1981. Paperback. New York: Da Capo Press, 1981. Compares in detail Hemingway's fictions with their film versions; lacks good film bibliography.

Lewis, Robert W., Jr. *Hemingway on Love.* Austin: University of Texas Press, 1965. Charts development of Hemingway's heroes from selfish to selfless love; perceptive despite overreliance on the Tristan-Iseult thesis.

Nahal, Chaman. *The Narrative Pattern in Ernest Hemingway's Fiction.* Rutherford, N.J.: Fairleigh Dickinson University Press, 1971. Emphasizes the alternating pattern of "systolic" (active) and "diastolic" (passive) action in Hemingway's fiction.

Nelson, Raymond S. *Hemingway: Expressionist Artist.* Ames: Iowa State University Press, 1979. Argues Hemingway's kinship to theories and practices of expressionist painters and writers.

Oldsey, Bernard. *Hemingway's Hidden Craft: The Writing of "A Farewell to Arms."* University Park: Pennsylvania State University Press, 1979. Companion to Reynold's *First War;* from manuscript materials discusses novel's titles, examines its "two" beginnings, categorizes its endings, and reprints the "original" beginning and the endings.

Peterson, Richard K. *Hemingway: Direct and Oblique.* The Hague and Paris: Mouton, 1969. Closely examines Hemingway's style and perceptively questions the purposes and effectiveness of his techniques.

Phillips, Gene D. *Hemingway and Film.* New York: Frederick Ungar Publishing Co., 1980. Paperback. Ungar, 1980. A briefer version of Laurence with a good film bibliography.

Raeburn, John. *Fame Became of Him: Hemingway as Public Writer.* Bloomington: Indiana University Press, 1984. Documents Hemingway's responses to reviewers and critics, arguing that the public personality dominated over the private artist in the 1950s.

Reynolds, Michael S. *Hemingway's First War: The Making of "A Farewell to Arms."* Princeton: Princeton University Press, 1976. A scholarly breakthrough, identifies the various sources Hemingway drew on; describes and quotes from the manuscripts, revisions, cuts, and endings; includes commentary on an interview with Agnes Von Kurowsky.

Stephens, Robert O. *Hemingway's Nonfiction: The Public Voice.* Chapel Hill: University of North Carolina Press, 1968. Follows up Fenton; methodically discusses, documents, and categorizes Hemingway's expository writing.

Svoboda, Frederic Joseph. *Hemingway & "The Sun Also Rises": The Crafting of a Style.* Lawrence: University Press of Kansas, 1983. Collates, describes, analyzes, and reprints samples from the notebooks, typescripts, and galley-edited materials out of which the novel arose.

Waldhorn, Arthur. *A Reader's Guide to Ernest Hemingway.* New York: Farrar, Straus & Giroux, 1972. Paperback. Noonday, 1972. Succinct, well-written overview of Hemingway; excellent but dated annotated bibliography.

Watts, Emily Stipes. *Ernest Hemingway and the Arts.* Urbana: University of Illinois Press, 1971. Shows the breadth of Hemingway's interest in and understanding of various pictorial artists.

Williams, Wirt. *The Tragic Art of Ernest Hemingway.* Baton Rouge: Louisiana State University Press, 1981. Argues that the development of Hemingway's fiction parallels the sharpening of his tragic vision.

Workman, Brooke. *In Search of Ernest Hemingway: A Model for Teaching a Literature Seminar.* Urbana, Ill.: National Council of Teachers of English, 1979. Paperback. Details an approach for teaching a 90-day seminar on Hemingway in the high-school classroom.

Wylder, Delbert. *Hemingway's Heroes.* Albuquerque: University of New Mexico Press, 1969. Perceptively differentiates the heroes in the first seven novels, with still the best essay on *The Torrents of Spring.*

Young, Philip. *Ernest Hemingway.* New York: Rinehart, 1952. Paperback. Rinehart, 1953. Enlarged and reissued as *Ernest Hemingway: A Reconsideration.* University Park: Pennsylvania State University Press, 1966. Paperback. New York: Harcourt, Brace & World, 1966. The second book for serious students, articulates and traces in the fiction the now-familiar wound theory of Hemingway's work.

5. Collections

Alderman, Taylor, and Kenneth Rosen, eds. *Hemingway notes.* Carlisle, Penn.: Dickinson College, 1971–74. Semiannual periodical, includes articles, reviews, notes, and bibliography.

Asselineau, Roger, ed. *The Literary Reputation of Hemingway in Europe.* New York: New York University Press, 1965. Conference volume 1: prints essays from the symposium of the European Association of American Studies, Bellagio, Italy, 1960; surveys of the responses to Hemingway by English, French, German, Italian, Norwegian, Swedish, and Soviet reviewers and critics.

Astro, Richard, and Jackson J. Benson, eds. *Hemingway In Our Time.* Corvallis: Oregon State University, 1974. Conference volume 2: prints twelve essays from the 1973 Oregon State University Conference on Hemingway, including the second "swan song" of inimitable Philip Young.

Baker, Carlos, ed. *Hemingway and His Critics: An International Anthology.* New York: Hill & Wang, 1961. Paperback: Hill & Wang, 1961. Excellent collection, prints twenty essays, three-fourths written in the 1950s, one-third by international authors.

———. *Ernest Hemingway: Critiques of Four Major Novels.* New York: Charles Scribner's Sons, 1962. Paperback. Scribner Research Anthology; includes two synoptic essays and from four to six now-standard essays each on *The Sun Also Rises, A Farewell to Arms, For Whom the Bell Tolls,* and *The Old Man and the Sea.*

Benson, Jackson J., ed. *The Short Stories of Ernest Hemingway: Critical Essays.* Durham, N.C.: Duke University Press, 1975. Paperback. Duke, 1975. Excellent anthology: an overview, a comprehensive checklist of criticism, and thirty articles on and explications of the stories.

Bruccoli, Matthew J., C. E. Frazer Clark, et al., eds. *Fitzgerald/Hemingway Annual 1969 {–1979}.* Washington, D.C.: NCR Microcard Editions, 1969–74. Englewood, Colo.: Information Handling Services, 1975–76. Detroit: Gale Research Co., 1977–80. Includes articles, reviews, notes, and bibliographic checklists.

Gegenheimer, Albert Frank, ed. *Arizona Quarterly* 33 (Summer 1977): 101–92; 39 (Summer 1983): 101–71. Special issues include nine and seven Hemingway articles, respectively.

Gellens, Jay, ed. *Twentieth Century Interpretations of "A Farewell to Arms":*
A Collection of Critical Essays. Englewood Cliffs, N.J.: Prentice-Hall,
1970. Paperback. Prentice-Hall, 1970. Prints sixteen items: articles,
chapters, and brief excerpts, showing the range of attitudes toward
the novel.

Graham, John, comp. *The Merrill Studies in "A Farewell to Arms."* Columbus, Ohio: Charles E. Merrill Co., 1971. Paperback. Reprints five
1929 reviews and six essays (mostly from the 1960s and anthologized
elsewhere), and includes Charles Vandersee's previously unpublished
"The Stopped Worlds of Frederic Henry," which raises excellent
questions about Frederic's narrative.

Grebstein, Sheldon N., comp. *The Merrill Studies in "For Whom the Bell
Tolls."* Columbus, Ohio: Charles E. Merrill Co., 1971. Paperback.
Reprints six contemporaneous reviews and eleven essays, mostly pub-
lished in the 1960s, and several anthologized elsewhere.

Howell, John M., ed. *Hemingway's African Stories: The Stories, Their Sources,
Their Critics.* New York: Charles Scribner's Sons, 1969. Paperback.
Reprints "The Snows of Kilimanjaro" and "The Short Happy Life of
Francis Macomber" along with thirteen previously published notes
and commentaries on the stories.

Jobes, Katharine T., ed. *Twentieth Century Interpretations of "The Old Man
and the Sea": A Collection of Critical Essays.* Englewood Cliffs, N.J.:
Prentice-Hall, 1968. Paperback. 1968. Gathers nine long and nine
short essays or excerpts, nicely allowing for sharply divergent interpretations of the work and opinions of its worth.

Lee, A. Robert, ed. *Ernest Hemingway: New Critical Essays.* Totowa, N.J.:
Barnes & Noble, 1983. Gathers ten new essays, seven by British
academics; Brian Way's provocative analysis of Hemingway's aesthetic
rescues the largely ruminant or tortuous pieces.

McCaffery, John K. M., ed. *Ernest Hemingway: The Man and His Work.*
Cleveland: World Publishing, 1950. Paperback: Avon, 1961. Reprint. New York: Cooper Square Publishers, 1969. The first anthology of criticism on Hemingway, reprints twenty-one reviews,
magazine articles, journal essays, and chapters from books written in
the 1930s and 1940s.

Meyers, Jeffrey, ed. *Hemingway: The Critical Heritage.* Boston: Routledge
& Kegan Paul, 1982. Selectively reprints in their entirety 4 obituaries
and 118 magazine essays and book reviews of Hemingway's works
through *The Nick Adams Stories,* three-fourths by American reviewers
and writers, one-fourth by British and a smattering of continental
authors; includes a 60-page overview of Hemingway and the essays,
and notes on each review.

Nagel, James, ed. *Ernest Hemingway: The Writer in Context.* Madison: University of Wisconsin Press, 1984. Conference volume 5: prints twelve essays from Northeastern University's conference of the same title in Boston, 1982; illuminating essay by Max Westbrook on Grace and Clarence Hemingway's relationship and the summer of 1920.

Noble, Donald R., ed. *Hemingway: A Revaluation.* Troy, N.Y.: Whitston Publishing Co., 1983. Conference volume 3: prints thirteen essays, eight presented seven years earlier at the 1976 Alabama Symposium on Hemingway.

Oldsey, Bernard, ed. *Ernest Hemingway: The Papers of a Writer.* New York: Garland Publishing, 1981. Reprints *College Literature* 7 (Fall 1980): i–x, 181–320. Conference volume 4: prints eleven essays from the 1980 Hemingway Boston conference of the same title, six drawing heavily upon documents, manuscripts, and correspondence in the Hemingway collection of the Kennedy Library in Boston.

Oliver, Charles S., ed. *Hemingway notes.* Ada: Ohio Northern University, 1979–81. Four issues of the semiannual periodical resurrected from 1974; includes current research, articles, book reviews, notes, and bibliography.

————. *The Hemingway Review.* Ada: Ohio Northern University, 1981–. Formerly *Hemingway notes,* expansion and change of title reflect the birth of The Hemingway Society.

————. *The Hemingway Newsletter.* Ada: Ohio Northern University, 1981–. Semiannual organ of The Hemingway Society, prints notes, news items, queries, and announcements.

Reynolds, Michael S., ed. *Critical Essays on Hemingway's "In Our Time."* Boston: G. K. Hall & Co., 1983. Includes contemporaneous reviews, ten essays on *In Our Time*'s unity, and old and new studies of individual stories.

Stephens, Robert O., ed. *Ernest Hemingway: The Critical Reception.* New York: Burt Franklin & Co., 1977. Gathers nearly 400 newspaper and magazine reviews of Hemingway's books through *The Nick Adams Stories;* sometimes in their entirety, often excerpted, occasionally paraphrased.

Wagner, Linda Welshimer, ed. *Ernest Hemingway: Five Decades of Criticism.* East Lansing: Michigan State University Press, 1974. Except for Edmund Wilson's brief, 1924 review of Hemingway's first two books, gathers essays from two decades: six from between 1951 and 1959, thirteen from between 1962 and 1972; but some valuable inclusions, despite nine essays that appear in other collections.

Waldhorn, Arthur, ed. *Ernest Hemingway: A Collection of Criticism.* New York: McGraw-Hill, 1973. Paperback. Besides own biographical sketch, reprints seven good overviews, three found in other harvests.

Waldmeir, Joseph J., and Kenneth Marek, eds. *Up in Michigan: Proceedings of the First National Conference of the Hemingway Society*. Traverse City, Mich.: The Hemingway Society, 1983. Conference volume 6.

White, William, comp. *The Merrill Studies in "The Sun Also Rises."* Columbus, Ohio: Charles E. Merrill Co., 1969. Reprints nine contemporaneous reviews and six essays collected in other anthologies of criticism.

Weeks, Robert P., ed. *Hemingway: A Collection of Critical Essays*. Englewood Cliffs, N.J.: Prentice-Hall, 1962. Paperback. Prentice-Hall, 1962. Reprints sixteen essays and excerpts that, despite the publication date, make this still the most provocative of the critical anthologies.

6. Miscellaneous Materials: Audiotape Cassette (AC), Film (F), Filmstrip (FS), Record (R), Videotape Cassette (VC).

Baker, Carlos. *Ernest Hemingway—A Life Story: A Biographical Interpretation*. New York: Center for Cassette Studies, n.d. AC: 27 min.

Ernest Hemingway—Rough Diamond. Lawrence, Kan.: Centron Films, 1978. VC: color, 30 min.

Fox, Paul W., producer. *Ernest Hemingway*. West Simsbury, Conn.: Wilson Educational Media, 1977. FS: color, 32 min, Hemingway in Paris, Spain, and Austria, 1921–26.

Grebstein, Sheldon N. *Ernest Hemingway's "For Whom the Bell Tolls."* Deland, Fla.: Everett/Edwards, 1970. Reissued: Mount Vernon, N.Y.: Gould Media, n.d. AC: 104 min. Lecture.

Hayes, Harold. *A Look at Ernest Hemingway*. Hollywood: Center for Cassette Studies, 1975. AC: 5 parts, 136 min. Part 1: Interview with Mary Hemingway and Jo August, curator of Hemingway Collection, about materials in the John F. Kennedy Library, 34 min. Part 2: Interview with Scottie Fitzgerald Smith and Matthew J. Bruccoli about Fitzgerald and Hemingway's relationship, 25 min. Part 3: Interview with Leicester Hemingway about brother and family, 26 min. Part 4: Interview with Helen Kirkpatrick and Charles Collingwood about experiences during World War II with fellow correspondent Hemingway, 25 min. Part 5: Interview with Ralph Ellison, James Jones, and William Styron about Hemingway's influence on them and other American writers, 26 min.

Hemingway, Mary, narrator. *Hemingway's Spain: "Death in the Afternoon," "For Whom the Bell Tolls," and "The Sun Also Rises."* New York: ABC, McGraw-Hill, 1968. F: color, 15, 19, and 17 min. Views people and places in Spain as Mary Hemingway visits the various locations for the three works.

Hemingway's Dispatches from Spain. Los Angeles: Pacifica Tape Library, n.d. AC: 54 min. Explains how Hemingway's journalistic dispatches from the Spanish Civil War reveal the politics of the struggle.

Hotchner, A. E. *Hotchner on Hemingway.* Cincinnati: Writers Voice, 1973. AC: 90 min. Talks about his fourteen-year friendship with Hemingway.

Huntley, Chet, narrator. *Hemingway.* New York: NBC, McGraw-Hill, 1965. F: B&W, 54 min. Bolsters the legend of the public Hemingway; nevertheless, and interesting period piece.

Hynan, Patrick. *Hemingway: A Portrait in Sound.* Toronto: Canadian Broadcasting Corp., 1973. R.

Kazin, Alfred. *Fiction in the Twenties. The Lost Generation—Ernest Hemingway.* Mount Vernon, N.Y.: Gould Media, n.d. AC: 28 min. Lecture.

Larson, Eric C., director. *Hemingway.* Tucson, Ariz.: Townsend/Larson Productions, 1984. VC: color, 55 min. Robert Townsend portrays Hemingway in February 1961 in an autobiographical monologue written by Sheryl Craig from Hemingway's letters with Mary Hemingway's collaboration; interesting conception.

Stephan, Donald E. *The American Experience in Literature: Five Modern Novelists: Ernest Hemingway.* Chicago: Encyclopaedia Britannica Educational Corp., 1975. FS w/AC: color, 18 min. Succinct overview of Hemingway's life and works.

Wylder, Delbert. *Ernest Hemingway: "Early Short Stories," "Middle Short Stories," and "Late Short Stories."* Mount Vernon, N.Y.: Gould Media, n.d. AC: 180 min. Lectures.

Young, Philip. *Ernest Hemingway's "A Farewell to Arms."* Deland, Fla.: Everett/Edwards, 1970. Reissued: Mount Vernon, N.Y.: Gould Media, n.d. AC: 110 min. Lecture.

———. *Ernest Hemingway's "The Sun Also Rises."* Deland Fla.: Everett/Edwards, 1971. Reissued: Mount Vernon, N.Y.: Gould Media, n.d. AC: 95 min. Lecture.

Index

Adams, Henry, 161; *The Education of Henry Adams,* 159
Adams, Nick; *see* Nick Adams stories
Aesthetic, prose, 14–36; central characteristic of, 34; effect of concept of time on, 108–27; involuntary shock of emotion in, 27; metaphor of violent games in, 15; mirror of Hemingway's art in, 50; relationship to the artist and the artistic process of, 75–76
Allegory, open-ended, 71, 78
American literature, function of, 105; challenge of, 141; concerns of the writer to, 147–48
Anderson, Sherwood, 6, 26–27, 154; *Winesburg, Ohio,* 26, 27
Archetype, definition of, 68
Art, authenticity, 14–15; meanings that evade conceptualization in, 71
Audience, Hemingway's view of, 15, 18–19

Baker, Carlos, 33, 49, 154
Barea, Arturo, 3
Beach, Sylvia, 160, 161
Bellow, Saul, review of *The Old Man and the Sea* by, 34
Berenson, Bernard, 154
Berto, Giuseppe, 149
Betsky, Seymour, 3
Bierce, Ambrose, "An Occurrence at Owl Creek Bridge," 19
Bishop, John Peale, 3, 7
Brague, L. H., Jr., 154
Bull fighting, aesthetic principle of, 17–19; use of metaphors of, 14–15

Camus, Albert, 105, 107, 149
Cargill, Oscar, on *The Sun Also Rises,* 139
Cather, Willa, *The Professor's House,* 169
Cave, Ray, 154, 155
Characters, Hemingway's typical, 6, 9, 38–39, 55, 67–68; emotional standards of morality in, 99; *see also* individual works: *A Farewell to Arms; The Sun Also Rises,* etc.
Chaplin, Duncan, 163

Ciao, newsletter, the early Hemingway in, 24
Code, the Hemingway, 38, 90–107, 129, 131–32, 135–37, 145, 151–52; characters' emotional standards of morality in, 99; criticism of, 102–5; definition of, 92–93; distinction between two versions of, 90–93; fusion with concept of time of, 126–27; philosophical basis of, 105–7
Code heroes, 38–39, 45; *see also* Tutor; Tyro
Cowley, Malcolm, "A Portrait of Mister Papa," 143–44
Crane, Stephen, 146
Cummings, E. E., 124

Death, Hemingway's views on, 12–13; possible expectations of, 168
Democracy, function of literature in, 105–6
Dietrich, Marlene, 158
Dignity, characteristic important to Hemingway, 47–48, 97–98
Dominguín, Luis Miguel, 158, 166
Dorman-Smith, E. E. "Chink," 160
Dos Passos, John, 151, 158, 159, 161
Douglass, Frederick, 161; *Narrative of the Life of Frederick Douglass,* 159
Dreiser, Theodore, 26
Dunning, Ralph Cheever, 161, 162

Edwards, Jonathan, 147
Eliot, T. S., 141, 150, 159, 169, 172; Hemingway compared with, 37–38; "The Hollow Men," 94–95, 96; "objective correlative," 28–29; *The Waste Land,* 37, 139
Emerson, Ralph Waldo, 69, 77, 100, 101, 105, 142, 146, 147, 148, 161, 168
Emotion, role of, 15; involuntary shock of, 27–28, 30, 66; objective correlative of, 28–29, 31–32
Epistemological fictions, 62, 78, 81, 130, 163–64
Evil, the role of, 104
Exemplar, the, 67, 167

Fable, the, 67

210